MEMOIRS
of a
MEXICAN
MISSIONARY

**LIFE EXPERIENCES TO INSPIRE AN
AUTHENTIC RELATIONSHIP
WITH GOD**

ARISBET S. CANTÚ

Memoirs of a Mexican Missionary: Life Experiences to Inspire an Authentic Relationship with God

Copyright © 2024 Arisbet S. Cantú

All rights reserved.

No part of this publication may be reproduced, copied, stored in a retrieval system, or transmitted in any form by any means, electronic, mechanical, photocopy, recording or otherwise without the prior permission of the author.

This is a work of creative nonfiction. While all the events and stories in this book are true, some names and identifying details have been changed to protect the privacy of the people involved. Any resulting resemblance to persons living or dead is entirely coincidental and unintentional. It is sold with the understanding that through this publication the author is not engaged in rendering legal or other professional services. This publication is not intended as a substitute for the advice of health care professionals. If legal or other professional advice or assistance is required, the services of a competent professional should be sought.

Scripture quotations marked AMP are from the Amplified Bible
Scripture quotations marked ESV are from the ESV Bible
Scripture quotations marked NKJV are from the New King James Version Bible

For reprint permission or speaking requests, write to overflowaris@gmail.com.

Paperback ISBN 979-8-35098-340-1

Cover and interior book design by Arisbet S. Cantú

"Nevertheless,

when the Son of Man comes,

will He find faith on earth?"

Luke 18:8

Dedication

A Dios Padre, Hijo y Espíritu Santo, todo es para Tu gloria.

Para mis regalitos del cielo, mis bendiciones de Dios, mi Chiquitini Nini Arixeny, Chalita mi Mariposita Xaeli y mi Bebe Bonita Titachi Yhnai. Ustedes fueron una gran motivación para terminar este libro. Son amadas con una profundidad inmensa, mis corazones. Que permanezcan las tres en el profundo amor de Dios siempre y lo mantengan en primer lugar al vivir día a día.

Me siento increíblemente bendecida de ser su mami.

Que cada una de ustedes viva apasionadamente por Jesús, y sigan el plan perfecto de Dios en sus vidas.

ഇരുയ

To God the Father, Son and Holy Spirit, all the glory is for You.

To my daughters Arixeny, Xaeli and Yhnai. You were a great motivation for me to finish this book. May you know the depths of God's love and keep Him first as you live life day to day.

I feel incredibly blessed to be your mom.

May each of you live out passionately for God and follow His perfect plan for you in your lifetime.

8

Contents

Dedication......7

Introduction......15

El Es / He Is......21

Keep Going......23

NICARAGUA

CHAPTER 1 - Miskito......29

CHAPTER 2 - Water......39

CHAPTER 3 - Malnourished......47

I'll have the steak, please. – A Narrative......55

DOMINICAN REPUBLIC & PUERTO RICO

CHAPTER 4 - Pa'lante......61

CHAPTER 5 - Living Worship......73

CHAPTER 6 - ¡Ay, Bendito!......83

CHAPTER 7 - Relationship, But a Good One......91

Witness - Experimental Dialogue......99

GUATEMALA

CHAPTER 8 - The Condition of Orphans......105

CHAPTER 9 - The Pact of a Union......119

Tsunami - Dialogue-Driven Vignette......137

EL SALVADOR & HONDURAS

CHAPTER 10 – The Time In Between......147

Consume......159

COSTA RICA
CHAPTER 11 - Pura Vida...163

CHAPTER 12 - Tombs...169

MÈXICO
Pa'curar...181

CHAPTER 13 - Tragos Amargos.......................................185

CHAPTER 14 - Dios Te Salve, Maria................................201

CHAPTER 15 - Worship Service......................................211

CHAPTER 16 - Cured..221

D.F.W, U.S.A.
Famine – A Narrative...231

CHAPTER 17 - Religious..235

CHAPTER 18 - Like Him...241

CHAPTER 19 - Bible Study..247

CHAPTER 20 - October...255

CHAPTER 21 - Thieves..263

SPAIN, FRANCE & ITALY
La Novia..281

CHAPTER 22 - Lavished..285

Flamenco...293

CHAPTER 23 - Sojourner...297

CHAPTER 24 - Work Of Art..309

CHAPTER 25 - Construction...319

LAS VEGAS, NEVADA, U.S.A.

CHAPTER 26 - Henderson...327

CHAPTER 27 - Casinos..331

CHAPTER 28 - Traffic...337

CHAPTER 29 - Free..343

CHAPTER 30 - Working Girls..347

Afterword: A Call to Salvation..363

Barcelona, Spain

Introduction

I want to give glory to God. What you are about to read are some experiences I've had in the mission field in Latin America and doing ministry in Dallas, Texas and Las Vegas, Nevada. You're probably expecting a sweet girl with a plain Jane hair-cut wearing an awful cardigan sweater (Christian), floral print blouse and boots (lives in Texas), and a heavy study Bible in hand (like, she actually reads it). Only one of those is true, the study Bible. I read it Genesis to Revelation at the age of fifteen for the first time after I had an incredible one-on-one experience with God.

I was invited to a Christian church youth service by a girl in my high school at the age of fifteen. When I finally went, I thought everyone there was crazy. It was a bunch of weird high school nerds (my teenage description at the time) jumping up and down to Jesus music. *'Wow, these kids are a bunch of freaks'*, I thought. I was raised Catholic and thought Christians were cultic people. But on that night, November 2, 2000, I decided to see what this girl from school kept inviting me to. Nobody spoke to me, and nobody touched me or prayed for me. It was a youth group service and some man spoke on a small stage in an upper room with lights dimmed. All I saw were shadows of people. I had no idea what the guy on the stage said or who he was. But I, being who I am, in my gritty, straight-up, get to the point character, confronted God in my thoughts.

Eyes open I blankly stared straight forward as if I was a bored and disinterested teen. I said for the first time in my life, *'God if you are real then take this away from me – whatever this is that I feel inside – and do it NOW. If you don't do it right now, You're fake, You don't exist, and all these people are just a bunch of freaks putting on a show. If you don't do this now I will never believe in You. But if You do it now, I will live for you the rest of my life.'* And as soon as I said *'life'* in my mind, I felt a powerful force move in from the top of my head and through the entire rest of my body. No one prayed for me and no one touched me. This powerful force felt like strong power that causes an extreme electrical like current in your body but doesn't hurt or kill you. It was as though the hand of God reached down from heaven and pulled something out of me. I can't explain or describe it with words except, supreme power, unlike anything

I have ever experienced before. Somehow, I was convinced deep within my spirit that there could be nothing more powerful than this. I cried like I have never cried out to this day. It wasn't like when you cry because you feel emotional or because of pain, it was *deeper within*, a transformation of sorts. I instantly felt new inside, like I finally became myself. The inner darkness, a form of depression, confusion, always frustrated internally and not knowing why – all of it left me instantly and completely for good. I was no longer burdened, no longer distressed, and finally knew what it felt to have inner rest. It was the power of God. I cannot deny that happened to me. It was an incredible moment when God answered with an overwhelming display of power, almost as if He had been anticipating this very moment in my life. I was set free.

I was born in Zihuatanejo, Guerrero México, but I'm really from the state of Michoacán. I was only born in Zihuatanejo because my dad visited and fell in love with the beach. I'm a Mexican immigrant who grew up in Oak Cliff, a hood in Dallas, TX. I'm a proud Mexican. I'm an artist. I love sports cars. I drive a blacked-out Chevy Camaro with black leather seats and sunroof. I wear high heels which some religious girls call 'stripper heels'. I love timeless style, and black leather anything. I chug salsa when I eat tacos. The spicier, the better. You can find me with a good book in hand at a local coffee shop in Dallas. I love ceviche. I place mind over make-up and I love learning. Faith, values, sincerity and ethical principles in a person are more important in my view, than their net-worth, associations, achievements, degrees, social status or material belongings. I'm purposeful on making a positive impact in the lives of others in a way that would go beyond material success. I care a lot about everyone I come in contact with and I want to see each person live life to their fullest potential. I love adventure. I prefer patio taquerias over fine dining. I hate salad bars. I love chocolate.

It's important that you know I'm a real person. Like *a real person*, not just another perfectly fake profile of a 'good Christian girl', or a missionary who would have been a nun as her second career option or a pastor's kid, you know or something like that. I didn't come from a perfectly loving Christian family. When I started going to a Christian church, my dad disowned me. "We are Catholics!!! If you keep going to that Christian church, you are no longer my daughter!" he yelled. "Well you did not die on the cross for me so that's fine!!" I yelled back as I walked out the door to drive to Thursday night youth service. I meant what I said. I felt sad for my dad; he had no idea how great the love of God truly was and how much God had transformed my life.

Some Christian authors project their lives as so perfect, however it's the full testimony of a believer that sets others free. If we were truly

INTRODUCTION

so perfect, Jesus had no cause to die. It's frustrating to see the perfect lives displayed by some Christians, because it leaves people outside of the church walls feeling as though they would never be able to measure up. If you know a good Christian woman or man, they have real problems and struggles. Yes, that priest, that leader you admire, the college professor with a doctorate and the mega church pastor with multiple campuses – all included. We are imperfect and that is the reality for all of us living and breathing. The only difference with a believer is that they have an advantage in their relationship with God which empowers them to conquer and overcome in a way that people who don't know God in relationship can do.

I wrote this book in hopes that these experiences would compel you to start or continue an authentic relationship with God. I hope to tear down every false image of God that others built up before you, which keep you from searching for God daily. May it all be destroyed, everything that kept you from coming to God whole-heartedly. To follow, you will read experiences and lessons that I learned as I traveled through countries, passionate about loving God and helping others. I hope some of these lessons and practical applications will help you as you navigate through life with a desire to know God. May they empower you to live freely, intentionally and authentically.

Religion is something many of us are born into, but living a lifestyle of truly knowing God - that is a personal decision you make daily. Relationship with God requires prioritized time fostering the consistent capacity to know Him. It's based on truth of Biblical scripture and serious personal intention. It's guidance and revelation of the Holy Spirit. But what does that mean? I hope this book helps you understand what it means. For many, faith seems to be something people step in and out of. Like your faith may be strong to believe you will get the job but it may fail when you have a family member dying of cancer. A simple definition of faith is *"trust in God's ability"*. You can't trust someone you don't know. You can't know someone you don't spend time with. You don't get to know God with a series of emotional experiences inside four walls of a religious building. You can go to church every week and be consistently faith-less inside, just complying with the image you need to portray for others. Religious. Wherever you stand, the secret is this:

Make time for God when no one is watching.

What is it that you give the most amount of time to? Consider giving time to knowing God. If you can't honestly say you know God personally, I urge you to pursue that relationship today. I included a prayer of salvation at the end of this book. If you currently don't know Jesus as Lord and Savior, and would like to make that commitment, I invite you to read that part at the end and connect with a good Bible teaching church in your area to continue your growth. You may read that and think, *'Yes, I go to church I already know Jesus.'* Sure, but I mean, *have you made Jesus Lord*? It's a yes or no answer only you would know.

    May you know the truth and have the courage to live out in freedom what God has placed in you – what most refer to as your 'life purpose'. Yes, you have one. May you never just sit in a church but know and worship God in a lifestyle as He has created us to. May you never bury and hide your gifts, because the world around you will be at a great loss. Finally, you should know I do believe what the Bible says is true. All of it.

Just visualize it.

    How incredible would it be, if Christ returned and found a generation, as the sands of the sea, *set free*.

Keep going!

El Es / He Is

El es unpredictable.
Y siempre in control.
El es the love of my soul.

Todos dicen I should leave Him.
Que es una locura to always believe Him.

El es celoso, He is good.
Incluso, He gets angry too.
Su persona frequently misunderstood.

Y la neta es que, I don't have to do what He says.
Pero al elegir la obediencia, I worry less.

Es confiable, He's unique.
Me escucha muy atento, every time I speak.
Y se le parte el corazón when my tears streak.

Le doy orgullo, and He loves me.
Le fallo, and He loves me.

El perdona, He forgets.
El me defiende, even when I'm not at my best.
Todo lo que El hace, He does it perfect.

El me reta to be more than what I want to be.
Y llama la belleza dentro de mí, you know, things I can't always see.

El cumple sus promesas, and never lies.
El es siempre fiel, and He's always wise.
Su amor por mi es grande, and those who truly know Him are not surprised.

Sin exagerar, loving Him is easy.
Pero no te equivoques, knowing Him is key.

El Gran Yo Soy, The Great I Am.

Author's Note:
I wrote this with English and Spanish mixed to reference the language of immigrant kids. Mexican children who grew up in the United States, that go back and forth from both languages. I prefer to either speak just English or just Spanish, but it looked best represented as both languages combined together for the poem.

Keep Going

I was 18 years old and dreamt I was in the middle of a jungle. I stood waiting to see Him. I wouldn't move until I saw Him and when I did, He ran. I ran after Him in what felt like a blink, no hesitation or thought process about the decision. As if I heard a gunshot go off and I was in an Olympic race, with that much fervor you see on those runners' faces and bodies, swiftly after Him. After Him as if He was the finish line. While His speed was lightning fast, I somehow was able to keep up. *How can I run so fast?*, I thought, and realized it was the Holy Spirit carrying me with His strength. He was leading me.

Suddenly, I was in a city. He stopped. I couldn't see Him but I knew He was there doing something. I waited for Him and looked around the busy streets of people rushing though life, dodging one another like in New York, on the go to the next appointment, to the next destination, to the next thing they had to do. Busy people doing so much they couldn't see one another and I stood observing and waiting...and waiting, and waiting. I then saw Him. He ran, and I ran after Him.

The Holy Spirit said "Keep going". It was all the instruction I had. He said, "Don't stop running after Him." and that's what I did. I was running after God.

We reached a desert, it looked like Dubai, it was a city in a desert, He had to stop there for some time, I stood there while He did something and I waited and waited until He appeared again, or better yet, until I could see Him pause, as a sign He completed what He was doing there and we ran again. We ran to another place, and another and another…

I wouldn't stop running after Him. I was chasing God around the world. Some places I could feel God's presence more than others.

There were times I worried He was not there, or I missed Him, but He was there and I knew I had to focus harder to identify Him. There were times I could see Him move clearly and followed His movements.

Each place was different in what people were doing. Some were busier than others. Some had fewer people. Some looked completely deserted and abandoned. The weather environment was different in each location and I had to show up prepared for the environment.

I awoke jumping off the bed with my heart racing. Although it was a dream, I got the message loud and clear.

This is our life as believers.

We run after God in every season, in every location and follow after what He is already doing. It's a choice not dependent on any circumstance we experience. It's recorded in scripture that Jesus said to his disciples, "...*leave everything and follow Me,*" without giving them time to figure out their matters. It's the same call for you and I. The act of leaving something or someone behind can take a literal form, for example, leaving a relationship, or a spiritual one, like severing the invisible bonds that might be holding you back from fervent devotion to God. Your success, the opinions of those you love, an unhealthy obsession with wealth, the idols you've placed in your life, or the ideas of the person you aspire to be—all of these things could potentially distract you from God's calling for your life. Everything will work out and all will be provided, just follow after Him.

We don't live and move on our own ability, but the Holy Spirit of God carries us through with His strength. It's not by our means, it's through His provision and power because we entrusted our lives over to God in Salvation.

Wherever you stand right now, in whatever location you find yourself in, run after Him.

Yield to Him. Most importantly,

Keep going.

28

CHAPTER 1

Miskito

"*Dawan latwan mai kaiki sa*" I said standing on what felt like an enormous, ancient wooden stage. Ancient. Starring back at me were the faces of Miskito Indians in the island of Waspan. It was packed. I just told them God loves you in Miskito. "Ao" they all replied, which means yes as all unitedly expressed agreement. I spotted the tribe leader from the stage. Waspan is home to an indigenous tribe of Indians called the Miskito Indians of Nicaragua. Without time to research, I signed up, went to the prep meetings and there I stood trying my best to share the message of salvation in Christ.

I was a student at a local Bible School in Dallas, Texas called Christ for the Nations Institute (CFNI). Unlike most students, I did not pursue Biblical Studies because I wanted to go into ministry – as in be some pastor's wife or take on any formal 'ministry' role of the type. My plan, unlike most of my classmates, was not to include ministry as a 'career path'. My parents are not pastors. I grew up a strict Mexican Catholic, and for me that meant being forced to go to church every Sunday. Religious, *religious*, as in my dad gave me the middle name Guadalupe after their saint la Virgen de Guadalupe. I graduated from an arts magnet high school and initially planned my career path in creative design enrolling in Cal Arts after graduating, adding a business degree or two ahead of it. I absolutely love business. Enrolling in Bible School was an impulsive decision when I visited the CFNI campus. I knew deep down it was where I needed to be next.

Because of the impact God had in my life at the age of fifteen, I wanted to use my future businesses to fund work that helps other people find God and have a genuine relationship with Him. I enrolled in Bible School to learn how to study the Bible, know more about who God was, and strengthen the foundation of my personal relationship with God so if any success came in the future, I would not mismanage it. I commended every one of my peers who pursued the calling to serve in a formalized ministry role, and was so inspired by their stories as many had gone through many hurdles to study and prepare for ministry. Each Summer we were offered an opportunity to travel and take part in humanitarian efforts abroad. What caught my attention about Nicaragua was the forgotten Indigenous Miskito tribe of Waspan.

We traveled through Managua, into the small town of El Cruce-ro where we would be lodging and serving at a children's academy. This academy was located within a small community on top of a high mountain. The road up the mountain was incredibly dangerous. There was just enough space for 2 cars to drive in opposite directions, and of course, no safety rails along the edge of the mountain. Our hosts were the missionary family, the Fullers. The Fullers had kids who were young adults and took part of most of the mission work. Their daughter Hope was gothic and read tarot cards on rides to church outreaches with her brother. The Fuller kids were disinterested in ministry work. Like many kids whose parents were in full-time ministry that I had met so far, there was an indifference in them regarding ministry. Not all ministry kids, but several I had already met were that same way. Hope pulling out the tarot cards wasn't a shock to me. She was best friends with Adrienne, our team leader. Adrienne was a slim Latina who I had just met when I signed up for this trip. She hardly wore any make up and had a very humble and polite way of being with an elegance to her mannerisms. The no make up and skirt thing came from being raised in a strict church denomination where women can't wear make up and have to wear long skirts to be seen as 'Godly' and respectable.

The team included about 10 students with one being a team leader and coordinating our itinerary with the local missionaries. Our luggage arrived about 3 days after we arrived. We went our first 2 days without running water and without clean clothes, the perfect way to start a missions trip. By the second day, it rained on the mountain and we were done. We grabbed our shampoo and all agreed we'd wash our hair outside as the rain fell from the gutters. I showered in the mornings and stepped out to incred-ible heat and humidity. Everyone would begin sweating almost as soon as we finished showering.

My house mates were South Korean girls I called the SoKo squad. "That is so cool, you're from Korea!" I said, to which they responded in complete scorn, "NO!!! What is wrong with you, we're from SOOUUUTH Korea. *South* Korea, ok, no Korea. Not North, SOUTH." It was as if I just cursed their mother. "I never said North, I just said Korea." I replied. I learned if you just say Korea then the North side is implied. I will rename them in this book as Ming, Yeeun, and Chen. They could not pronounce my name and called me "Wai Song Yani" which meant 'sister Wai Song' in Korean. They said that I looked like a famous South Korean pop sing-er. Ming explained, "Yes! You know, she is in South Korea, like American Britney Spears, Wai Song!" They all laughed and agreed and called me that the entire time. "Whatever, I'm not googling it, I believe you." I said. I was the only one in the room with a phone that worked but I didn't tell anyone it worked. Thank you T-Mobile. I wanted to unplug completely and unless it

Street Evangelism, Managua Nicaragua

Wood working Class *The Children's School students*

was an emergency, then I would use it. We stayed in student lodging, which were rooms of metal bed bunks, about 6 beds per room. The beds were very uncomfortable, and it was common for us to find spiders and huge bugs creeping in the room day and night. Managua has massive bugs that should scare any college girl but I didn't have the energy for that and killed them without hesitation. I became a hero for the SoKo girls who would run and jump behind me every single time.

    Managua reminded me of Mexico in so many ways. When you step outside, you get that Mexico rancho smell of wood and trash burning. Also the poverty in many areas, the corrupt government, and the humility of everyone I met. The people were very kind and hospitable. There was an election going on in Managua where José Daniel Ortega was running to become president. I asked Manuel, our driver, his thoughts on Jose Ortega. "That man is a dictator who takes advantage of the poor. He is evil and corrupt. But no party wins here, because everyone is bad." One Sunday, we were leaving church service and I noticed there were political representatives of Ortega, driving branded beat up pick-up trucks and other vehicles. I asked Manuel what was going on and he said, "They are bribing people in the neighborhood for their vote." In the United States, a crooked politician would go about that in a more discrete manner, but in Nicaragua it was not hidden. He said, "People here are so poor, they will happily accept money to cast a vote."

I slept covered in my hot sleeping bag, with the zipper shut almost all the way closed, only exposing my nose to avoid spider bites. The food was a culture shock, but I consumed everything handed to me out of respect. I genuinely enjoyed every meal and any offering the people served us. They had what they call "gallo pinto" which was black beans and white rice mixed together, and it was good! They did not eat spicy salsa, and there were no tortillas. One day we had to eat an American home cooked meal at the Fuller's home with some of their American friends. I stepped into the kitchen to ask the church volunteer lady if I could help her cook. She said no, but my mother taught me to always serve in the kitchen even as a guest in someone's home. Whether it was cooking or cleaning I was raised to lend a hand and help the women, and so I insisted. The volunteer lady accepted my help and had me making "cubed steak". I had never heard of it. It was delicious and humorous that I learned how to cook American cubed steak in Nicaragua.

It was a rocky time in that my team members began to doubt the family cared about the locals. I kept my thoughts to myself. They shared how they felt Mr. Fuller did things that didn't make sense. At one point, he had us cleaning and polishing a car as "punishment". When a couple of students from our team demanded to know why, he said we did not properly communicate to him that we were going to visit a church one day. Because we didn't run that by him, we had to clean and wax a car he hoped to sell. Also, the team was confused by where our meal money went. The Koreans were mostly upset and demanded to know why the Fullers were not covering all of our meals when we had already pre-paid them prior to arriving. I stood back and watched everything without sharing my input because I knew there was no point in arguing with Mr. Fuller. Adrienne, our leader, was in a hard position and couldn't step up to Mr. Fuller as our leader either. Being so much younger than Mr. Fuller and physically half his size on top of that, it was unrealistic for us to expect her to. She preferred to ignore it and pulled one of the older students to determine what they could do and how they would lead us despite the circumstance.

Adrienne tried to manage the complaints as best as she could among the group but the Koreans saw quickly they were not going to get their meals paid. I knew Mr. Fuller was wrong for not providing us the meals, being college kids and especially our foreigner friends. That's the only thing I spoke up about on behalf of the Koreans. I was grateful I had a job and was able to buy whatever I wanted, but they were international and limited with money. I'm sharing this because this is the reality. Christians are not perfect, even if they run ministries abroad. Mr. Fuller needed a mentor, a ministry leader who could help him and keep him accountable and it was highly likely that he had no one. In the Christian community, we have everything from good-hearted, God devoted believers to corrupt abusive leaders, to extortioners, to human traffickers, you name it. We sometimes focus ontitles, see ministries running well enough and believe everything is ok, but fail to see that there is work to be done in leaders to keep their lives right with God privately. My perspective was, that even if I find out how messed up people are, I'd pray for them and focus on God. No one, regardless of their role, will always represent God accurately. Understanding this is very important, and I learned this very early on after committing my life to God at the age of fifteen.

A few days after the meal situation, Mr. Fuller asked us to meet him for Bible Studies a few times during the trip and take notes. He said that we were to always keep God and the ministry first above our family. We glanced at one another in disagreement, except the Koreans. The SoKo squad was so over this guy that they were not even paying attention. But those of us who were listening, disagreed. He continued to teach that he placed his wife and kids as second priority below the work of the ministry. He said "the work of the ministry" is above family. I noticed he did not say 'God', he said the 'work of the ministry'. Basically, work is above family. Before I had a chance to comment, one of my team members Larry, quickly and abruptly interrupted him from continuing his teaching to disagree. The SoKo squad suddenly sensed disturbance in the force and paid attention. Larry continued by saying that he studied the same scripture and believes that family should come first before the work of the ministry. I said in my mind, *'Oh God here we go. Larry chill out, let's just keep it moving so we can get out of here.'* But Larry couldn't hear my thoughts and Larry wouldn't let it go. Very quickly, another team member Ally interrupted both of them to agree with Larry and she was upset. Soon every young college missionary stood up to Mr. Fuller to say that your first ministry is your family. I stood back and looked at Mr. Fuller with a silent, *'You know it's true sir'* look on my face. Everyone came for him and the last thing he needed was some Latina telling him something. I knew that even if I said anything it was pointless. Words wouldn't work in that moment and only God could get his attention. At a previous Bible Study his teaching title was, "4 Legal Ways to Make Money." I checked out at the title. So here we are now and as everyone addressed Mr. Fuller, I spoke to God in my mind – *'God, come down and talk to him. And please God, let there be good, strong coffee tomorrow.'*

We spent our mornings and evenings in time of worship. There was a guy from Japan which I truly respected. He was reserved, but I knew he had so much wisdom. He was maybe in his mid 50s. His name was Yoshi. He encouraged us all to not focus on the problems but instead worship and praise God. He emphasized how fortunate we were to be there and be used by God to speak life into the people of Nicaragua. I was right there mentally. I made time to wake up early in the mornings before my team mates to attend the wood work art class the kids took from the academy. My goal was to hear about their lives, encourage them and learn the artistry of wood crafting. We learned how to make jewelry boxes. We began by drawing out our design and transferring it to the wood box using wood cutting tools. It was more than art class, they were learning a skill they could use to make money by selling their crafts to tourists.

May 20, 2006 we headed to Volcán Masaya very early. The volcano emitted a gas that felt like it was choking you. I thought it was an exciting reminder that life is short. We took time to explore the volcanic grounds before we headed out to evangelize at a common plaza in the city. We met all kinds of people there as we visited churches and public events. Between taking Malaria pills that made us sick, prayer services, church services, hanging out with the school kids – it was a full itinerary every day. I was excited about seeing a new culture and learning about the people.

I did not realize what I was really getting myself into. A few days later, we boarded the tiniest and oldest plane I had ever seen in my life to this day. "This is it!?" The SoKo squad exclaimed in cold shock. Their faces

The tiny plane. - Managua, Nicaragua

Miskito homes - Waspan, Nicaragua

turned pale at the realization there was no exit out of this plan. We all had to board the plane. They rambled in super-fast Korean which none of us understood. "It's not safe, it's too little…oh my God we're going to die!" they said a few words in English. Although it looked like any light wind would tear the plane apart. I was not at all concerned. I just trusted that whoever was the pilot knew what he was doing and flew this frequently enough. The plane ride was *rough*, and that is an understatement. We literally could feel every gust of wind that tugged at that tiny little plane and were tossed forcefully in any given direction. We were on our way to the island of Waspan.

May 24, 2006, in the island of Waspan, we woke up and headed for Rio Coco. We met a guy named James who helped at the island's children's orphanage. James spoke to me about his life in Nicaragua, politics, and what the people were like. I wanted to soak in as much as I could. He also taught me common phrases I could use. Hello is 'naksa' and goodbye is 'aisabe'. 'Nahkisma?' means, 'How are you?'. During a meal, I picked up a fork and he told me the word for fork was 'park'. It was interesting. In about 3 hours we arrived to the village we were going to visit and were met by a group of kids who ran up to the boat.

May 25, 2006 I woke up so tired in Waspan. I went for a walk with a few team members looking to see what the everyday life was here. There was miscommunication among the leaders and we missed out on spending time with the new orphans at the village. We bumped into two of the leaders who were shopping for the children's clothes at one of the merchant shops. We bought the kids shoes and were invited to go to the orphanage last minute. Everything there was the middle of nowhere. Homes were surrounded by palm trees, and were propped up by long sticks that looked unstable on the soggy dirt ground. I imagined the Amazon in Peru possibly looked similar. We were asked to go pray for a man who was sick. We arrived to his home, and the house looked like what you would see in a movie. It was put together by sticks and palm leaves as part of the roof. The man's bed was mostly layers of blankets. It was a very tiny home, with a main room that included the kitchen, and then a back room. I was so fixated on this man's physical condition. He was more dead than alive and the woman who was caring for him was overwhelmingly worried. Where was the hope? When people got sick they had nowhere to go. There was no ambulance, no pharmacy, no medical teams they could get him to, and loved ones were overwhelmed with the inability to do anything but sit at their bedside.

When we spoke at the church on our first day there, the tribe leader for the Miskito people stood up in the assembly and said, "I thank you for coming to visit our community. We welcome you, we're honored with your presence and thank you for all of the gifts of clothing you have brought. But I beg you to please tell others in your country that we are dying and need medical help. Our community members are sick and we need medical help. Please bring doctors and nurses to help us, I beg you." We got to see his reason for urgency very quickly. As I walked around the island, I consistently asked myself, *'how do they survive here?'* These people were forgotten. Everyone at every location we visited had the same chilling stare on their face of desperation, sadness, hopelessness and hunger. There was a lack of joy except is some of the children. I handed the kids bracelets I had made for them in my free time back home. They were plastic beads tied with stretchy string from a jewelry making kit. I measured the length on my niece's wrists imagining most kids may be their age. The bracelets fit the kids perfectly and their joy was priceless. I couldn't stop smiling at their excitement to wear them. The women looked overwhelmed like they had worries to last an entire lifetime. They hardly spoke.

It was as though we just stepped into a time machine a hundred years past the current time. Many of the children had terrible skin rashes. A great amount of them had 'worm belly' and it was in one word: devastating. I felt overwhelmed with sorrow for them. The leadership told us prior to arriving that we were not to touch or come in close contact with the Miskito Indians as we had high risk of catching sickness and disease, some of which could be deadly. While attending CFNI, we heard a girl caught a disease on a trip to another country and was in her death bed. It's serious and the school did everything to prepare us and prevent that from happening. We were required to take a test and interview before being allowed to travel as part of a team. After that you had to take the immunity shots required for the country you would travel to.

Traveling around the jungle in a beat-up pickup truck, suddenly we hit something and got a flat tire. If you can imagine it, we were driving over sewage, weeds, tall grass, muddy waters, unable to know what we were driving over at times and then suddenly we found a dirt road. We were on the dirt road and all we could see was jungle all around us. As we waited for the men to figure it out, a young girl about the age of ten emerged from the trees. She was dirty, messy hair, tired eyes, but a beautiful welcoming smile. She was holding a baby comfortably on her arms resting on her hip. This baby had a horrible rash on her face and head. A rash I've never seen on anyone. The baby's hair was incredibly thin, with some patches of her head missing hair. She had 'worm belly', and was crying painfully. It happened so fast. I wasn't thinking. I walked over to them and extended my arms in the unspoken gesture asking may I hold the baby? The girl smiled sheepishly at me and handed her over to me.

I grabbed the baby from her hands and cradled her tight like I did my nieces. The baby stopped crying as I stared at her face and I asked God for her wellness and that her sister would have a happy childhood. I was lost in prayer at the sight of the baby's physical condition. I wanted her to know she would be ok. I wanted her to be healed right then. Everyone around me disappeared, until I felt my team members' fear and shocking stares. I looked up and they all stared at me with wide eyes. No one said anything but everyone was thinking the same thing. Their eyes told me, *'You're not supposed to touch them.'* I smiled back at them with carefree joy as if to say, 'Look guys how cute is this baby!' My thought was honestly how could I not? This was a tiny helpless and sick baby in the arms of a ten year old child emerging from a freaking jungle. Like first of all my thought was, *'What in the world are babies doing emerging out of a jungle like this...'* And secondly, aren't we here telling people God is a healer? Aren't we proclaiming to this nation that Yahweh – the Great I Am - is powerful and He is the God of the impossible? After a few minutes of silence, and stares, one girl from my team stepped forward towards me and asked, "May I hold her too?"

As we proceeded our journey in the jungle, on frequent occasions we saw women and girls of all ages, walking up and down hills within the jungle holding jugs of water. I was amazed to see how such tiny women could carry these large buckets of water up and down the hilly jungle. Many women looked to be in a state of malnutrition and fatigue but somehow pulled all the energy in the world to make that happen.

"How long does it take them to do this until they are done for the day?" I asked James. "Well it takes them all day almost, but it is a very important task. Water is very important for their survival here," he explained. "Seriously…" I said amazed, "And it's not even purified."

"Yes, but their bodies are accustomed to it." he replied.

I want to stop here.

I want to talk to you about water.

CHAPTER 2

Water

Water is one of the most vital substances on Earth and there in Waspan, clean drinking water was not available. Our bodies are made up of 60% water. Babies average about 78% water and a fetus in their mother's womb average 95%! Water keeps us alive and helps with our blood flow. Water helps to purify and detoxify our internal system. Water covers 70% of the world's surface. [1] Wherever there is water on Earth, there is life and without water, we don't exist.

Genesis 1:2 says, *"Now the Earth was formless and empty."* Between Genesis 1:1 and Genesis 1:2, Satan entered the Earth. The scripture continues *"Darkness covered the deep waters and the Spirit of God was hovering over the surface of the waters."* The world was a swampland. Chaotic, without order and void of all good. Satan had just showed up according to scripture and darkness is an implication that God is not present. This is our exact condition without God. Chaos, disorder. Polluted waters.

The scripture explains that the Holy Spirit hovered over the waters. He was working and putting things in order, separating waters from the land and organizing things in their place. Psalm 104:30 describes that the Holy Spirit *"renewed the face of the ground"* and in this same way, when you allow God into your life, this is the first thing you will notice that will happen within you. The chaos that once was, starts falling into order. Without your involvement and your understanding, things within your heart and mind and deep inside your being begin to change and you experience re-order. It looks like a changed mind. A new perspective. More optimism. A desire for good. A state of peace and a reason for hope. Order.

1 John 5:6 describes Jesus as *"This is the one that comes by water and blood."* As I bring up water, I want you to know that detail. Jesus is described as entering into the earth by water and the Holy Spirit is also described with water. There is water in baptism and it demonstrates the purifying power of God over a person being baptized as described in Matthew 3:6. At the cross, Jesus was pierced at the side and blood and water flowed. Blood signifies the payment for sin, and I conclude that water is the purifying power of God through the work of the Holy Spirit. Just as Jesus promised

---

1   Source: USGS.gov, https://www.usgs.gov/special-topics/water-science-school/science/water-you-water-and-human-body

the woman at the well in John 4, *"But whoever drinks the water that I give him will never be thirsty again. But the water that I give him will become in him a spring of water [satisfying his thirst for God] welling up [continually flowing, bubbling within him] to eternal life."* Again in John 7, Jesus continues his talk on water,

> *"He who believes in Me [who adheres to, trusts in, and relies on Me], as the Scripture has said, 'From his innermost being will flow continually rivers of living water.'"*
> *- John 7:38-39 AMP*

Water is clearly understood to be the sanctifying, quenching, comforting and healing work of the Holy Spirit and that the sufficiency is everlasting. This water is never ending and Jesus commands us to *"come and drink"*.

1.8 billion people worldwide drink water that is contaminated with feces.[2] Have you seen those charity commercials on TV asking for donations, with footage of malnourished and sick babies with big bellies and tiny thin arms and legs? Part of this percentage included the people I met in Waspan and I was able to see visually the effects that take place in a person who drinks contaminated water. Their water was contaminated with parasites. Typically, this happens to people in areas of famine, generally with poor sanitation where the parasites enter through the dirty water into their bellies. Parasites consume the vitamins the person needs in order to grow and be healthy. So, they have to eat more to get nutrients and by doing so they feed the worms more. They have to get rid of the parasite to be healthy.

---

[2]   2023. Water, Sanitation, Hygiene 'a Human Right', Crucial for Health, Prosperity Worldwide, Speakers Stress at Conference'S First Interactive Dialogue. United Nations. https://press.un.org/en/2023/envdev2052.doc.htm#

El Rio Coco - Waspan, Nicaragua

WATER

It's the same with many people in or out of the church. They read scripture without the Holy Spirit's involvement. Some merely use their own understanding, with no desire to know God. Some read it to use what they read in efforts to gain a business relationship, in search of profit. Others to merely gain knowledge for the purpose of debating others. Others use knowledge of scripture to support their bad behavior, while others use the same verses to condemn other people. Some to make themselves feel better that they checked a 'good person' box. Still others read it and distort it's message to obtain dominance over other people and manipulate them. It's the same as drinking contaminated water. It's full of parasites.

Parasites because there is an intoxication of the purity and perfection of God's spoken word, which is inspired by the Holy Spirit. Have you sat through a church service and heard a pastor say something like, "If you don't tithe, you will not go to heaven." And then quote a scripture chapter after the statement. That's a parasite. It doesn't sound right to you, but he used a scripture and he is the pastor, so you may believe that it must be true. You just drank contaminated water. Then, you get on YouTube, someone shared a video with a title like, "Will you be part of the remnant?", or "End Times, Only 14,000 People Will Make It to Heaven". They quote a few scriptures in the video to support what they say. You finish watching that one and then another interesting title similar to that one comes up, and another, and another. You keep drinking contaminated water and spiritually, you're getting sick because these ideas even with partial truth cancel out God's truth in your life.

Have you ever seen a really sick person? Like someone who is so sick they don't partake in any activity? Sick people don't do anything. They stay in bed. Little to no activity. They don't move and can't work. They have nothing to show for long periods of time because they are so sick, they can't do anything. That's what a spiritually sick church looks like. The people who attend don't move, they have nothing to show for years of church going. There's no spiritual growth and there is no impact.

Jesus said, *"I offer you living water"*. John 7:37-39 Jesus shouted, *"Anyone who is thirsty may come to me!"* Not your pastor, not your leaders, not your parents, not your teachers. Ultimately the source is Christ. *"Anyone who believes in Me may come and drink! For the scriptures declare, "rivers of living water will flow from his heart and belly."* When Jesus refers to living water, He is talking about God's Holy Spirit who enters your life after you come to God's saving grace through faith in Christ as Savior. Here, we see Jesus speaking prophetically because at this point and time, He had not yet resurrected. You and I are living after Christ's death and resurrection which made it possible for us to drink living water and have a relationship with God through Christ and the Holy Spirit's guidance. Despite clear warnings against false doctrines in scripture, individuals both affiliated and unaffiliated with the church continue to rely on unreliable 'contaminated' sources and hope for good results.

John 4:14, Jesus says to the woman at the well, *"Whoever drinks this water will soon be thirsty again, but whoever drinks the water I give them will never thirst again. Indeed the water I give them will become in them a spring of water welling up to eternal life."* The Holy Spirit plays so many important roles and He is so overlooked in the church. The Bible describes His role as our counselor, comforter, teacher, our guide towards the truth. He is key to understanding and interpreting scripture and the result is that our soul and spirit are completely satisfied.

There's a big problem with constantly drinking contaminated water. It's deadly. People get Guinea Worm. If an already infected person with an open Guinea Worm wound enters a pond or well used for drinking water, they will spread that parasite to the water and continue the contamination and infection into a community.[3] There are people who spent years accepting messed up theology, with open wounds, entering in the church and spreading the contamination to others. Many are pastors and leaders. Maybe some were hurt in or out of the church. Many have a vague understanding of God because they don't read the Bible. Whatever wounds they carry, along with a false understanding of God or no understanding at all, it's inevitable that people surrounding them would be affected too.

There are people everywhere just spreading contamination and it looks really good on the outside. The worship sounds great, the service production looks amazing – but there is no solid teaching of scripture, no life transformation happening in the lives of people who attend the church. It looks unhealthy. Years pass and it looks the same. Stagnant. That's the first problem, but the second problem is that they want to function with an open wound which will contaminate others. This could be an attendee, a visitor, a member, a leader or a pastor. Preachers and teachers are responsible to deliver the complete, pure and perfect word of God to others but could be practicing out of open wounds that influence them to deliver half-truths to the church body.

Jesus said, *"Woe to you, teachers of the law and Pharisees, you hypocrites! You clean the outside of the cup and dish, but inside they are full of greed and self-indulgence. Blind Pharisee! First clean the inside of the cup and dish, and then the outside also will be clean. Woe to you, Pharisees!"* Jesus was saying here, listen, address how sick you are inside. You preach from a wrong motive because you're not right within. You're looking at the word and misinterpreting it, adding your own message to it and contaminating everyone who hears you! The Pharisees were looking at Jesus, the Living Water, the entire time and still remained completely unphased. Jesus further addressed them and their

---

3   2024. About Guinea Worm. U.S. Centers for Disease Control and Prevention. https://www.cdc.gov/guinea-worm/about/index.html.

Miskito people - Waspan, Nicaragua

behavior, describing how they looked so religious on the exterior but were spiritually dead inside. Matthew 23:27-28, Jesus exclaimed, *"Woe to you, teachers of the law and Pharisees, you hypocrites! You are like whitewashed tombs, which look beautiful on the outside but on the inside are full of the bones of the dead and everything unclean."*

    There's not only the deadly effect of contaminated water, but Parasitical Disease. Parasitical Disease can be spread when people swim in or have contact with contaminated waters. Some people live believing their environment will not have an effect on them. It's deception. Some think they are stronger and just being around contaminated things and exposing themselves but not consuming will keep them safe. You're already open to accepting things because your mind is so receptive to whatever the environment is presenting to you. It's just inevitable, and in a matter of time you'll look back and wonder – how did I end up here?

    The Samaritan woman in John 4 had a good question. After Jesus commanded the woman to in essence, serve God, saying in John 4:7, *"Give Me a drink"*, she replied with a question. Like many of us, her initial response in behavior is to question God. Her first question was related to her identity, and pointing out how unqualified and unworthy she was. *"You are a Jew and I am a Samaritan woman. How can you ask me for a drink?"* (John 4:9). She was saying, 'I can't serve you because I'm not worthy of serving you. I'm not even a Jew, I'm not good enough for you to even talk to me.' Many people are left with the same belief today– *they are not good enough.*

    Her next question comes after Jesus expressed she doesn't know who He is and if she knew, she would ask for living water. She asked in verse 11, *"You have nothing to draw with and the well is deep. Where can you get this living water? Are you greater than our father Jacob, who gave us the well and drank from it himself, as did also his sons and his livestock?"* This is her explaining that she doesn't even know the scripture. She lacks an understanding of the true nature of God, unaware of His character, His expectations, and even the appropriate ways to worship Him. She had only partial understanding based on what other people had told her. Contaminated water. The parasitical water she drank was served to her by her ancestorial lineage.

Like the Miskito tribe, they spent hours a day carrying and drinking contaminated water because that is all they have ever had and that's all they know. Jesus then continued to show her what the truth was. He said, *"Whoever drinks of this water will never thirst again...the water I give will become a fountain of water springing up to eternal life."* Right there at that moment she got it! Her spiritual eyes were opened and her response was *"Sir, give me this water!"* Because she was thirsty and her lifestyle was evidence of it. He quickly addressed her problem. John 4:16 says that He told her, *"Go, call your husband and come back." "I have no husband," she replied. Jesus said to her, "You are right when you say you have no husband. The fact is, you have had five husbands, and the man you now have is not your husband. What you have just said is quite true."*

As a recap, first she had the issue of living with partial truth of God. Secondly, this affected her lifestyle which Jesus made it a point to address. As I previously mentioned, the Holy Spirit works to bring our chaos into order. He cleans us up! It takes time but some of the work needing to be done inside us came from years and generations of messed up family members. He addressed her condition – but not in a critical and condemning way. He offered it as an ailment, revealing He was the source.

I really want you to notice something. After Jesus addressed that she had no husband, her response was not shame! Her response was to clear up another lie she had always believed! Isn't that amazing!? She wasn't trying to explain herself or clean herself up once she faced Jesus. She was interested in knowing the truth about God. She said in verse 20, *"Our ancestors worshiped on this mountain, but you Jews claim that the place where we must worship is in Jerusalem."* Jesus filtered her water and responded, in verse 21,

> *"Jesus said to her, "Woman, believe Me, the hour is coming when you will neither on this mountain, nor in Jerusalem, worship the Father. You worship what you do not know; we know what we worship, for salvation is of the Jews. But the hour is coming, and now is, when the true worshipers will worship the Father in spirit and truth; for the Father is seeking such to worship Him. God is Spirit, and those who worship Him must worship in spirit and truth." - John 4:21 - 24 NKJV*

You cannot worship a God you do not know.

It's important for you to be aware of this critical step. Many rely on a general revelation of God, that is, knowing of God based on what others have told them or what they heard from someone standing on a pulpit in a church. The critical step we can't skip is that we must have a personal revelation of God within our spirit. Many people struggle in and out of churches because of this missed step. A general understanding of God leads people to stay away from a church or truly committing to the faith until they clean up their lives. You can't clean up your life from the outside. The cleaning up part *is not done by you*, it is done by the Holy Spirit of God inside you. The starting point to know God is found in complete truth of who God is as the Bible explains.

Maybe you have been drinking from contaminated sources, so your image of God is all messed up. The Bible itself can be confusing when you first start to read it. The Holy Spirit's job is to help us understand the scripture. That's where you have to begin, drinking clean water. You have to start pursuing God with acceptance of His word in it's purest and clearest truth, not contaminated. You can't mix in practices of pagan religions, or mix in your desire for what you wished it to say.

The good news is the truth of Gods' word is readily available to us now more than ever.

The best part is you can start today.

CHAPTER 3

Malnourished

June 1, 2006 I awoke completely unprepared for what I was about to experience. We were headed to go to our next assignment and visit a community they called the "Dump Community". The woman in charge as our guide jumped in our van and prepared to review the plan. "Okay, you are about to meet and serve the Dump Community. All the supplies are packed and on the way. We have a church group who will be joining us today. This group has worked with us in this ministry before." She was very organized and mission minded. She was a sweet white lady who wore no make-up, with a worn out t-shirt and comfortable running sneakers. Her presentation was that of someone who was completely dedicated to the work of the ministry. I could tell service was important to her. She sat on the front passenger seat of the van, as the driver began to drive, she turned to look at us and explained, "We are going to then serve them a plate of beans and rice…and," I interrupted her to say, "Just beans and rice? I'm sure we can buy them some meat too. Can we stop by the store on the way there and pick it up?" She replied, "Nope, that is more than enough, trust me." and she finished reviewing our schedule. We continued towards a dirt road that led to an entrance of a landfill. There were kids who greeted us at the entrance, and as we drove in, I saw mounds of trash, piles and mounds of trash, it was endless. Among all the mounds were tiny homes put together by trash, large pieces of aluminum and other different discarded materials like plastic and cardboard. I had never seen anything like it, even in the poorest areas of Dallas. There was fog from the smoke and dust in the landfill, so much debris and piles of burning trash in certain places. Kids ran around barefoot, everyone's clothes were dirty and people looked like they had never showered. They had no access to really anything.

We arrived to the spot in the landfill where we would set up. We helped the team prepare to serve food and set up chairs and tables. The church group began to deliver a short message of encouragement and salvation to the community members who would join us. The chairs were placed in a circle and a guy set up a portable speaker to hook up a microphone and his guitar. Mostly women and kids attended. The amount of kids was incredible. I was just at a complete loss for words at the reality that tiny babies lived there, and mothers, with so many kids. I saw a thin teenage girl

47

holding her first baby, and in my eyes she was a child herself. As we settled down and everyone was in their seats or huddled around, the local church group started their presentation with signing songs and giving a devotional. I tuned out to the presentation completely, consumed in thought about how much help they needed and how our efforts seemed...insignificant. Don't get me wrong, I know that sharing the message of salvation and hope in Christ has immeasurable value. What I mean is – they had no homes, no access to food or running water, and I felt overwhelmed that we were there giving a presentation, handing out a meal and toys then leaving and they were left to live another day in a landfill. Kids and tiny babies would stay here. I wanted to pack them all up and house them somewhere. The dangers they must face just living out there. I couldn't believe it was real.

    After the presentation we served each person a plate of rice, beans and pasta with bread. Our mission teams were handed the shoeboxes filled with gifts and toiletries. Pure joy filled the faces of each child as they opened their gifts. I wished I could give them the world. Then, I noticed this girl. She had a tank top that used to be white with a tribal design on it and stained as much as a car mechanic's shirt. She wore blue swim shorts that fit loosely and fell below her belly button. Her hair was messy but pulled back and parted at the center with half of it tucked to the side.

The Landfill Community - Nicaragua

Like everyone else, her skin was dark from all the dirt. She didn't necessarily stand out from anyone else really, but I could not lose sight of her. She had a certain look on her face, something in her eyes like I had never seen before in anyone. Despair. Hunger. Malnourishment. She was lacking everything. Existing but not living. Nothing to look forward to. Basic needs unmet. Sick. Impoverished…needing all the help in the world and forcing on a smile for all these strangers who traveled to serve her community. Suddenly, I saw her throw up everything she had just eaten. I ran to her along with our guide and a couple other people. "We need water! Give her water!" someone yelled franticly as others rushed for napkins to help her clean up. "Oh my God, what happened is she ok?" I asked our tour guide. "Yes she will be fine." She said. "Does she suffer from a sickness?" I asked her. "No, it's just a lot of them are not used to eating actual food. They typically eat whatever they can find. Her stomach could not handle eating even rice and beans. It was too much for her and she couldn't keep it down." I stared at her as she explained this to me and realized she was not in any way shaken by it. She's seen this happen before countless times and she can handle it without falling apart. Just another day in ministry. You could see the shock in other people, the worry and concern, and many stood speechless as they observed everyone in the community – but not her. Once we saw the girl was ok, she moved on fast to get everyone else fed and taken care of. She checked on each team member volunteer to make sure someone had something to do. I write this in tears as I remember her. She's a woman whose name I can't even remember but who made a remarkable impression in my life. Someone I can say I truly admired.

Fast forward to a few years later. I was a young professional in Marketing working at a big insurance company. The profile of this company was impressive, yet most of my co-workers *hated* their jobs, with the exception of a few top producers. I was a new hire and the way they spoke negatively about the company to each other made me so nervous about the decision I made to take the job. They complained about leadership, particularly my boss, who was the regional manager. My co-workers described the company and the culture like they were in a prison they voluntarily stepped into every day. '*Crap*', I thought, '*What did I get myself into? Why are these people so miserable? Clearly they know something I don't.*' I decided to focus on exceling in my work and taking it a day at a time.

One day I stepped into a meeting with a Producer co-worker. The office secretary warned me to be careful around him because he was "inappropriate" with women. I don't go by what people say about other people especially when it's negative. Who knows what their history was and I overheard the secretary gossip to others before. But so far, she seemed to be right about this guy. He always stared at me like he was hungry. In

Mexico, we call this *'hechandose un taco de ojo'*. It won't make sense as a literal translation – but something like 'His eyes are eating a taco'. I stepped in and stood at the door. "Hey there, what's up." I began…as I stood in his office with my project notepad and pen.

He began to explain how he wanted me to get him new business through an aggressive marketing campaign. "I need more clients, but I want this to be an aggressive alert." As he described the specifics, I saw something I'd never seen in anyone's face before. "We're going to instill fear in them!" he demanded, "Write it in a way that they will know it's urgent and they need to be afraid of a breach!" Like a pig who hadn't fed for days and was aggressively going after leftover slop. "Say whatever you have to say in there, *but make them feel it,*" he clenched his teeth and tightened his fist – "If they don't call me right now they're going to lose everything!" His eyes were ravenously hungry. "And email it to every client in the system, I don't care if they're assigned to anyone else," He wasn't looking at me anymore, but he was looking at something though. He was looking past me at invisible dollar signs. He didn't care who he had to run over to make it happen, even if it meant running off with his colleague's clients. He asked me to include them, and he could convince them to transfer over to him as their account rep. He was money hungry.

As he continued to rant, I heard a silent pitch in my head that silenced his voice completely. Suddenly, and very clearly, I heard God tell me, "Remember that girl in Nicaragua?" and a flash of her image shot through my mind. "Remember how you saw her?" And the memory returned as if she stood before me again, the chilling stare on her face, the forced smile, the torn clothes and then…the vomit. I heard God explain, "That's exactly how I see him. He's malnourished."

I froze completely. I saw it. This guy was already incredibly well off financially, to the point he could show up to the office and play golf all day without a complaint from the regional manager - yet he was desperate he needed more, and more and when he got more, *it still wouldn't be enough.* It wouldn't satisfy his hunger. Despite what I physically saw as wealthy, I understood God saw who he really was – an impoverished, malnourished man who lived in a dump yard spiritually and had no access to real food. Spiritually malnourished and impoverished. One day closer to death, surviving on scraps, nobody can outwardly see – but God sees it every time He looks at him.

God felt for him the way I felt for the girl in the landfill.

I wished I could move heaven and earth to provide her needs. I wished I could get her to health again and somehow I could give her a home. I desperately wanted to rescue her and was completely torn inside just observing her physical condition along with everyone else in her community. I'm confident God feels worse, on another level we as human beings could never understand, for those who are spiritually malnourished. I finally understood why Jesus made it a point and pursued the tax collector, the prostitute, the work-a-holic fishermen, the adulterous woman caught in sin and thrown at his feet, etc. He didn't come for the healthy, Christ came for the sick, and if we are honest, none of us are well without Him.

The girl from the landfill community. - Managua, Nicaragua

This is the heart of God. *Everyone.*

It's something religious people do not understand. They don't understand the heart of God for the world around them. They'll look past their bank teller, the guy who does their taxes, their co-workers or the waiter at the restaurant. They notice a stripper, a felon, a drug dealer, or a guy who shows up to a bar, and make it a point to stay away from them and look the other way. Some see the way a woman dresses, or how she wears her make up, or at a man's short comings and look down on them. Even the smallest difference from themselves, anything that doesn't fit their perception of 'good' or 'Godly', it doesn't even have to be much. In Dallas, you can go to a middle-class church and observe how they look down on others who are not on the same tax bracket. Some churches go as far as requiring women to only wear skirts and not wear makeup – all for acceptance. Not only are the men in those churches conditioned to judge women in and out of their church based on those requirements, but it conditions the women from their congregations to judge other women outside of their church and feel superior. It's baseless. It's basic nature for a religious person to determine a woman is unworthy or does not belong based on the outfit she wore to church. Many are judged very quickly and are not pursued by the members of these church ministries whose mission is to reach the lost.

At the same time, many can look at a pastor and their family, a missionary family, prestigious leaders in our communities, and think highly of them, but they could be living like hell privately. I came to a new realization of how God sees people. It's easy to see a poor orphan and have compassion and move heaven and earth to supply their needs. It's clear to everyone – religious or not – to rally together and fundraise for a community who suffered loss after a natural disaster like a tornado or a hurricane. Everyone understands the desperate need of those people. But it takes the power of the Holy Spirit living inside you, it takes the love of God poured over you, to see a money-hungry wealthy executive and desire to move heaven and earth to get him to meet God in relationship. Like how Christ must have seen Matthew, the tax collector. I couldn't look at this co-worker, or anyone, the same way after that moment. The lady at work who gossiped and ran over co-workers, or the pastor leading who mistreated and manipulated the members. I was more cognizant of God's frustration with the Pharisees.

Knowing the scriptures, and being responsible to teach Biblical law – the Pharisees had no excuse as to why they were imposing religious rules on people that were empty, and look down at those who would not or could not comply to their rules, all the while leaving people spiritually malnourished. They neglected to teach the things that mattered to God. This was John the Baptist's cry, *"Prepare the way!"* as in preparing people spiritually to receive the 'manna from heaven', that is the spiritual nourishment that would come to all of us through Christ our Savior.

"Man shall not eat by bread alone, but by every word that comes out of the mouth of God," Jesus emphasized in Matthew 4. How long can you go without eating? Not long, right? Because when you have skipped a meal or two you started to see the effects and impact on your body. You lose focus. You're weak. You're not yourself. Imagine that impact on your spirit. If the word of God is food for your spirit – what's the condition of your spirit going so many days, months, years, without consuming the word of God. I don't mean knowing a few Bible verses, or hearing a few on Sundays at a service. That's like when someone offers you a bite and you don't really want to eat it but are like, meh ok I'll taste it. I mean *consuming* His word by taking the time to read, learn, understand, study and apply it.

I think it's amazing that of all the things Jesus could have done after conquering death and the grave, He appeared to the disciples at the sea of Galilee and shared a meal with them.

"Jesus said to them, "Come and have breakfast." None of the disciples dared to ask Him, "Who are You?" They knew [without any doubt] that it was the Lord. Jesus came and took the bread and gave it to them, and likewise the fish. This was now the third time that Jesus appeared to the disciples, after He had risen from the dead." – John 21:12-14 AMP

Of all the things Jesus could have done; He shared *a meal*. Two things are definitely true here. First, that Jesus in His essence seeks relationship with us. Second, that food is spiritually just as important as it is in the natural. Critically important. Jesus was getting ready to connect the importance of these two things. After they finished eating, Jesus asked an urgent question to Peter – the disciple who had previously denied Jesus three times. The question to Peter was, *"Peter – do you love Me?"* We know it's urgent because Jesus asks this same question to Peter back to back, three times. The scripture leads to the instructions Peter must follow in response to his love. John 21:17 says,

> *"Peter was grieved that He asked him the third time, "Do you [really] love Me [with a deep, personal affection, as for a close friend]?" And he said to Him, "Lord, You know everything; You know that I love You [with a deep, personal affection, as for a close friend]." Jesus said to him, "Feed My sheep."*
> *- John 21:17 AMP*

Jesus was addressing the spiritual. Jesus revealed the evidence of our love for Him by saying, *'feed spiritually those who I died to save'*. Peter didn't ask things like, *"What do you mean? What food? Who are these people? How do I feed them, how often, and for how long?"* Peter also didn't ask, *"Does it have to be everyone? Can it just be the people I like and get along with? Can you give me a pass on my enemies?"* If you're a believer, you have this same responsibility.

Picture the girl I described in Nicaragua again. What if we showed up to her village and asked her to feed the entire community? That is incredibly ridiculous, right? We wouldn't consider placing that expectation on her because it is completely unreasonable and illogical. She's starving herself. She has no food to share, and no resources to produce or buy food whatsoever. How can you feed someone when you're impoverished yourself? It's impossible. That's exactly what is going on in many churches around the world today. The community is not being fed, and it's a ridiculous expectation to ask them to reach their community when they are missing *"every word that comes from mouth of God"*. In the same way, it's incredibly unreasonable to place high expectations of ethical and moral value on a generation who was never taught even how to consume *"every word that comes from the mouth of God."*

Food is important to survive and in America, we know how to eat. Take time to answer these very important questions for yourself.

Are you spiritually malnourished?

Are you living the life of 'it's never enough'?

You would know. When your spirit is deprived, your soul, mind, will and emotions - begin to die.

I'll have the steak, please.
A NARRATIVE

I love steak. It's nice when you go to a restaurant and are served. But more often, you must serve yourself.

Sometimes you're eating with company, but other times you're alone. Sometimes it's easy to cut with a fork, and easy to consume. Juicy and flavorful, it goes down easy - mmm!

But sometimes it's tough, hard to cut, hard to chew, hard to swallow. You ask, "Can I get some sauce on this?" You have to add something to help you feel better about consuming it.

Then other times, it's so hard to consume, you give up and set it aside.

These moments, most people reach for a side, a small portion of some side dish to get them through the hunger pains. Others reach for dessert, because forget nutrition, they will settle for a quick sugar high as if they had a satisfied meal.

Either way – no one swallows a steak whole. If you're too confident, you can choke and regurgitate it. Once you spit it back up, it didn't stay in your body to offer any nutrition or benefit. If someone asked you what you ate, you can't honestly say,

"I had steak for dinner."

When people choke on steak, the first thing most will desperately reach for is water.

Yesterday I choked on steak. I was paralyzed.

I couldn't breathe.

He walked up to me as I struggled.

He gave me a drink of water.

I apologized. "I'm sorry," I blurted out. I was a complete mess, as I attempted to take in some air, "I eat steak all the time, I was so confident, and sure that - "

"You're ok." He interrupted.

"See…" and He began to pick up the cutlery to demonstrate how to properly cut a steak.

As if I never learned to begin with.

"This is how you consume steak. You take one piece at a time, and chew on it. Take your time."

Devour the Word.

Author's Note:

This short narrative is about reading scripture. Different places in the Bible describe that we should consume the word of God. In this story, the steak is Biblical Scripture. It continues with the different scenarios. Some Bible scriptures is easy to understand, accept and receive. The verses make you so happy and satisfy your soul.

But other scriptures are hard to understand, accept or even believe. The message is too strong for you to take in. Looking for sauce, is when you try to mix in other religious practices that are easier to accept, or seeking other people's opinions that make you feel better about the topic to try and accept the hard message. You can't accept it by itself, you have to find other sources to accept what the truth of the Bible has said.

I'LL HAVE THE STEAK, PLEASE.

Water represents the Holy Spirit.

The Bible is clear that the Holy Spirit helps us to receive God's word in our spirit where we can easily understand and 'consume' it. The Holy Spirit helps us accept it when we, in our natural capacity, cannot accept it, struggle to believe it or fight to accept it.

When you regurgitate it, this is describing when you hear scripture and understand it, but you really do not want to apply it to your life.

You refuse to apply it, so it's the same as you never consumed the word to begin with.

And if someone asked you, you couldn't honestly say you believe what the Bible says. You can't say you accepted it in your life.

By the very act of refusing to put it to practice you're telling God,

"I don't agree with You."

Your spirit was not nourished.

You didn't have steak.

Dominican Republic & Puerto Rico

CHAPTER 4

Pa'lante

Dominican coffee is STRONG. I mean strong – just like the people. Dominicans are fighters and survivors, in pursuit of the good life. You can see it in their eyes, rising to each day with rich optimism despite the greatest of life's obstacles going against them. You can hear it when they sing doing basic tasks, and the passion in their tone. You feel the joy that exerts when they dance bachata and merengue music. They dance freely like no one is watching, without limitations, and without a care in the world. One thing I loved instantly - they have coffee all day, every day. I absolutely *loved* that. The moment you walk into someone's house, you become family. They spoke to us as if they saw us grow up. They greeted us with joy and a tone of endearment as though we had known each other our entire lives. Open arms, lots of smiles, confident loud voices, laughter, joy and as I turned someone was walking up to me with a platter full of small espresso shots and offered me the most delicious dark, rich coffee. Then they'd reach over my tiny cup with what looked like a small two inch rock in their hand and a tiny cheese grater, and grated "pimiento" (pepper) into my shot of espresso. I thought it odd to put pepper in coffee and it was not something I expected, but it was so delicious. The pimiento gave it a special flavor like I'd never had before – and I drink a lot of coffee. They drink it with or without milk and the locals drink it straight with no sugar or cream.

When we arrived to the Dominican it made me think maybe that was what Cuba might look like, based on what I had seen in movies, except the cars were newer models. It was very tropical with large palm trees. Cool Cuban style hats and shirts were worn by many of the local men. The flowers were bright and beautiful with hydrangeas of all colors in many places. I admired how beautiful the foliage was wherever we went. This trip was very organized. A woman greeted us after we landed. She moved at a fast pace, made a call, checked on her team, greeted us with a genuine smile and asked how our travel went. She was a woman on a mission. "Llevate a este grupo en la wawa", she said to one guy and it looked like she had a thousand things flying across her mind at once. Fast-paced, she was giving orders to men and they did everything she asked. "Soy la pastora," she said to us. In translation she said she was the pastor of the church we were going to serve in. Her husband was also referred to as pastor, but we perceived she drove the ministry forward. She was a no-nonsense type of businesswoman, always on the move and passionate about sharing Christ with everyone who would listen to her. She was a woman of character and the type that did not care what anyone thought about her. She was herself no matter who was watching. This woman was completely opposite of what I had observed from most pastoral wives. Often, pastor's wives seemed like they were restrained and were their husband's shadow. They maybe led the prayer ministry or played the piano. You know with a meek-like character where they didn't say much and presented themselves as though they were living perfect lives. Not this woman. She had been through some things and wanted to tell the whole world Christ saved her soul with a demand, "Join me! See how God will do it for you too!" I admired her tenacity.

We jumped in the wawa, what they call pick-up trucks, and traveled to the town of Higüey. That was where we would be working and where the local church was located. The pastors owned a villa nearby and that was where we lodged. It was a mansion like villa with a winding road that led to the main entrance. The road was surrounded by a lush but unkept garden. As we pulled up we saw a large outdoor covered patio on the lower level of the two-story Colonial style villa. All the rooms were to be shared. The women were split into two groups and lodged in separate rooms. The guys and lodged separately, of course. There was a small store down the street that looked like a tiny shack. I believe it was part of someone's house, similar to some homes in Mexico where they open the street facing room of the home to sell things. There were palm trees everywhere and the tiny road that led there was almost hidden. It was savagely beautiful and reminded me of the island of Waspan in that it was as though we had traveled years back. The jungle was pitch dark at night with palms looming over our heads in what seemed several feet taller than during the daytime.

On our first night, we were each to go out to one of the local church leader's homes for Bible Study. We were tasked to go in groups of two, and one of us was to lead the teaching. I was paired with and older woman, Clara, maybe about 50-ish. She was a very sweet and meek woman who mostly (and wisely) listened and smiled at everyone. I led the message in the home group that night and was amazed at the church community. They all appeared to love God *passionately*. I had not seen anything like it before. I really have to go into a detailed description here because I really want to communicate what a tight community of believers they were. They worshipped God deeply, with a reverence. Many had recent stories of what God had done, and not just a few people, but several. The church members were self-motivated. No one had to cheerlead them on. The pastor was not a charismatic person which they idolized. There was a reality of heaven and hell preached and a mutual urgency among everyone to bring as many peo-

Dominican locals giving a special presentation. - Higüey, Dominican Republic

Church construction with a local Haitian.

Me, preaching on Mother's Day.

ple into the faith because of their personal testimonies. They were so aware of the urgency to have a relationship with God. They expressed in prayer the importance of not depending on self or others but to truly live trusting in God for everything. Even the youth were self-driven. They were like their own separate church where they would call each other up through the week and organize evangelism on their own. They were not afraid to share the Gospel with anyone and did it freely on their own time, without a youth pastor to direct them. While there, I don't remember finding out who the youth pastor was. Teenagers of all ages could share scripture and pray for others without being told. The pastors didn't act like they were perfect and didn't expect perfection of the members. They wanted authenticity. The pastors also didn't give members orders to volunteer, serve, evangelize, or give money while they kicked back in the comfort of their privileged leadership roles. Pastors and leaders were out there doing the hard work and sweating like everyone else alongside the members. The pastor's wife didn't care what she looked like. She showed up to do ministry in shorts and a muscle shirt. Her running shoes were always dirty.

Another night at a Bible Study, as people prayed, you could tell that they all independently had a personal prayer life. They had been through some storms and survived. They each could pray for others freely on the spot and knew scripture. We weren't in a church, we were in someone's home. I had never been to a gathering, even in a church, where everyone collectively prayed with such confidence. Usually it's a handful of people in a church that can pray, you know like 5% have a solid prayer life and expresses a confidence with desire to pray for others. The house was packed tight and there was nothing comfortable about it! It was sauna room hot in there with no AC. There was no food being served, no spread on the kitchen counters or dining table, considering everyone's allergies. Everyone was there with just their Bibles and ready to hear whatever message God wanted to share with them through whoever was teaching. The desire to be there in that type of setting had to come from personal relationship with God and the fact it was so many people that packed out this house amazed me. No one was watching the time and as we took off there were still people who stayed to keep praying for one another. I saw it all and was at a complete shock. Because how do these people keep going with such passion, excitement and fervor as they suffer through so much?

Pa'lante. This is a word Dominicans live by. It means at any cost, regardless of what has happened to you or has not happened for you,

Bible study. - Higüey, Dominican Republic   *Church service. - Higüey, D.R.*

Dominican art for sale by local artists. - Santo Domingo, Dominican Republic

regardless of your current circumstance, or regardless of whatever you are currently facing right now - you have to press on, move forward and give life all you can. This word destroys any victim mentality from taking root in your mind. They say it to each other all the time. "Pa'lante, pa'lante, vamo pa'lante" and they say it with a smile. Nobody gets a pass here on crying about their misfortune.

One thing I notice about each country I've been to is that even though people don't know each other, the territory carries the same kind of vibe. Whatever the culture has accepted just passes on to the next generation and the next, and the next, and it naturally becomes the voice of the country. Here I see a lot of people who survived a lot of deep pain, and the excitement that they made it out. They see hope ahead consistently without any reassurance of a good result. The Christians had assurance in God, but even the Dominicans who didn't believe in God still had confidence everything would work itself out. Then, other people were stuck in dark places, as if they had mental chains. Not literal physical chains, but I observed they dealt with a private pain within, a heaviness, as if they were imprisoned to thoughts. We went to a hospital where we prayed for patients in their patient rooms. I spoke to people in waiting rooms as their sick loved ones were cared for and I saw them burdened. We went to Iberia, a grocery store to pass out flyers for an outreach event and even in some people who looked outwardly as though they were missing nothing – you could see it. A war going on within each person.

Have you ever spoken to someone who has been through something incredibly difficult? Someone who went through a painful life experience that left them in a completely broken state? Try to tell them to keep going and move forward. It's borderline offensive to some. You may get a response like, "Who do you think you are? You don't know what it's like. You don't know what I've been through." But even if you can't understand, you can see that inward fight they are going through is dark. Although you may not have experienced some intensely painful life experience, the truth is that we are not all much different. Go all the way back with me to Genesis chapter 3. This is where the conflict started: in Eve's mind. Contemplating a thought, deciding it was true, coming into agreement with it and then she proceeded to take action on it.

One thought.

*"Now the serpent was more crafty (subtle, skilled in deceit)
than any living creature of the field which the Lord God had*

made.

And the serpent (Satan) said to the woman, "Can it really be that God has said, 'You shall not eat from any tree of the garden'?" And the woman said to the serpent, "We may eat fruit from the trees of the garden, except the fruit from the tree which is in the middle of the garden. God said, 'You shall not eat from it nor touch it, otherwise you will die.'"

But the serpent said to the woman, "You certainly will not die! For God knows that on the day you eat from it your eyes will be opened [that is, you will have greater awareness], and you will be like God, knowing [the difference between] good and evil." And when the woman saw that the tree was good for food, and that it was delightful to look at, and a tree to be desired in order to make one wise and insightful, she took some of its fruit and ate it; and she also gave some to her husband with her, and he ate.

Then the eyes of the two of them were opened [that is, their awareness increased], and they knew that they were naked; and they fastened fig leaves together and made themselves coverings.
– Genesis 3:1-7 AMP

Who would ever say that one thought is a weapon that can be used by you – not someone else, *you* - to destroy not only yourself but others around you? That's exactly what happened in the book of Genesis the moment Eve took action on just one thought. It's the same thing that happens with each one of us. How many thoughts, whether you experienced trauma or not, do you contemplate daily? It's difficult to put a number on them because there are so many. The main detail to focus on about Eve's one thought was that the thought that destroyed her was a lie. Satan knew he was lying. Wanting to be like God himself, he was living out the miserable consequence of acting out on his own toxic thought, *"to be like God"*. By the time he dropped the thought before Eve, he had severed his relationship with God and was cast out of Heaven. Satan knew the thought *"to be like God"* was *impossible*, he was struck out of Heaven for it himself.

Also, consider this. Eve had no past trauma. She was living in paradise. She was missing absolutely nothing. *"You will be like God, knowing the difference between good and evil."* was completely unnecessary in her current environment. Still, she believed the thought in her mind first, the unseen, and then saw with her eyes the tree. The fruit was there before the thought came into her mind, but she never saw that it was good until after she accepted the lie.

Sometimes we see outward behavior and address that outward behavior when the real problem is not in what we can see. The reason she didn't eat it before is not to be credited to self-discipline. It's credited to an opposing thought. She thought differently before. We live as though our thought-life doesn't matter. We consume all day long on electronic devices as though none of the messages will have an impact on who we become. We listen to people who gossip and lie about others thinking it will not affect us in any way. No one can see what we keep in our thought life, but our lives reveal what we allowed ourselves to mediate on. No one can see the thoughts we choose to accept, yet eventually all will see them expressed through our behavior. If anyone is convinced that their thought life doesn't affect them or others around them, they are self-deceived.

One thought changed Eve's identity just as one thought changes yours today. *One thought* led to broken relationships with God and others, just as your thoughts could be the cause for broken relationships in your own life today. One thought can keep you separated from God today just as one thought separated her from God. Genesis 3 describes the destructive weapon of one thought and the entirety of scripture reveals to us that today we all are facing an unseen war.

> *"For though we walk in the flesh [as mortal men], we are not carrying on our [spiritual] warfare according to the flesh and using the weapons of man. The weapons of our warfare are not physical [weapons of flesh and blood]. Our weapons are divinely powerful for the destruction of fortresses. We are destroying sophisticated arguments and every exalted and proud thing that sets itself up against the [true] knowledge of God, and we are taking every thought and purpose captive to the obedience of Christ..."*
> *– 2 Corinthians 10:3-5 AMP*

Based on scripture, we are continuously warned about an unseen war that does not involve physical weapons which are being used against you. Focus on what the scripture says in 2nd Corinthians 10:3-5, and you can see that the weapons we are to destroy are *"arguments"* and *"lofty opinions raised against the knowledge of God."* In other words, *thoughts*. Those are the weapons coming against you.

Here's an example. You grew up hearing conflict with your parents.

You hated it. Although you couldn't in your young mind understand it all completely, you knew it was not supposed to be that way. As you grew up, thoughts came in and out of your mind consistently as your child mind attempted to resolve what you were experiencing. One of the thoughts you kept hearing was, *'It must be my fault'* and another may have been, *'I'm the problem'*. Then you said with your mouth one day, "It's my fault," aloud. Then, all of a sudden you start behaving like a problem. Now you're an adult, and as an adult, you're stuck living a life based on those thoughts. This guy shared with me this was his life experience and he grew up believing it was his fault his parents hated each other. He wasn't the reason at all of course, their problems were completely beyond him, but he decided to accept that he was the problem and lived by it. He was short-tempered and conflict would follow him. Instead of rejecting it as a lie, he agreed with it. That thought is a weapon constantly working against him in his life to cause chaos, destruction and disorder. That belief attracted people towards him who agreed with his belief too. As hard as we try, we cannot hide in our behavior what we truly believe in our minds. In the same way, Eve couldn't help but act on the thought. In the same way, we move on thoughts we are convinced of. Look around you. Your life today is a result of every thought you have accepted.

Imagine this for a moment. You're standing with me at the massive front porch of this Dominican villa. You look around and all you see is jungle. While this jungle looks beautiful, you begin to recognize that it has been forgotten. You know, forgotten as in unkept. No one has been around to keep up maintenance on the landscaping or any of the plants. Vines grew uncontrollably over time, choking the plants in it's path. It's for the most part, naturally wild. I walk you further down the paved path to show you that some of these beautiful plants were intentionally planted. There is evidence of a unique array of hydrangeas, together with the unintentional weeds, overgrown grass and other plants that sprouted in the most random places. Some plants, no one knows how they got there because they were dropped randomly by birds, they sprouted and took root.

Years passed and it grew savagely out of control, all growing together with what was once intentionally planted. Because the owner of the home did not take care of it over several years, this is the result. The same is true for our minds. We must take intentional care of the thoughts or "seeds" dropped into our minds to make sure that they don't take root in our hearts. As soon as an opposing thought is introduced, if we do not maintain our thought life, they will grow like vines over several years choking everything in it's path, causing damage and destroying us completely. One major difference between this jungle and the paradise Eve lived in was that her environment had order. Everything in her paradise was intentional-

The jungle. - Higüey, Dominican Republic

ly there and maintained. God walked with her and Adam daily. The environment had upkeep.

Ask yourself today what is it that you believe and take time to identify the areas in your life where you experience consistent conflict. Write them down in a journal. Ask God to point everything out to you directly and He will show you the source of where those beliefs came from. Now the people or experiences which deposited those thoughts may be important, but *not as important as what you did with that thought in your mind.* That part was, and is currently, your responsibility. Ultimately, no one went into your thought life and forced you to accept it. The great news is that you have complete control of maintaining your thought life today.

Pa'lante.

The beauty of the word is that there is hope ahead and you can get up and keep going. Despite any circumstance, experience or setback, there is a way out of the chaos. Peace is attainable. Isaiah 26:3 shows us how to obtain constant peace, and it is a collaborative work accomplished and completed in our mind.

> *"You will keep in perfect and constant peace the one whose mind is steadfast [that is, committed and focused on You—in both inclination and character], Because he trusts and takes refuge in You [with hope and confident expectation].*
> *– Isaiah 26:3 AMP*

The collaboration is between you and God. This scripture explains that constant peace is a result of one person who has made the decision to keep his or her mind committed and focused on God. There is a reason why someone would do that and the reason is specifically because he trusts and takes refuge in God (with hope and confident expectation).

Pa'lante, pa'lante vamo' pa'lante. After sharing a conflict or problem with someone, you may hear them advise you to just 'let it go' or 'move on.' I've noticed that for many, their inability to move on has nothing to do with their lack of information, resources or even money. Most often, our inability to truly move on rests in the thoughts we have been convinced of. Do the exercise of asking God intentionally every day to show you what about your life is out of place and what beliefs you need to correct. It will not be the easiest thing you do because it is hard work to undo what you have believed for most of your life. I encourage you to do it and go past 'let it go', past 'get over it', and past 'it is what it is'. Instead, move forward in Christ's victory which He died for you to live in today. The type of victory that doesn't allow you to look back or re-play history.

The scripture describes in detail the mindset to live by and it's described as the "mind of Christ". I encourage you to study on it in the Bible. Philippians 2 addresses this mindset that is available to you and I *right now.*

> *"So if there is any encouragement in Christ, any comfort from love, any participation in the Spirit, any affection and sympathy, complete my joy by being of the same mind, having the same love, being in full accord and of one mind. Do nothing from selfish ambition or conceit, but in humility count others more significant than yourselves. Let each of you look not only to his own interests, but also to the interests of others. Have this mind among yourselves, which is yours in Christ Jesus."*
> *– Philipians 2:1-4 ESV*

Encouragement, comfort in the form of love, affection, sympathy, complete joy and humility by the act of considering others as higher than yourself -all are included in having the mindset of Christ. Specifically, the mindset description includes *"participation in the Spirit"*. Here the requirement is that you agree with the Holy Spirit of God. Typically, you wouldn't participate in something with someone that you do not have agreement with, so coming into agreement with God is critical.

"And the peace of God, which surpasses all understanding, will guard your hearts and your minds in Christ Jesus.... Finally, brothers, whatever is true, whatever is honorable, whatever is just, whatever is pure, whatever is lovely, whatever is commendable, if there is any excellence, if there is anything worthy of praise, think about these things."
- Philipians 4:7-9 ESV

So here we see a snapshot of the mindset we are to have. Paul is urging the church to adopt this mentality. Focus on those thoughts and adopt that mentality, applying it into practice. Paul is expressing, this is what it looks like and it is available today. We get to decide on our mindset.

Some people say, *'Get your mind right'*. Except the problem with that statement is the implication that it's you who will accomplish this by yourself. Your effort alone will not make it happen. Your effort, rituals, yoga, and meditation are not the source of this mind renewal; it's entirely God's work through Christ and the Holy Spirit within you. The Bible is clear on this. Anything you do on your own is a temporary fix that quickly goes away and has you chasing the next self-care treatment, the next high, the next retreat, the next person to date, the next mentor, the next workout, the next degree, the next church, the next...fill in the blank with whatever you chase after to help bring you mental peace.

To put your mind in order, and to get your thoughts corrected you have to come in agreement with God about each and every matter of life. The Holy Spirit of God will transform and renew your mind. Your part is to yield to God in agreement. Remember again the warfare we are undergoing, as described in 2 Corinthians 10:4-5 *"For the weapons of our warfare are not of the flesh but have divine power to destroy strongholds. We destroy arguments and every lofty opinion raised against the knowledge of God, and take every thought captive to obey Christ"*. Yes, it will take time and intention on your part but it's worth your lifetime. Right where you are, evaluate your thought life.

What have you been thinking about and what thoughts have you accepted?

What does your life and the way you live, currently say you believe?

Be willing to allow the Holy Spirit to renew your mind, and be willing to come into alignment with God's truth as you discover it in scripture.

CHAPTER 5
Living Worship

The first sacrifice you make when you come to God is yourself. We clearly see this in the lives of people who make a complete transformation that is undeniable to those who know them best. They do not remain the same. I was ten or eleven the first time I heard someone give me their testimony of how they gave their life to Christ. I was in 5th Grade I consistently finished my work before the other kids in my class, so I used to just sit at my desk quietly waiting. My teacher began to notice that I'd finish my work fast and started asking me to help her do her filing and other tasks. She'd pay me a dollar or two, even though she didn't have to do that. I was happy to assist and felt a sense of pride to get to help her. It was an honor to be a kid and get to help your teacher with her work. Plus, I thought it was fun!

One day I was filing for her and saw her open her purse to take out her lipstick and re-apply it without using a mirror. "Wow", I said in amazement, "How do you do that without having to look in a mirror!?" She smiled back at me and replied, "Well I do it so many times, I don't really need a mirror anymore." She was maybe in her mid 20s or early 30s. She was a beautiful black woman with an immaculate sense of style. She wore professional A-line skirts always meticulously ironed. Her dressy work tops and high heel pumps were always perfectly paired.

On this particular day, she continued to tell me how she was applying her lipstick at church and the way she said she wouldn't miss church service, I knew it was especially important to her. I wondered why she would go to church on purpose, I mean it didn't make sense that finally you're an adult and you can do whatever you want - *and still go to church?* Crazy. My parents forced me to go to church, so it was weird that she spoke of God and church in that way. Catholic church services were unbearable for me. Curious I asked, "Why do you want to go to church?" She looked at me and began to tell me her story, "I didn't take God as seriously before until something happened to me. I used to know this guy. He was not a good guy and I began to want to get away from him. He began to follow me around and I became fearful. I mean, I was so afraid of him and when he was going to show up again. He wanted to be with me and wouldn't take no for an answer. I asked him to leave me alone and he was aggressive. Nothing worked.

I was so afraid. It got to the point where I just walked into church one day and I asked God in prayer. I prayed to God and asked Him to help me and get the man to leave me alone and just forget about me completely. I really meant that prayer from the depth of my soul and do you know, I never saw or heard from that man ever again. I have since committed my life to God. I know God is real and I know God did that for me."

I attentively watched her facial expression as she told me in detail what God did. I saw the fear in her face as she spoke of that man not leaving her alone. I saw her fight back tears as she spoke of her overwhelming feeling that it was completely out of her control. She was tormented. She didn't say it, but I perceived the man was about to kill her. He wouldn't take no for an answer and her face said it all as if that was her next statement but she couldn't say it aloud. Clearly she was wise enough to not reveal that detail to her student. Now as an adult woman, I'm surprised she felt close enough to me that she told me the story at all. I know it was a God moment intended for me. No one could have stopped such a ruthless man, but God. She was convinced it could only be God's hand, and so was I.

By now, I've heard several people give an account for what God had done for them, inside and outside of a church building. In these missionary trips I made the clear connection of being convinced of the goodness of God to the point you entrust your entire self over to Him. A living sacrifice. In these trips, I got to see people live out what that kind of life looked like.

Nothing about these trips was luxury despite the country I went to, simply because we didn't go to serve the wealthy. I slept in a sleeping bag and carried very little belongings. I packed my Mexican passport with U.S. Residency card, a journal, my Bible, a few bills in local currency with a bank card, toothbrush, sunblock, chapstick, deodorant, a camera and my cell phone with charger. Most of my beds were hard surfaces even if it had a mattress. I always packed the thinnest and least amount of clothes as the countries I went to were in Latin America where Summers were hot.

The days went by fast and body aches didn't hit until we get to our sleeping bags at night. In between the Bible study meetings, we do a lot of what we call street evangelism which just means we share the gospel message to strangers on the streets. We also usually have a local church we partner with where we preach and serve that local community, visiting families, dropping off groceries, and other humanitarian-like work.

On this trip to Higüey, it included manual labor doing construction work as the new church was being built. Whether you decide to plant roots and commit to live the rest of your life in a country as a missionary or not, I highly encourage people to take a short-term missions trip. I once heard a missionary give a talk at a mega Baptist church in Dallas. The guy was older,

Cleaning day at the villa. - Higüey, Dominican Republic

maybe in his early 30s and came across scornful as he told the group of us young adults that if we weren't going to commit to live our lives in another country as a full-time missionary then we shouldn't bother to go. His perspective was limited and possibly even damaged by a personal offense he held on to. I completely disagree with his point of view. Even if you spend one week out there, the person who will be impacted the most is you. It completely transforms your mindset, your heart and life. Based on scripture, everyone back home, wherever home is, all those people are your mission field. You will bring what you learned back home and impact other people's lives in such an amazing way. Your life will be enriched and you will learn to value what truly matters in life.

May 20, 2007, a team member came up to me and asked me to join her as she was asked to preach later at the church. When we arrived she shared a message along with her testimony and I prayed for people. All of a sudden as I stood there, I felt God nudge me to step outside. I did and there was no one there. I began to pray over the congregation inside and the ministry, and when I opened my eyes, a young teenage girl walked up to the church. I greeted her and felt she was the reason I had to step out, to get her attention. Without hesitation I asked if I could pray for her and I shared a message of God's love for her life. Although she knew of the church and started going she had not taken God seriously. She cried and I asked her if she wanted to surrender her heart to God, and she did. Many experiences like that happen out in the mission field and I was frequently reminded of God's perfect timing for us.

Observing and learning that culture opened up my worldview to see a new reality. Along with the differences, I noticed many similarities. Like other Latin American countries I visited, they had little shops that sold everything from paintings to food, to shoes, clothes, you name it. These were little markets, like those we have in Mexico and some areas in Dallas. Whatever you need you'd find it there. Some of us took the opportunity to pray for people as we shopped. We walked into a store that sold art and a few other items. I saw a wall filled with art done by locals, mostly of naturescapes showing palm trees and the beach. All of a sudden the store workers and my team members broke out in dancing and singing a Spanish corito (gospel song), "Alabaré, Alabaré" with tambourines. Dominicans were just joyful people.

    I was asked to teach Bible Study, like many of my teammates, at home groups. One evening I taught on the book of Romans. I asked two of my team members to join me to help pray for people. One of the older young adults named Staci, was a single mom who made the sacrifice to be there. I really admired her. Her heart was beautiful, I mean she truly was a gem of a person. Radiant. I could tell she had suffered through some things but I don't like to pry into people's business especially when it's painful, unless they themselves decide to share something with me. I never learned any details of her past, yet I knew it was difficult. At the home group we met a girl who said she wasn't ready to take God seriously in her life and there was another young girl had issues with her stepdad. They asked us to pray for them and the girl who missed her dad asked for her birth father to show up in her life again.

    I met a lot of youth like this in the Dominican. Young people who felt isolated and were raised by a single parent or stepparent, without a

Date Un Giro Outreach Event. - Higüey, Dominican Republic

Church service. - Higüey, Dominican Republic

relationship with their biological father. I saw my sisters out there, fatherless and struggling. "We're not so different," I said, "My dad lives in my house, but he's very absent from my life and the lives of my siblings. He doesn't know much about me at all." I told them that to make them feel better, although it wasn't the exact same thing they faced. Maybe seeing your dad around the home is still better than knowing he's completely gone. We assured them that regardless of the circumstance, that God offers us hope in every situation.

One event we helped execute was an outdoor event called *'Date Un Giro'*, which means to make a 180 degree turn in your life. The general message here is saying give your entire life to God and you'll see your life transform completely. These were outdoor events where the church set up a stage outdoors with a line-up of performances, salsa music and someone giving a message with a call to salvation. The event ended with people dancing salsa, merengue, and bachata fit for the culture in an outdoor block party. Our team took part in helping as much as possible in any area that the church members needed help in, including inviting bystanders to come to the event, and then sharing the gospel and praying for people who decided they wanted to surrender their lives to Christ. I stood backstage with team members observing the sea of Dominicans listening to the presentation message.

There was a good crowd of people who gathered in the main stage area and several others who stayed on the grass surrounding the main area. Even more people stood further back out on the outskirts to listen. Many people made the commitment to surrender their lives to God. I began to see all of the church members, the tight knit church family, run over to people,like soldiers at war, placing arms around strangers and praying for them, giving them hugs, and encouraging them. You can't witness this without crying. People left their cares and whatever burdened them in the arms of complete strangers who cared for them. Hope and joy filled their hearts as it reflected in their faces. The dedication and commitment of the church members was inspiring. I had never seen a church like this in U.S. or anywhere. I couldn't believe it existed.

We repeated this event on a smaller scale another day. I was out walking with some of the team members inviting people who were outside at a park. I noticed these two guys on a bench. I went up to them to invite them to the event as it was about to start inside the nearby church building. As soon as I stepped up to them, I realized they were narcos (drug dealers, traffickers, etc.). You'd think I'd quickly turn away, but no. I interrupted their conversation and gave them the flyer. I invited them to stop by the church event, waiting on their "no" as soon as I extended the invite. I saw the gun on one guy's side as they both looked up at me in silence. Ok for sure right here at this point I left right? No. Once the word no came out of one guy's mouth I took a seat and shared the gospel with both of them, my *'make-it-quick, get-to-the-point'* version. I ended it with, "You don't need to go to this, you don't need to step into this church. You can surrender to God anytime, just you, when you're alone. I hope you decide to do it at some point and soon. Everything else that comes after the decision, God will lead you and tell you what to do every step of the way." They heard me, I saw it in their face. It wasn't me who did anything, it was all God. They both said "Ok." They said nothing else. I got up and moved on to the next person. Later, those guys showed up at the doors of the church's event as it started. As soon as they stepped to the door a male leader from the church walked up to stop them and not let them in. They knew who they were. I saw the men signaling me out by pointing over to me as if to say they wanted to just talk to me. But by then several other men gathered from the church asking the two men to leave, and they did. That wouldn't be the last time I shared the gospel with drug dealers. Many people think money keeps them from living a life for God. It's not the money, it's identity. It's the power and respect, centered in pride. It's not much different from any other person's reason to live life without God at the center. Whatever the reasons are that keep people from surrendering, they are all empty.

You have to be so convinced God is good and He is who He says He is in order to surrender your life completely, and many people struggle with this internally. Many fill up the church pews, sit in doubt and never take this step. Many settle in between faith and doubt. Lukewarm. In Revelation chapter 3, Jesus warned the church at Laodicea a firm warning against the position of indecision, against being lukewarm. It's dangerous. Think of how much damage follows someone who is indecisive. As practical as a driver unable to decide between two lanes, dodging vehicles left and right to finally exit seconds before the lane ends. Chaos. A man who can't decide between two women will leave a mess around him and destroy his family, just from that one area of indecision. Business deals have gone wrong and money has been blown because one decision-maker couldn't make up his or her mind. In my work experience, companies lost money, they lost talent and resources because the decision makers didn't make up their mind or waited too long to decide.

What good can come from not making up your mind?

"I know your deeds, that you are neither cold (invigorating, re-freshing) nor hot (healing, therapeutic); I wish that you were cold or hot. So because you are lukewarm (spiritually useless), and

> *neither hot nor cold, I will vomit you out of My mouth*
> *[rejecting you with disgust].*
>
> *Because you say, "I am rich, and have prospered and grown*
> *wealthy, and have need of nothing," and you do not know that*
> *you are wretched and miserable and poor and blind and naked*
> *[without hope and in great need]" - Revelation 3:15-16 AMP*

It's offensive to God to be undecided about Him.

However you get to the point of surrendering your life as 'living sacrifice' to God, no one can avoid that step if they desire a genuine relationship. On the other side of that decision is the beginning of a daily 'dying' to self. It's a process of transformation where the person is made new. Many who are offered to take God seriously hesitate in that they know they can no longer stay the same. They believe the version of themselves without God at the center, is somehow superior.

If I could point to the area which changes the most when you surrender to God, and is constantly renewed, *it's your mind.*

CHAPTER 6

¡Ay, Bendito!

a Isla del Encanto. Tuesday May 29th, 2007 I woke up at 7:00 a.m. in Higüey, ready to fly back to Puerto Rico. I grabbed pizza for breakfast at the airport and chugged black Dominican coffee like a local. The island of Puerto Rico is referred to as 'La Isla del Encanto'. You quickly get the sense of the pride Puerto Ricans carry. The way Dominicans have strong coffee, Puerto Ricans have strong attitudes. Some anger, some passion but everyone carried a badge of pride for the culture, displaying their flags everywhere you look. Don't ask anyone anything about the American government unless you want a fight. The history here of countries who showed up to overtake them by force left wounds and they had to fight to keep their identity. It's too much to get into with any local. Puerto Rico suffers by the tragic storms that come in and destroy everything they worked so hard for. Then they're left to start over and re-build. The worst part is that when storms take over, we frequently hear in the news how little resources and assistance they are given in order to re-build. Even as part of the U.S., they struggled to get the assistance they needed and so many people held strong political opinions.

When we landed, I was stopped by immigration because my U.S. Residency card was expired. I went through the interrogation from immigration police, or who we call 'La Migra', wondering what the outcome would be. *'I'm not a felon, but it is expired'*, I thought, *'Could I really be detained here? Am I getting deported to Mexico for this?...'* An officer asked me, "Where you from?" He asked without looking at me and focusing on my documents, "It says Zihuatanejo, Guerrero but I was only born there. I'm from Michoacán, and I live in Dallas, TX". I don't have that Mexican accent when I speak English, and I hoped that helped me out a little with the agent. "Why is your Residency card expired?" I'm just myself, so I said, "...I really have no excuse for that. I knew I should have done it and didn't prioritize it before leaving with the group." I was honest. He finally looked up at me after I said that and held silence as his eyes scanned mine. "I don't have an excuse." I said again. My parents were always afraid of police and every person in uniform was basically La Migra to them. When we drove around in Dallas in the 90s and a cop car was in the area, my dad would yell, "¡Agachense, la Migra!", then all of us kids would hide under the seats

Musicians and Performers - Viejo San Juan, Puerto Rico

rolled up as small as we could.

Even after I got a Residency 'green' card I was still scared of police. I grew up in the hood and nobody likes the police there either, so that didn't make my perception of any law enforcement officer any better. I imagined when police showed up to a nice middle-class neighborhood people were relieved. Whenever police showed up to the hood that wasn't the case. It wasn't just because they were casually making a pit stop to grab a snack at the corner store, like Chief Wiggum did on the Simpsons.

The immigration officer responded, "Wait here" and walked away to check my background. I saw the row of illegal migrants arrested and lined up sitting on the floor. "What are you going to be doing in Puerto Rico?" he asked. "I'm a student, we came here to do missionary work for a few days, then we are heading back to Dallas."

They had me wait for what felt like forever, coming back one at a time to ask me one question then saying I had to wait. Coming back, another question, walking away and leaving me to wait. It's intimidating on purpose and despite my composure, I was preparing myself for detainment. Finally one officer walked back up and said, "Ok we don't do this for anyone" which told me they've done it for others. He continued "but we're going to give you a courtesy extension on your residency card. Listen to me," Sharp eye stare... "The moment you land in Dallas, get it done." It was the way he said it, I had never heard anyone sound that firm about anything. A single drop of sweat fell, la gota fria. Relief came over me and I stepped out to the driver who waited for me outside. He explained that everyone left and couldn't wait for me to resolve the issue, especially since they weren't sure if I was going to be released. I apologized for the inconvenience and seriously meant it. It was an ugly reminder that one poor decision could have ended worse. An oversight, neglecting our responsibilities or even things that are seemingly insignificant to us in the moment can bring a set back also to people around us.

One day we were traveling to do ministry and made a pit stop at a corner store for gas. Tall palm trees, in a barrio, nothing out of the ordinary. That's where I met her. I walked up and saw a girl standing near the entrance. She had medium olive brown skin, a beautiful round face, but it was aged. Her skin damaged by the sun. She was probably 20 but looked 30 only because you could tell she had a rough life of maybe drug use and possibly living on the streets. You see this in Oak Cliff, especially the South side. There was nothing particularly shocking to me about her. She was most likely a working girl. She was angry. Not angry like most people are angry, where it comes and goes. She settled into angry like anger was her home and her permanent personality. That kind of angry. The kind only deep trauma can lead someone to. I began to glance around to see if I could spot a guy nearby watching her and quickly stopped myself because it didn't matter. I chose to focus on her.

As I approached the enrance I greeted her and she looked angrily to the side telling me without words to get out of her face. She wouldn't look at me. I didn't force the girl to talk to me, but I also didn't walk away from her. I wondered how many people had already done that in her life. Women in her position are usually so mistreated and gone through so much trauma they lose their voice. Like they are used to not speaking up at all about basic things. I was definitely not going to expect words out of her. I began to share the love of God with her, as if I was reciting a book I memorized. "I just want to tell you this," I said and continued, "God's love for you is perfect. It cannot be measured. The Bible says no height, no depth, nothing created, no person, no power can separate you from His love." Then I felt led to specify further and speak on God's love as a husband.

The scripture in Isaiah 54 flashed in my mind and I knew it was the Holy Spirit asking me to share it with her, about specifically God's love as a husband. "There's a scripture that says "For your Maker is your husband, The LORD of hosts is His name; And your Redeemer is the Holy One of Israel; He is called the God of the whole earth."

She finally looked at me.

Suddenly, what was anger turned into a look of nervous fear as she finally looked me in the eyes. That was it. The Holy Spirit reached her heart. Her eyes welled up with tears. I continued, "It's like the love of a perfect husband, if there was such thing as a perfect husband, who loves his wife perfectly. God exceeds and surpasses that image in a way we cannot even imagine fully in this lifetime. God wants you to know you are valuable to Him." She fell apart, and her hands went up to cover her face as she began crying profusely. "The Bible describes you as the apple of His eye, He knew you before you entered your mother's womb, your value is so high God sent his Son to die so you could be close to Him in a personal relationship. God desires a relationship with you." I wrapped my arms around her. Another team member had walked up with me to pray for her. I told her my quick version of the Gospel. The fast version with the emphasis on the love of God. She agreed and we prayed.

I encouraged her to find a local church. "Ask Him to show you who He is. Look for a church that can help you know God personally..." As I spoke she would not stop looking at me straight in my eyes like she believed everything I said and the biggest tears falling but she wouldn't stop starring at me in my eyes. Finally, as I was about to leave, I felt the Holy Spirit tell me "Give her the ring". I honestly didn't want to give her my ring, but I didn't think twice and in obedience I said, "I want to give you this." I proceeded to take off my most valuable piece of jewelry at that time. It was a sterling silver ring that said worship in different languages engraved around the entire ring. I wore it on my ring finger. I explained to her how it was my most valuable piece of jewelry and how much I loved the ring. I mean I *loved* that ring, it meant so much to me. (I later tried finding it online and never found it again.) I explained to her that I knew God wanted me to give it to her as a symbol of her value to Him and His love for her. As I placed the ring on her finger, I felt how tough her hand was and I saw her scars. I slid the ring to her ring finger, and guess what? It fit her *perfectly*. She finally smiled the biggest smile and let God into her heart. I hugged her so tight and together with my team mate, we emphasized she find a good church to help her stay on course with God. She agreed she would. She wasn't given assistance or a way out. I don't know what God's love as a husband specifically meant to her and I could not have come up with that on my own. It was all God pointing at something in her heart.

While her circumstances had not changed in the natural, I knew her life just changed. Light filled her face. She looked like a different person. She actually smiled a genuine, big smile. Whether I saw her again or not, I knew God would take care of her. He was, after all, the one who brought her back to life. Like Lazarus. Whatever has died inside us, God can bring back to life.

We went to a local Christian T.V. station as a team where we were asked to share a message God placed in our hearts and I spoke on Lazarus. So much was accomplished in Lazarus being raised from the dead in John 17. Jesus explained it was for the glory of God. Whether you know what it is to lose someone you loved or not, loss is not limited to losing a loved one. According to researchers, loss occurs when there is a permanent change in our circumstances or perceptions, especially after we undergo

The girl at the gas station. - Puerto Rico

major life changes. Loss can be related to death, but loss also occurs around painful or disorienting experiences which do not involve death and we can experience genuine grief over tangible or intangible losses.[1]

This is why the miracle in John chapter 17 is so relatable to all of us. The thing that stands out to me often is most people focus on Lazarus. Clearly he needed the miracle, he died, but the miracle was not for Lazarus' sake alone. It was for everyone standing by who observed it happen. It was for his sisters, Mary and Martha. It was for the loved ones who mourned with them. It was for the loyal Disciples who followed Jesus there. It was for the religious Pharisees. It was for the on-lookers, the crowd of people who were un-named. It was for those who walked over to see what all the commotion was, to later have something to talk about at the local market. John 17 reads as follows.

> *"So when Jesus arrived, He found that Lazarus had already been in the tomb four days. Bethany was near Jerusalem, about two miles away; and many of the Jews had come to see Martha and Mary, to comfort them concerning [the loss of] their brother. So when Martha heard that Jesus was coming, she went to meet Him, while Mary remained sitting in the house. Then Martha*

---

1   Shelvock RP, CT, MACP, MA, Mark . 2022. Grieving When No One Has Died Grief Is Not Exclusive to Death; Other Losses Occur More Often Throughout Life. Psychology Today. https://www.psychologytoday.com/us/blog/navigating-the-serpentine-path/202210/grieving-when-no-one-has-died

said to Jesus, "Lord, if You had been here, my brother would not have died. ... "After she had said this, she left and called her sister Mary, privately whispering [to her], "The Teacher is here and is asking for you." And when she heard this, she got up quickly and went to Him. When Mary came [to the place] where Jesus was and saw Him, she fell at His feet, saying to Him, "Lord, if You had been here, my brother would not have died."

When Jesus saw her sobbing, and the Jews who had come with her also sobbing, He was deeply moved in spirit [to the point of anger at the sorrow caused by death] and was troubled, and said, "Where have you laid him?" They said, "Lord, come and see." Jesus wept.

... "So Jesus, again deeply moved within [to the point of anger], approached the tomb. It was a cave, and a boulder was lying against it [to cover the entrance]. Jesus said, "Take away the stone." Martha, the sister of the dead man, said to Him, "Lord, by this time there will be an offensive odor, for he has been dead four days! [It is hopeless!]" Jesus said to her, "Did I not say to you that if you believe [in Me], you will see the glory of God [the expression of His excellence]?" So they took away the stone.

And Jesus raised His eyes [toward heaven] and said, "Father, I thank You that You have heard Me. I knew that You always hear Me and listen to Me; but I have said this because of the people standing around, so that they may believe that You have sent Me [and that You have made Me Your representative]." When He had said this, He shouted with a loud voice, "Lazarus, come out!" Out came the man who had been dead, his hands and feet tightly wrapped in burial cloths (linen strips), and with a [burial] cloth wrapped around his face. Jesus said to them, "Unwrap him and release him."...So then, many of the Jews who had come to [be with] Mary and who were eyewitnesses to what Jesus had done, believed in Him."
- John 17:38-45 AMP

The situation was bad. Hopeless. The guy had been dead for four days. Consider that detail, the length of time it took before God showed up. It stinks. Dead things stink. I thought of the girl and wondered how long it had taken for God to show up in that way for her. So much was dead inside

¡AY, BENDITO!

her and seeing a Mexican girl walk up to her with Jesus in her mouth didn't make sense. I didn't know what she had been through or how many years she had suffered. Like Lazarus, many would have said she shouldn't have had a chance to smile again.

I want to shift your focus to everyone around Lazarus. There was only 1 dead man, but there were many more surrounding him who were alive. Jesus was thinking about all of them when he said, "for the glory and honor of God, so that the Son of God may be glorified by it." Maybe not because they were nosy, not because they had nothing better to do, but possibly because they are watching to see, will God show up? If He showed up for a dead man, then surely, He could show up in their own situation.

I was hoping to get that same message across at the T.V. studio, but I had a very short time. I learned some of the station execs had problems going on behind the scenes. I wasn't given details, just that they needed prayer for the T.V. ministry. It's so easy to look at the need as isolated to just one individual or one group of people, like the leaders. I did my best to share the message of Lazarus on air that night. I couldn't emphasize the importance of the impact from the miracle of raising dead things to life being for everyone who is watching. Whatever issues they were having to cause a delay or to completely shut down that station – *dead* – it was overwhelming to them because they looked at the situation in isolation. Each to his own misery. Just like in John 17, each bystander had their own isolated response. Mary and Martha had some resentment as they said, "If you would have been here sooner Jesus…" and the disciples were clearly walking over there in fear with Thomas finally commenting his ride or die statement, "Well, we will go and die with you there."

But if, for example, each of those T.V. media leaders allowed themselves to take a step waaaaay back and consider the glory of God, it would no longer be isolated. Instead, a completely different response would come from each of them as they experience the conflict. As an example, if I were one of them, and I was isolated considering myself only in this problem, I may possibly be consumed with frustration. If someone in the team for example, cut me out of a decision that meant the station was shutting down, I'd be angry, naturally. But God demands the spiritual action out of us. The spiritual requires that we stop to consider the glory of God.

Imagine a bird flying over a region and seeing a million things going on at once. We say "a bird's eye view" when we ask someone to see the big picture. It means a view from above, the ability to look at something from a very high place so that you see a large area instead of what is simply in front of you. I would look at the thousands of people being impacted by the loss of just one broadcast on that station. If I focus on all of those people who are bystanders, I'd behave differently behind closed doors and in public. As I went through the chaos internally, I would realize this is about the Glory of God and surely God has His hand in this end. And if I truly believed this, knowing His character, God may decide to raise it from the dead, just as Christ did with Lazarus. But either way, whether God does that or not, I can be at peace internally.

¡Ay Bendito! This is a phrase Boricuas use like in astonishment. I imagine it's appropriate when you witness the glory of God. It blankets the earth. When you witness it, it leaves you speechless. In the same way seeing a natural wonder leaves you speechless and in awe.

What are you going through?

What are the dead areas in your life?

Who has shown up around you to observe?

Have you considered it may be "for the glory of God"?

What if Jesus did not raise Lazarus from the dead? What if He just showed up and comforted those mourning, said a few words as a loved one would in a eulogy at a funeral…What if He said nothing, and all they had was His presence, standing by their side in that difficult time of mourning.

Would it still be to the Glory of God? Jesus is still Jesus after all. God is still God. The Holy Spirit remains the same.

Think of a moment when you felt God didn't show up. Is it possible the tragedy overshadowed your ability to see the glory of God?

If you were there and Lazarus was not raised in front of your eyes, would you be able to see the Glory of God anyways?

It's up to you.

CHAPTER 7

Relationship, But a Good One

Just because someone says that they have a relationship with God – it doesn't mean it's a good one. While there may be many indicators, you can really tell by the way someone prays. Some pray repetitiously, "Father God...Father God...Father God..." nervously searching for words they can't find. Others can only pray a pre-written prayer, unsure what words are worthy enough to say to God. Some beg a lot in their prayer. Others only pray when they face a near death experience. Some pray really loud, possibly because they believe God is far away in the heavens, as if God can't hear a whisper. Others pray in silence. I would say most people today recognize there's an insecurity in their relationship with God simply by their prayer life, or the lack of. It doesn't matter if they quote a little Bible verse here and another verse there mixed in.

Imagine if I sit next to you for coffee, and as you address me, you repeat my name about 10 times in one sentence. "Hey Arisbet, thank you for meeting with me today Arisbet, Arisbet you're such a good friend Arisbet, you know Arisbet, I'm thankful for you Arisbet, the other day Arisbet..." Sounds like nervous stuttering. I would first ask, "Are you ok? Why do you keep saying my name?" I know my name - when will you start to actually talk to me? I would come to the determination that you're insecure and unsure about what you are saying to me. It's usually when someone is a stranger that you don't have much to say, right? Imagine you want to have a relationship with me and you really want to talk to me yourself but you feel you need to go through someone else in order to reach me. What would you say our relationship is at that point? Would you think you know me? Would you consider us to be close if that's the only way you could reach me?

This is how I observed many men that were held at Teen Challenge and the churches we visited in Puerto Rico. Wednesday May 30, 2007 we left at 7:00 a.m. to go to Teen Challenge as our team leader preached a message to the guys who were part of the program. It was like a halfway house, where the guys just got out of prison in Puerto Rico and they entered their program to transition them back into the community. It is a faith-based organization so they share the gospel with them as part of the program. The room was small and it was full of guys that still walked in like they were

Preparing to serve a meal to the men at Teen Challenge. - Puerto Rico

incarcerated. Our group leader, who I believe was also a pastor, preached on the demon possessed man in Mark 5 and shared his personal experience of how Teen Challenge also was part of his story. The organization helped him out of a broken life when he was younger. The general message was, that if God could set this demon possessed man free of all the demons that oppressed his life, and if God was able to set his own life free from all the torment he personally experienced in his past – then surely God would set each of them free.

Sitting there watching the ex-inmates walk in and sit. As the pastor preached, I observed the men's reactions. Many with their posture hung, lowly and slouched. Many appeared disengaged. I wondered what they did to end up in prison. The message was over, and the response was quiet. I wondered if they struggled to believe the message, or maybe their minds were on other things. Maybe they did believe it, but they were used to suppressing emotion and it was all internalized. God knows what they were thinking. Everyone started to walk out, and I stepped out to this courtyard looking area. There was a guy sitting on the floor and I saw my brother. I walked up to him and introduced myself. He opened up to me and told me about mistakes he made that led him there, "I messed up a lot, but I want to get my life together, I got into a gang, I don't want that life anymore…and now my dad's sick. He just had a heart attack." Although he thought he was in a bad place, I thought he was in a great position. Solitude. A place where no one else has your attention but God. It could only get better for him from there.

Despite how far away he perceived himself to have been from God, I know he was in that moment closer to God than many churched people living a comfortable life are. I told him I'd pray for him and his dad and encouraged him to pursue a relationship with God. If he committed himself to it, he could avoid prison a second time and it was possible. "You really cannot do it alone. If you rely on your strength you will end up back here. It has to be God and a relationship with God to really help you live a good life for yourself first and then for your family." I hoped he believed me, but he looked to be drowning with worry. He was desperate to get out of there. He gave me a card with a message in it before I left, saying thank you. He asked me to pray for him and his dad every time I looked at it and I keep it at home in my wooden jewelry box from Nicaragua, full of memories.

Prayer that is fully devoted and a private conversation between you and God, is incredible. It feels like peace and security. It brings comfort. In heart felt prayer, you enter a space with God where you are complete. God is a loving father ready to listen and ready to speak to you. Based on how Jesus described prayer, it's not meant to be mechanical or forced. It's just you being you. It's not meant to be a performance. Some people refuse to pray even when asked. Their relationship with God is broken. No one who professes to have a good relationship with God should refuse to pray for you or with you. While people can fake something like talent to worship on a stage, talent to preach a good message, no one can fake the fruit of the Holy Spirit as described in Galatians 5, which is produced out of a good relationship. *"But the fruti fo the spirit is love, joy, peace, longsuffering, kindness, goodness, faithfulness, gentleness, self-control."* This is developed by the Holy Spirit working within us as we commune with God.

Like my brother, these guys were each overtaken by something. If

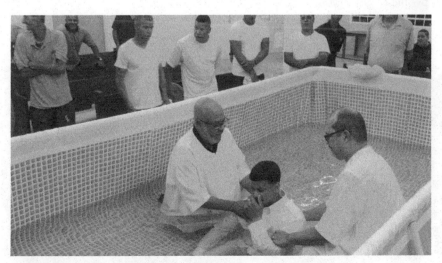

A young man getting baptised at Teen Challenge. - Puerto Rico
Photo Credit: Teen Challenge, Puerto Rico

anyone tried to point to what went wrong for them, they may talk about a missing father or mother. They may point to a traumatic experience they had as a child. There are careers built around figuring out what goes wrong in the lives of inmates and felons. The studies continue and the reasons are always inconclusive to one precise cause. Many people approach God in conversation to get answers, to understand cause of pain. Understanding the cause of our pain ends when we allow God to enter into our hearts to remove it. That can take several conversations, over many years.

Jesus expresses in John 10 verse 27, *"The sheep that are My own hear My voice and listen to Me; I know them, and they follow Me."* The reason we follow after Christ in relationship with God is as result of knowing His voice. Conversation, or prayer, is fundamental. A truth you have to be convinced of is that God created humanity with the intention of relationship in conversation. He wants you to talk to Him and He directly speaks to you without an in-between person to relay the message.

Truly knowing God's voice and sharing something on his behalf is not guessing or assuming. Often, a common challenge for many people I meet is that they say they have trouble hearing from God for themselves. Even those who spend years in church say they struggle to know when it's God or when it's not and it becomes easy to rely on the pastors and leaders to tell them. I believe it is simply a lack of personal time spent with God. God doesn't want for you to live confused and not know what He's telling you. I know without a doubt that God prefers to tell you directly as opposed to sending someone to tell you something. At times God will use other people to tell you something, absolutely! But based on scripture, the heart of God is to have relationship directly with you – not through other people to get to you.

Many people say prayer changes your situation but I say prayer changes your position, *'la oración cambia tu posición'*. I've seen many people

Teen Challenge facility tour. - Puerto Rico

discouraged because they pray or beg God in conversation and don't see their situation change. What they cannot see is that something did change, and that is the position in which they stand with God internally. By calling out to God in prayer they moved positioning in the spiritual realm. A visual I like to compare it to is that of someone surviving a deadly storm.

Imagine standing outside on the streets of Puerto Rico when suddenly a severe storm approaches and you see it coming for you a few miles away. The storm is not leaving, in fact it strengthens and worsens as the seconds pass. You realize shelter is a few feet away, and you dash towards it. The storm is still raging out there but suddenly you're covered. Your action of taking shelter, *that's prayer*. It did not eliminate the storm. What changed is the position where you stood. You once stood in direct proximity to the storm, easily impacted and potentially taken by it's force. But when you made the choice to run to shelter, despite how the storm may have worsened or weakened or dissipated outside, you remain secure. That's what prayer does. Conversation with God changes your position as you take refuge in Him. He is our shelter, Psalm 46:1. Our strong tower, Proverbs 18:10.

Imagine you stand in a tornado shelter, and you hear the power of the tornado coming. You know it's destroying everything in it's path outside of that shelter. You would absolutely feel fear. Many people look at Christians confused like why are you afraid I thought you believed in God? I thought you "prayed" about it? Listen, fear will absolutely hit you as you observe destruction happening in real life. You would feel worry and concern even though you stand in shelter. All those feelings will come up, but you have reassurance that you will not be destroyed by the storm. We see this confidence in Mark 4, as Jesus slept through the storm while the disciples freaked out. At the face of a deadly storm they ran to wake Him up and yelled in verse 38, *"Teacher, do You not care that we are about to die?"* Christ was expecting that their relationship up to that point would have been sufficient for them to not only have remained calm, but let Him sleep it out. But it wasn't. Christ expressed frustration in his response, asking *"Why are you afraid? Do you still have no faith and confidence in Me?" (Mark 4:40 AMP)*. You may be facing something so bad it feels like you're dying right now. You may have cried out, "God don't you care!??" How is your relationship?

Just like those fear-stricken disciples, even if you don't see your prayer answered or situation change – each conversation with God causes something to change within you and it happens right away. Prayer is key to a good relationship with God. God shows up when you start talking, and deep within your spirit you feel His presence start to change you from within. Destroy the image that prayer is primarily for making something happen for yourself or someone else. For example, when you pray only for healing or a miracle. So many people's relationship with God involve a prayer life of "please God, give me this, give me that". Do you know someone who only looks for you when they need something? As much as you would want a good relationship with a person like that, it will not be a good meaningful one. So, destroy the intention behind prayer that bargains for God to do something for you first before you seek to know Him.

God doesn't need anything from you or me, or anyone.

He is all sufficient by just existing. A good barter would involve two parties who each have a vested interest in the exchange. It's ridiculous to attempt to barter with God and even if you try and God hands you what you've asked for, it's because He willed to. But if you spent your prayer life bargaining with God, it would not lead you to a good relationship with Him. That's a transactional, business relationship that you must maintain a personal distance in. Like a good client who gives you a lot of business, they may get a birthday card from you, or a luxury executive gift or experience as a reminder that you're there. If you want to secure rapport, you would show up and give time out of your day, but limited access to your heart. That type of structure with God is equal to no relationship and God wants all access to your life. Not because He needs something from you, but because He loves you.

If when you pray you sound like you are begging all the time – that's an indication of an identity issue. Only orphans beg for things. We are called children of God, so if you had a good relationship, you wouldn't show up begging especially for things that we have already been promised and given by God. How crazy would it be to see a child begging their parent to open their closet full of clothes or access to the refrigerator full of food that their good father provided?

You have the chance to get your prayer life right today. It's this simple – talk to God with a desire to be your honest self and speak to Him as you would speak to a loving Father. You don't have to sound programmed. You don't have to hide your feelings. You're mad at Him? Start by telling Him that. He knows who you are and nothing you will say will surprise Him. Don't pretend to be religious. Also, saying that you're going to do "x" if God does "y", when you know you're not going to fulfill your promise, is aimless in your pursuit of a good relationship with God. Pray with the greatest desire to get to know Him above everything else. Wouldn't you agree that the tightest relationships you have are with people who are completely themselves, transparent and honest with you about who they are? Dishonest people naturally place space between each other and the result is distrust. God wants you to trust Him and the only way you'll get there is by getting to know Him in conversation and quality time spent reading the Bible.

One mega church in Puerto Rico where we served was massive. It appeared as though a sea of people sat behind us as we prepared to join them in worship service. The pastors were a striking contrast to the pastors in the Dominican in that they and their leaders dressed dapper sharp. The order of the service was a completely thought out production. We were asked to pray for people as usual and I saw how people would walk up with their worries and needs. The evidence was on their perplexed facial expressions. Sadness, depression, sorrow. Some people approached us with the idea that God would listen to us more than He would listen to them. While we were complete strangers, they had greater faith that God would hear us more, as if there was something special about us praying. It's also similar to how people go to a pastor or a priest believing their conversation with God holds a higher priority, which is simply not true. I wanted them to know there was nothing special about us, and God heard them when they cried out to Him alone.

Whenever I say that to people who ask me for prayer abroad or at home in Dallas, I can tell they don't believe me. They don't believe they can pray for themselves and God will hear them the same. They think all the bad they have done in their past keeps God from hearing them. Many believe because they failed God they're not worthy of speaking to God. I wish they understood that according to scripture, they are the ones God wants to hear desperately from. Throughout the Old Testament we read time and time again, God wanting those who have turned away from Him returned into His care. 1 Peter 3:7 does say that a man's prayers will be hindered if he mistreats his wife, but that could be resolved if he has a conversation of repentance with his wife and with God. Even if his prayers are hindered, it doesn't mean God didn't hear him. Reconciliation with God begins with a conversation. Inner healing of the soul begins with a conversation. All the prophets were sent out to gather God's children back to return to Him, relaying a conversation, "thus says the Lord your God..."

If you are waiting to understand the Bible, God or His ways before you try and come to God in a genuine conversation – you'll reach the end of your life and never speak to Him sincerely. One of the most chilling things Jesus said in the Bible can be found in Matthew 7:21-23.

> *"Not everyone who says to me, 'Lord, Lord,' will enter the kingdom of heaven, but the one who does the will of my Father who is in heaven. On that day many will say to me, 'Lord, Lord, did we not prophesy in your name, and cast out demons in your*

> *name, and do many mighty works in your name?' And then will*
> *I declare to them, 'I never knew you; depart from me, you workers*
> *of lawlessness."*
> *- Matthew 7:21-23 ESV*

Prayer changes you. It changes your focus from inward to upward. As an example at the dissatisfaction at a job, people may say, "God I hate this job! Give me a new job, a better job, a better boss. Where should I work? I need better pay, I need a better work schedule, I need more benefits, I need…" When you are in a committed relationship of prayer with God you have already come to a realization that prayer has to be kingdom minded. So, it turns into "God I hate my job. Show me how to glorify you in my work. Create in me a new mind, a new outlook. Give me patience and grace for people I can't stand. What I want is another job, but if it's not Your will, help me to glorify you in my job." It's aligning to what Jesus did in the garden and throughout His life. He went everywhere having that kingdom mindset about prayer. Wherever Christ went, and whatever He did was based on what He had already spoken to God about. Down to the Garden of Gethsemene, He prayed, *"Let this cup pass."* Which means death on the cross was going to be difficult, and then followed it with *"But nevertheless, not My will, but Your will be done."*

Ask someone to pray for you and listen. I hope you know, just because someone says they have a relationship with God – it doesn't mean it is a good one. At the end of your life, imagine stepping up to meet God in person in eternity and that being the first meaningful conversation you have with God. Seriously, picture it. Standing in front of God, at a loss for words and ready to hear what He has to say, finally, for the first time. How would you feel? You spent a lifetime without talking to Him. You may be shocked He exists. What will be your excuse? No matter what your background is, what your culture history is, how you were raised, what your setbacks were, if you had too much or too little, there will be no excuses as to why you spent a lifetime in silence towards God. That is an important run-on sentence you should read again.

If you have not already started talking to God, begin today.

If you wait to reach the end of your life on Earth to say anything –

Jesus made it clear, it will be too late.

Witness

EXPERIMENTAL DIALOGUE

Appear and Testify.	No.
Why?	Because.
	I didn't see anything.
	My mom told me she saw Him and He helped her out the other day. - But she always needs help.
You received a subpoena.	I can't.
Why?	Because. I didn't hear anything.
	He did knock on my door again this morning when I woke up I glanced to look and it was Him.
	- But I didn't open it, I had a lot to do today.
Why?	Because...
You will be held in contempt.	I told you I can't.
Why?	Because...
	I don't know the guy.
	My neighbor knows Him. He said that he's a good person. A lot of people say that. - But I personally don't know him like that.
Approach the stand.	No.
	...

> This is a crime.

Author's Note:
This short narrative is about how people are asked to testify and be a "witness" for Jesus – but they can't. How can they be asked or expected to be a witness to something they never experienced? Or about someone they really don't know?

We take the justice system seriously.
Someone cannot take a witness stand and an oath to tell the truth, the whole truth and nothing but the truth when they can't honestly testify on what occurred.

I see this play itself out within the Christian community. People don't witness because they didn't see anything.

Many church goers physically attend a church service but are not personally present in a private life with God.

The words See, Hear and Know in the narrative are marked in red to reference how Jesus explained the critical importance of people having spiritual eyes to see, spiritual ears to hear in order to know Him as Savior while He taught the masses.

> *"In them is fulfilled the prophecy of Isaiah: 'You will be ever hearing but never understanding; you will be ever seeing but never perceiving. For this people's heart has become calloused; they hardly hear with their ears, and they have closed their eyes. Otherwise they might see with their eyes, hear with their ears, understand with their hearts and turn, and I would heal them.' But blessed are your eyes because they see, and your ears because they hear." - Matthew 13:14-16 ESV*

Christians all over the world are missing on the witness stands every day and in moments where their testimony matters most.

The demand from the attorney to take the stand in the narrative is a reference to the Holy Spirit, who urges believers to speak up. Anyone who identifies as a Christian does not get special privileges to be excused from the witness stand.

They hear too much even with a Sunday only attendance to claim ignorance. This is where the subpoena comes in.

The statement 'This is a crime' refers to how Jesus declares in scripture and describes a life sentence in eternity.

"Every tree that does not bear good fruit is cut down and thrown into the fire...On that day many will say to me, 'Lord, Lord, did we not prophesy in your name, and cast out demons in your name, and do many mighty works in your name?' And then will I declare to them, 'I never knew you; depart from me, you workers of lawlessness.'"
– Matthew 7:19; 21-23 ESV

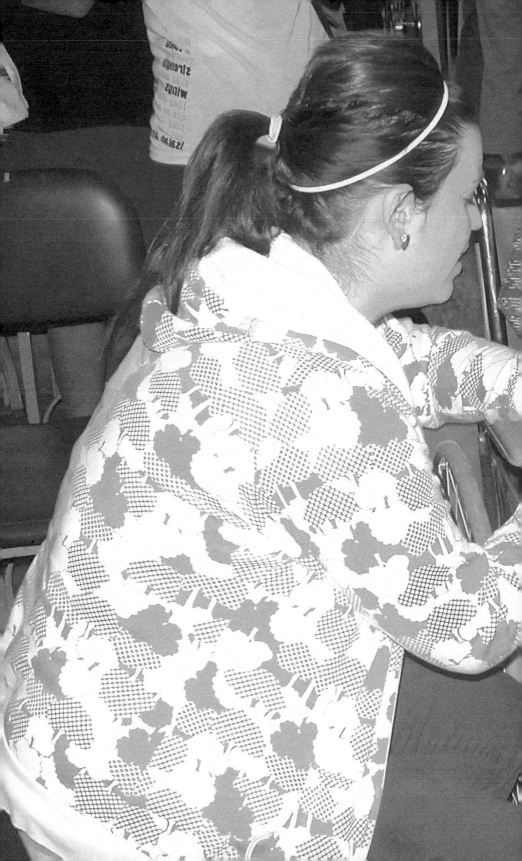

CHAPTER 8
The Condition of Orphans

"His brain is so damaged he can't speak to you" said the worker as she handed me a ball to begin play therapy. I couldn't. He was excited to see me, a new face, a new friend. *'Don't cry,'* I told myself as my eyes filled up with tears. I hid my face with my curls as I swayed them to one side. I struggled to hold him close. He looked to be 6 but was probably older. His body curled up naturally in a fetal position, which he held in place with strong tension. This was his permanent condition. His left wrist was permanently bent and he struggled to stay still because of the disease. The children's orphanage in Guatemala looked like an eerie building from a 1940s movie. You know those old hospitals from the early 1900s, small, with many rooms and an open courtyard area. Everything happened fast there. Staff moved quickly through a main hallway and in the rooms caring for the kids. That orphanage was special though. The kids there each had a special need, suffered from an illness or had some sort of disability. Children, all ages, with some form of physical or mental deficit. I had never been placed in this kind of situation before and the organizers couldn't possibly brief us enough to prepare us for what we were about to see.

We were supposed to play with the kids and I was handed a small soccer ball. As I held the little boy in my arms, I thought *'God this is impossible. There's no way I can properly communicate here.'* After handing me the child, the worker didn't give me any other instructions. I asked God to be the translator and help us understand each other. When you have no words to express what you feel, He can translate for you. I saw this little boy smile and play with a ball in my arms. No dialogue was exchanged but his laughter and excitement to see a new visitor made me happy. I don't have children but couldn't imagine what it must feel like for the parents behind each child in there. What happened to the mothers and fathers? I learned some of them handed their child over and were never seen again, while others did visit from time to time. I imagined most mothers were grateful to find out about this place because living in poverty, it would be impossible to properly care for a special needs child. But the fact is, this is an orphanage. That word discloses there was an act of abandonment. Without knowing details of pay structure or volunteer volume, I recognized that the people caring for the kids there had managed to make ends meet. Whether they got paid

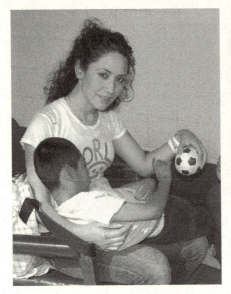 

The boy in the orphanage. - Guatemala   *Mayan mother with baby on her back. - Guatemala*

or not, they made sure each child was properly cared for and loved.

    I tried my best to imagine good parents. Parents in a difficult position who were heartbroken and torn to have to hand over their child. Parents who visit. I looked at my teammates who made it to this visit and they each had a similar reaction. Shock and complete sadness but forcing out a laugh or a smile. Maybe it wasn't forced, maybe it was genuine and they were stronger than I was. It's heartbreaking for the obvious reasons and the struggle the facility must have with few resources. I wondered about the potential exhaustion of the staff who were probably overworked, especially if they didn't have enough volunteers to help.

    Years later in 2015 I was doing Bible Study ministry in Dallas and visited a small start-up church. One night I dreamt that I was going to visit the woman pastor at her home. I walked into her house and it was falling apart. The walls were made out of thin wood panels, and everything about the structure was unstable. It was dark inside because she didn't have light connected or didn't pay the light bill. The only thing I can compare it to is the house from Charlie and the Chocolate factory – the 2005 film with Johnny Depp. It looked like Charlie's house in that movie where everyone lived in one room and the house was falling apart. Just like that, but worse. Thin aged wood planks put together with worn out nails made up the walls and ceiling. I was just visiting the pastor woman's house and as I walked in I was very careful where I stepped as the floor was broken and patches of thin wood revealed an exposed and incomplete foundation.

    "Good morning," I said to her from the door with concern. "Oh

THE CONDITION OF ORPHANS

hey Arisbet, I'm just making breakfast for the kids." She replied. She looked busy and rushed. She was standing next to her stove making a meal. As I approached the stove, what I saw made me sick to my stomach. She had a big pot and what she was making was not food. It had trash and dirt in it, I could see bits of rice but it looked just like dark slush. Then one child walked up to her with a bowl, and then shortly after another walked up with a bowl and so on. Each child was malnourished and they had skeletal figures. Their clothes were incredibly dirty and torn. None of them were wearing shoes, their feet dirty and callused. They were sad, no facial expression and almost lifeless. They had no energy, they could barely walk in as they approached for food with their small bowls. It looked like they were homeless and I heard the Holy Spirit explain to me and said, "They're orphans". I couldn't keep my eyes off of the pot of food though. "That's not food" I said, "You can't feed them that…" she ignored me as I watched in shock as one by one the children took the food to eat it. "Where are their shoes?…" I asked. She gave no answer, and began to get nervous. "Why are their clothes so dirty?…" I continued. She was uncomfortable at the fact I noticed something was wrong. She smiled and pretended I didn't say anything, looking busy boiling the slush and serving it to each child as they walked up to her. I was only visiting and because she ignored me, I walked away and left.

The dream showed the spiritual condition of her church, and many other churches all over the world leading members who are not adopted in the faith. They do not know their Heavenly Father personally in relationship. Pastors everywhere are dropping whatever message or "slush" they could come up with and calling it a "prophecy" or "the word of God" to members, and they remain orphans in the faith. In another ministry, at a potluck one of the church pastors joked he hadn't written his sermon for Sunday but would just throw something together the night before. It was not surprising to hear that from him as he worked with complete indifference to the church and the church members.

> *"But to all who did receive Him, who believed in His name, he gave the right to become children of God."*
> *– John 1:12 ESV*

The Old Testament reveals God promised He would reconcile humanity to himself and restore the very things that Adam and Eve gave up. The most important thing they gave up was relationship status. We are adopted into God's family because of Christ's redemption and resurrection. Through accepting the Gospel message, the gift of Salvation in Christ, we

The orphanage in Waspan. - Waspan, Nicaragua

enjoy all the privileges, obligations, and inheritance rights as God's children. In Romans 8:15, adoption indicates that the believers who were once enslaved to sin, were given this adoption by God.

Not only were we estranged from God before this adoption through Salvation, but we were also enemies. Jesus explained in Matthew 12:30, *"Whoever is not with me is against me, and whoever does not gather with me scatters."* That means we cannot be neutral with regards to Christ. Many people today think that as long as they live a morally decent life and don't bother anyone and are not out there committing crimes, abusing drugs, or causing trouble that they stand in a position of being good with God. This is deception. If you have an inner disposition that God is irrelevant to your daily living, it's equal to being in opposition to God.

> *"Since, therefore, we have now been justified by His blood, much more shall we be saved by Him from the wrath of God. For if while we were enemies we were reconciled to God by the death of His Son, much more, now that we are reconciled, shall we be saved by His life. More than that, we also rejoice in God through our Lord Jesus Christ, through whom we have now received reconciliation."*
> - Romans 5: 9–11 ESV

Passivity and complacency is a response of rejection towards God. Self-sufficiency is a position of opposition towards God. Indifference and disinterest in God is, in essence, a form of opposition to Him. The Bible teaches us that if we stand anywhere outside of a heart fully surrendered through Salvation in Christ, we are left orphans and our spiritual condition is at best, *impoverished.*

THE CONDITION OF ORPHANS

Grocery bag distribution to the Mayan people. - Guatemala, Guatemala

Jesus' conversation with the Pharisees in John 8 reveals that some who proclaim to know God as father, can be mistaken. In John 8:37 Jesus said, *"I know that you are Abraham's descendants; yet you plan to kill Me,"* that is, although they were born into a lineage of faith, their behavior is evidence that they don't belong to God the father. The scripture continues, *"because My word has no place [to grow] in you [and it makes no change in your heart]."* (John 8:37 AMP). There are people who can hear scripture or read it and it has no effect or impact in their lives. This very thing is what Jesus used to show them that they were not true sons of God. The word of God didn't take root or grow in their spirit and hearts. He called them descendants only as part of the lineage of the father of faith, Abraham. Similarly, there are people today who feel confident in that their parents are pastors, or missionaries, or leaders in church ministries, but that doesn't give anyone an automatic pass.

Many people are falling back on the faith of someone they're related to, that praying mother or grandmother, or that friend they can always run to when they need some 'Jesus' in their life. If this is you, consider these words Jesus spoke to the Pharisees in John 8:39. They answered, *"Abraham is our father."* Jesus said to them, *"If you are [truly] Abraham's children, then do the works of Abraham and follow his example."* He was speaking to men who were devoted to meeting and gathering to recite God's word religiously, and daily. This is revealing that going to church and being able to recite a Bible verse is not enough. Serving in ministry and clocking in hours doesn't give you a pass into relationship as son or daughter either. Jesus is calling out their hearts and points to their actions taken. Their behavior is evidence that their father is not God.

My friend Angela sharing the Gospel in the Mayan village. - Guatemala

> "This is not the way Abraham acted. You are doing the works of your [own] father." They said to Him, "We are not illegitimate children; we have one [spiritual] Father: God." Jesus said to them, "If God were your Father [but He is not], you would love and recognize Me, for I came from God [out of His very presence] and have arrived here. For I have not even come on My own initiative [as self-appointed], but He [is the One who] sent Me.
>
> ...You are of your father the devil, and it is your will to practice the desires [which are characteristic] of your father. He was a murderer from the beginning, and does not stand in the truth because there is no truth in him. When he lies, he speaks what is natural to him, for he is a liar and the father of lies and half-truths."
> - John 8:39-44 AMP

By the time I saw the orphans in Guatemala, I had already been to two other orphanages in Nicaragua. If you take time to observe, no matter where you go, you'll notice similar behavior.

Orphans have a deep longing for acceptance and identity. Many know very little about their fathers and mothers. Rejection is deeply rooted within them. Performance is a way they feel they can get accepted and will do whatever it is to be accepted and praised. In some places where we did children's ministry, the children performed by singing songs they couldn't even understand because they were in a different language, but they would sing and smile really big and it was part of that performance mentality. In Nicaragua one day, I walked around this gym where the kids were practicing singing the song "I Have Decided to Follow Jesus". The missionary leader saw me walk up with a video recorder and she told them to sing louder for the people to see and donate. I thought, *'Oh no, don't tell them that!'* I stopped recording and just watched them. They looked at her with desire for acceptance. They didn't know what they were saying. They spoke Spanish.

Orphans are insecure and deal with envy by comparison. At one of the orphanages in Nicaragua we saw a young girl who had the most strikingly beautiful eyes. They were one-of-a-kind blue green and brown, very clear as if you were looking at the most crystalized ocean waters. Every last one of us walked over to her to admire her eyes and tell her "Wow! Your eyes are so beautiful!" and I saw the envy on the other kids faces. Some looked jealous and sad as if her having beautiful colored eyes meant theirs were ugly. They desired what God gave to someone else.

Whatever you give an orphan, they will accept because they don't have confidence in that they may receive anything tomorrow. The scarcity mentality keeps orphans in a position to accept everything they are given. Everything looks good to them and they will consume whatever is presented in front of them. Orphans are guarded and don't trust easily. Their fear of people will keep them from doing many things in freedom.

This is the exact condition of people everywhere in and out of the church. They are spiritually orphans. Outside of the sonship of God, there is no rest. Like the orphan, they don't know their Heavenly Father and have a deep longing for acceptance and identity, looking for it everywhere they turn. Especially within the church culture, performance is the way many feel valuable. Their means for acceptance involves checking off boxes and fitting the requirements placed on them by others, not by God. They stay busy doing ministry and look to each other and leaders for acceptance. The same way the Pharisees lived with fulfilling the standard of man and not meeting the standard of God, rejecting Christ in their work. Their identity is found outside of adoption as sons. Without understanding the identity of son or dauther in Christ, no one can successfully follow after Christ. The lack of trust in God demands

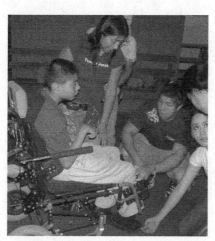

Wheelchair distribution. - Guatemala

self-sufficiency, requiring them to make decisions in their lives first and then ask God to bless their choices. Spiritual orphans are led by their own understanding and suffer the consequences.

There are Christians filling the pews who perform believing they will receive right standing with God and remain struggling in identity. They carry hearts of offense, wearing their brokenness and shame as a badge of honor. Many people today boast and adopt character and identity God did not give them. If you tell an orphan they are valuable, they wont believe it. Orphans look ahead and see hopelessness. Sons and daughters without any natural assurance look to the future and know it will be a good future. They carry an expectation and hope in their souls. Like the orphans, there is a plague of envy and jealousy among many people in and out of the church. They destroy each other because of comparison, spreading gossip about others, splitting congregations up and splitting families apart. Within the church, it looks like a church body with a revolving door of people coming in and out and the church doesn't grow. They thrive on shame and live from a position of guilt. There is always the risk they will get rejected if they do anything wrong. Women tear down women out of envy. Men don't show up for other men out of pride. The same root that took Satan out of God's kingdom is taking the souls of men out today. Pride. You ever notice a family with a missing father? The children are left broken and divided.

How do you know you're a true son or daughter of God?

"For all who are allowing themselves to be led by the Spirit of God are sons of God. For you have not received a spirit of slavery leading again to fear [of God's judgment], but you have received the Spirit of adoption as sons [the Spirit producing sonship] by which we [joyfully] cry, "Abba! Father!" The Spirit Himself testifies and confirms together with our spirit [assuring us] that we [believers] are children of God."
John 8:14-17 AMP

We know because we *"allow ourselves to be led by the Spirit of God"*. When you whole-heartedly commit your life to God, the Bible says you are sealed with the Holy Spirit (Ephesians 1). The Holy Spirit is now living within you and you get to allow the Holy Spirit to lead you. John 8 continues in verse 17 by adding, *"the Holy Spirit himself testifies and confirms together with our spirit [assuring us] that we [believers] are children of God."* There is a confidence we have that we know without a doubt because we have His assurance and no one can take that away from us. We have all been given

THE CONDITION OF ORPHANS

this opportunity but many people remain idle and do not accept it. Many people in the church remain like the Pharisees and while they can be found within the church buildings regularly, reject Christ in their hearts daily. They fight the word of God within themselves so much, it's a form of spiritual persecution of Christ in their hearts. Most people know how to talk about God's love but many don't know what it is to live and abide in it daily. A daily experience, an authentic awareness of God the Father's undying love for you. You have to be honest with yourself. Because if you identify as a believer, you will remain in a religious cycle with no breakthrough. If you're not a Christian, and all this is new to you, you will continue living the life of 'it's never enough'.

Isn't this true for the world today? We're served messages and ideas every day to help feed our needs and desires and we consume and consume and the world is still left dissatisfied. It's never enough and being hungry for more we have created the worst case of mass consumption in history. Our landfills remain in crisis, telling the story of our struggle and inability to satisfy ourselves with material belongings. The stories of lives lived in a condition of *'it's never enough'*.

Knowing God as father changes everything. Sons and daughters have no fear of people because they hold a genuine fear of God. The words spoken by God carries more weight and value than words spoken by others. They carry a peace that transcends understanding and don't second doubt themselves as they are led by the Holy Spirit. No one can bully them into doing things they know God didn't call them to do. Sons and daughters have an assurance of receiving provision daily. Their understanding of God gives them a confidence in knowing their own identity and living it out. They don't look for God to get a gift, simply spending time together brings contentment. While orphans receive love by earning it, sons and daughters in Christ know they are loved by grace alone without having to check off boxes. Grace is unending. They don't have to do anything to earn love, they live in awareness of God's love poured out in their hearts daily. Jesus' induction into ministry included affirmation of Sonship directly from God and the Holy Spirit. As He was being baptized by John, the skies broke open and God said from heaven, *"This is my beloved Son, in whom I Am well-pleased."*

> *"When He had been baptized, Jesus came up immediately from the water; and behold, the heavens were opened to Him, and He saw the Spirit of God descending like a dove and alighting upon Him. And suddenly a voice came from heaven, saying, "This is My beloved Son, in whom I am well pleased."*
> *- Matthew 3:16-17 NKJV*

Overlooking the view from the mountains of the Mayan village.
- Guatemala

Notice this detail. Jesus had not yet completed one miracle work. No one had been healed from an incurable disease. No lame man had walked and no diseased leper had been miraculously healed by His doing. When this baptism affirmation moment occurred, Jesus had not clocked in hours of preaching time in the synagogue yet. He had not been rejected by those who were supposed to celebrate Him yet. He had not yet been sought after to be murdered for doing the will of God yet. He hadn't resurrected His friend Lazarus for the glory of God yet. He hadn't died on the cross to reconcile the world back to God yet. None of that had happened yet and he was already fully loved by God. Before doing any 'ministry work', Jesus was already a beloved son whom God was pleased with. This certainty of acceptance and love of God without having to perform or do anything is fully understood by people who have been adopted in the faith.

I wish I could accurately describe the level of poverty that the orphans in one of the orphanages of Nicaragua lived in for you. It was severe. There were no resources and although the missionary family ran the place, it was evident they lacked the organization and ability to bring in the children's most basic needs. The look on the orphans' faces and their inability to laugh genuinely like any healthy child I saw back home was haunting. Whatever they had seen and experienced up to that point, no human being can undo with medication or any therapy plan. While teams can visit and provide donations, no volunteer, no staff member, no doctor, no missionary, no pastoral care worker can go deep into their core and restore them within. Regardless of how qualified they may be.

When I think of the state and condition of many churches in Dallas, in the nation, I mean in the world – and how members walk in and out

THE CONDITION OF ORPHANS

of the church spiritually – they suffer from the same condition.

Many pastors today are not running churches, they are running orphanages.

Like the orphanage in Nicaragua, pastors everywhere are struggling to lead ministries, relying on their own efforts. They perceive themselves capable and forget that despite their best credentials, only the power of the Holy Spirit can do the work in people. The confidence in material provision is seen as Mega church budgets in the millions go to build a beautiful building, while neglecting the spiritual build up of the foundation in the body of members. A lot of money will go to programming and stage presentation, the largest LED screens, the perfect Christmas program, while year round people are not loved, embraced, taught or discipled. Visitors all over the world enter church services, become members and remain orphans.

But I remember and hold on to the assuring words Jesus spoke to us in the book of John.

> *"If you love me, you will keep my commandments. And I will ask the Father, and he will give you another Helper, to be with you forever, even the Spirit of truth, whom the world cannot receive, because it neither sees him nor knows him. You know him, for he dwells with you and will be in you.*
> *"I will not leave you as orphans; I will come to you."*
> *- John 14:15-18 AMP*

In the view of orphans, the care giver who receives the child is the game changer. That care giver changed their identity from orphan to adoption into a new family. No longer an orphan, now a son or daughter. Where there was lack, now there is abundance. Where there was sadness, now there is renewed joy. From abandonment to support in a newfound community of loved ones.

In the faith, the care giver is the Holy Spirit through the power of Christ's death and resurrection. We are called children of God, with the Holy Spirit given to us and abiding in us forever, as Jesus described above in John. People sing songs like, "Holy Spirit rain down" and "Manifestation of the Holy Spirit" and accept emotional experiences indulging in their feelings, when the Bible says the Holy Spirit is a person and His presence remains in us always. Like a best friend who has all the answers and never leaves your side. He never leaves us.

It is clear to see why so many people come to God when they

are at rock bottom and have no way out. When you are suffering through something alone and suddenly look up, it's easier to recognize the living God who redeems you as a loving father. God's love transcends salvation of your physical being and reaches your inner spiritual core, the you that no one can completely see. Sons and daughters live from a position of love they received. They are not trying to get it from anyone or anything else.

As children of God we discover that the fully manifested love of God is the power of God. Some people may think the greatest power of God was manifested through raising people from the dead or performing miracles. Most everyone would share the opinion that the height of Christ's power was made evident in resurrection. I believe the greatness of the power of God that was displayed on Christ's death on the cross is overlooked. The power to forgive while being persecuted and mocked by those who should have celebrated you. The power to willingly surrender your life for someone else who didn't deserve or value you.

Physical suffering is one painful reality, but Jesus not only underwent physical suffering on that cross, He suffered emotional pain. The suffering reached his soul as only one of His disciples was left standing at the foot of the cross. Despite having family, only His mother stood there until his last breath. While He healed many and preached to masses, seeing a small few standing at the foot of the cross in his final moments likely brought Him profound sorrow. All that, together with the resurrection, is astounding power. All of it was done because of love and to reconcile us as sons and daughters. Who could measure up or match Him? No one. No position, no material possession, no career, no spouse, no amount of money, nothing could ever match the love of God. His love holds incredible power.

A final thought is that the position of Orphan implies there is no relation. You can't keep showing up to church trying to relate to God from the spiritual position of an orphan. If you do, your life will say to everyone that God must be a liar. Many believers are confused by how they could possibly not be a son or daughter. I've heard people give testimonies of how they went to church for years, some have been raised in church, but one day something happened in their lives and finally in their heart they took the step and surrendered their life to God. They continue to share with excitement all the areas in their life that changed. If you listen closely to these testimonies, you never hear them give themselves credit. Quite the opposite, you hear them recall the shift in their lives with complete amazement as if it were a miracle and completely done outside of their effort. No one can tell them it was not God. You can't logicize them out of their faith and belief, as though it was good vibes, luck or by force of the universe or whatever other theory. They are convinced beyond any doubt it was God's

THE CONDITION OF ORPHANS

presence and power.

That's adoption.

Not only does God see you, He is the best caregiver. He brings complete restoration to you and gives you a position of heir as son or daughter in His heavenly kingdom. It's not a promise for when you die, that is, when your physical body perishes. It's a promise for you while you still live on earth. You entered into a heavenly spiritual kingdom of personal freedom and abundance in Christ. Invite Christ as lord of your life. You can finally rest and receive as a son or a daughter of God right where you are.

Your position to sonship is immediate.

CHAPTER 9

The Pact of a Union

I was excited about all the work we had planned for on our excursion to the Guatemalan mountains. We were scheduled to fix wheelchairs for handicap children. We prepared for a long workday and traveled to Guatemala city, through areas which were poverty stricken. We traveled into the mountain villages and stopped by the market to buy 25+ bags of food we would distribute to families in the neighborhoods. These small neighborhoods were nestled on the side of a mountain, like some pueblitos in México. I saw kids walking everywhere with worn out clothes, dirty faces, messy hair, no shoes and big smiles. The markets were busy with the sound of Latin music and comadres[1] gossiped amongst each other as they worked, cleaned fruit and cut vegetables to prepare them for sale.

It made me happy to see women living in community. Despite what many may consider to be living in poverty, they were rich in community and full of joy! They spoke fast as they worked, so it was hard for me to catch what they were saying but just a name here and there followed with laughter. Everything was moving fast and people yelled after me to buy produce as we walked by. I saw rows and rows of food, hand grown by these hard working locals, along with the faster than New York City pedestrian traffic of people needing to urgently get somewhere on the streets.

I was so eager to get going to visit families and pass out food but I wouldn't get to join in after all. Ruby, my American teammate had broken her ankle and our team leader thought it was best for her to go to the pastors' home and rest or possibly help the women prepare food for the team's lunch. Nobody volunteered to stay with her. Who wants to stay in a home kicking back and miss the greatest trail hike adventure of climbing a mountain to pass out food!? I felt bad for Ruby to be at the pastor's house alone without any way of communicating as she only spoke English, so I volunteered to stay with her.

The pastor's house was on that same mountain village and the hike was tough for Ruby but I helped her up along the way. We entered into a tiny humble home that may appear to most American visitors as a home with little means, but I knew they were actually some of the most well off

---

1   In Latino culture, comadre refers to the relationship between a mother and her child's godmother. It can also refer to a special bond between intimate female friends.

'Las Comadres', the women in the market. - Guatemala, Guatemala

residents of this mountain. The kitchen had an old iron stove, the kind you would see in the homes of cerros in México. I have a special love for Latin kitchens, it feels like home and I felt so grateful to ever experience cooking a meal with Guatemalan women. Not just any meal but a wedding meal, what an honor. The smell of tortillas quemadas took me back home because my mom's house smells just like that. I'd often be getting ready to go out and suddenly the smell of burned tortillas made it's way into my bedroom. I'd swing my bedroom door open to yell out, "Mom! The tortillas are burning, I'm going to stink like tortillas now!" and quickly run out to open a door or two, turn off the stove and wrap my long hair in a towel. The women were making tortillas and were surprised to see me make them so easily. However, the Guatemalan tortilla is not wide and thin like the Mexican tortilla, smaller in circumference, about 4" in diameter and thicker too. It's about the size of a Mexican gordita, a little larger than a Salvadoran pupusa but with nothing inside. One of the women was the pastor's relative, Camila, which I believe was his cousin and the other a church member. Afterwards, I helped sell products in their small family store. It's like the stores you see in neighborhoods in pueblos in México, where the family lives in the home and the store takes up a room in front of the home.

  The team returned and looked physically exhausted. We were to have lunch and prepare to be guests at a wedding, which was very exciting. Camila and I had become friends instantly it seemed, she was so kind-hearted and joyful. She let me into one of the bedrooms so we could talk about the wedding. Of course, the main question out of my mouth was, "What are you going to wear Camila?" She walked over to the closet and brought over this beautiful 3 piece traditional Guatemalan outfit. It included a skirt with many colors, long in length but perfectly fit to stop at your ankles. It came with a white blouse which had a beautifully colorful hand-sewn floral design decorating it like a necklace. The blouse was worn tucked inside the skirt and the skirt was then wrapped around and tied together with a traditional Guatemalan belt. Camila looked at me and said, "I have one for you to wear!" She looked in the closet and pulled out another one for me. I felt so beautiful and truly honored that she allowed me to wear something so valuable to her. We have very similar traditional clothing in México, and it felt like being around family. We were preparing to celebrate a wedding, the pact of a union, and one of the most beautiful celebrations anticipated within any Latin American community.

Before the wedding started, we stopped to pick up the couple and bring them back to the home where there were other friends and family waiting for us. The custom is for friends and family to walk together with the couple to the church. As we began the walk down the mountain, people stepped out of their homes and joined us on the way to the church. Everyone in the community placed so much time, effort and cooperation into the celebration of a union. The wedding ended and everyone walked back up the mountain together to enjoy a wedding feast.

This is when I met Maria. Our team leader asked me to pray for a young girl who suffered from an illness. When I walked over to one of the outside rooms, there she was, a young Guatemalan girl. She was a young teen with a lovely warm smile. She wore her beautiful long black hair in braids with red ribbon bows. She sat with her mother hunched over, wearing permanent worry on her face. She struggled to give me a welcoming smile as I approached them. Since they spoke only their indigenous

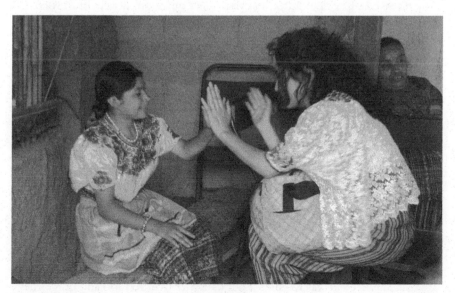

Patty cake with my Mayan friend. - Guatemala

My beautiful Mayan friend. - Guatemala

language I had a local translate for me from Spanish.

I started by being a friend and taught her how to play patty cake as we waited for the translator. I asked what was wrong. The mom explained that Maria suffered from torment and a disease that nothing could cure. I began to pray as I usually do, seeking the Holy Spirit's understanding about the situation. As I prayed, I noticed she was wearing a bracelet around her hand and a necklace. They were made of beads and had a human skull on it. I asked her mom what was the purpose of the bracelet and she said it was a gift given to her by someone in the community for protection. "Oh protection?" I asked, "Yes," she said, "Protection from death so she wouldn't die from the disease." How does a death skull protect one from death? In México many people also believe this and worship a skeletal figure cloaked in female form. They call it 'La Santa Muerte' which means, 'The Holy Death'. People offer pledges or offerings in hopes to have their miracle granted or mainly to prevent the death of someone.

Not to be mistaken with blatant satanic worship, many Latinos in different countries come in agreement with these types of spirit beliefs mixed in with Christian faith in hopes to reach a certain outcome. In Maria's case it was *'If my daughter wears the jewelry with a skull on it, she will be protected from death and receive the miraculous healing of her disease.'* Whether the Santa Muerte, or a skull dedicated to some Guatemalan spirit idol, trusting in this alternative source is not the way to reach her desired outcome.

I explained to her mother that the jewelry did the complete opposite and brought further spiritual bondage to her daughter. "It's a form of idolatry, to place our faith on a death saint or an object above God alone. Only God can fully heal and only God will protect her." I explained to them that all she needed was to entrust her daughter over to God and pray believing with confidence that God's word will not fail her. I encouraged her to

A bride and groom on their way to the church on their wedding day. The community of people walked behind them carrying gifts. - Guatemala

have faith and believe God for her miracle. Maria's mother agreed, took the jewelry off of her daughter and handed it to me. I continued praying for Maria and after I prayed, we talked a bit more before I walked away holding Maria's jewelry in my hands. I remember looking down at the skulls, which to me looked powerless. They were mere pieces of plastic and metal, given presumed power only by one person's faith. Maria's mother was already a believer in the Christian faith yet she still placed her faith on these skulls. Moments like these in the mission field magnified an awareness of how Christians in the faith will still desperately search for an alternative method, another way, aside from just God alone.

    Another night, we went to an outdoor church service. There was a make shift portable stage set up like a small outdoor concert. It was late and dark out, and the pastors who were hosting us in Guatemala were going to preach. Our missionary team was invited to help pray for people after the service at what Christian churches refer to as "the altar call" at the conclusion of the sermon. During an altar call, people who may need prayer walk up to the altar for a minister or leader to pray for them. The sermon ended, and all of a sudden a good amount of people from the crowd began to form a line to get prayed for by the Pastor's wife. I saw as some of my teammates approached the people in that line offering to pray for them and the people declined their offers firmly. "What's going on?" I asked a team member. I really only asked my teammate the question to validate what I believed was going on. "Well, they are saying that they only want the pastor's wife to pray for them so that their prayer gets answered." I stared at the whole situation stunned, watching my team members get denied one by one by the local Christian church members. There it was, I saw it again, people trusting in an alternative method, with full faith on getting to God by another way. I didn't get close to the line of people as soon as I observed this occur.

I focused in on the pastor's wife though. I wondered if she knew. They not only admired her in the pastoral role she held, but they considered her to be the source of their healing miracle, the source of their answered prayer. She was the alternative way. If she did not speak it to be it wouldn't be. She smiled at them, the line noticeably in front of her, and she was beaming with joy. *'Does she know?'* I wondered…and I stared from afar. Does she know they have made her an idol? They didn't believe, as the Bible teaches, that anyone can pray because the power is held by the Holy Spirit alone and we are merely vessels in Gods hand. They believed that in order to get an answer from God, only she could obtain it on their behalf. Idolatry. The same way some Catholics believe in a saint that can be the only one who they can pray to in order for a specific miracle. There are many saints in México, like San Judas Tadeo, which people believe that each hold a unique ability to get their specific miracles form. You need healing? There's a saint for that. You need children? There's a saint for that. You need financial blessing? There's a saint for that. Many Mexicans also rely on witchcraft and believe God will bless them despite their faith in that alternative way. The same way Maria's death skull jewelry was ineffective, these alternative methods fail because the person has removed God from His highest position.

Starring at the pastor's wife, I wondered all the possibilities that kept her from stopping the people from rejecting the missionary team members. Maybe she learned this as an acceptable form of leadership which her denomination demonstrated for her where they keep pastors in a hierarchy above everyone else. Maybe that norm was why she didn't stop them. Despite the gleam on her face, I hoped she would awaken to the tragic problem she faced ahead of her with those people.

If they keep running to her as the source, they will keep missing God.

Ministry is not successful unless we are urgently redirecting people to go directly to God themselves. I imagined action I hoped for, I envisioned in hope that she would suddenly pull the mic in front of her and speaking aloud in boldness, *'God is not limited to just me! The Bible says you have been given power yourself! If you have been truly saved and are a Christian, the Bible teaches you're sealed with the Holy Spirit. The Holy Spirit doesn't need to come down, He already did that, He now lives in you! When Jesus healed the sick and burdened, the Bible says He told them frequently, 'your faith' has healed you. Your faith! Where is your faith placed upon? Mark 9, Jesus said if you can believe, all things are possible to him who believes". After He said this, the man who hoped for his child to be healed admitted his faith was weak, that child's father cried out to Jesus in response, 'Lord help my unbelief!'...You see these students? All of these students have traveled from all over the world and dedicated their lives to study in a Bible school, they can pray for you!'*

I don't know something like that. I wanted to see something in her that bothered her about seeing the line of people reject prayer from the missionary team members, but she went on and prayed for the line as other ministers, including her husband, stood aside. I don't mean to shame her in any way, and in the end only God knows our hearts. I share this to highlight this critical error in some ministers who accept this behavior from people where the result leads to idolizing them.

Idolatry is seeded in the belief that there is another way, another source to get you the result with God. If you believe ideas like, *'If I wear this item, then God', 'If this person prays for me, then God', 'If I do all of these good things, then God'*...you risk removing God from the highest position and place that object, that person or your personal effort in His place. It should just be God.

An idol, by definition from scripture, in Hebrew is the word *'pesel'*. It refers to an idol or image, false gods or objects of pagan worship and are described as a person, place or thing, an image made in the likeness of man or animal, made of wood, stone or metal, which are created by man. (Strongs 6459 *Pesel*; Strong's Hebrew 6091 *Atsab*; Strong's Hebrew 1544 *Gillul*.)[2] When God instructs *"You shall not make for yourself an idol"* in Exodus 20:4, we learn that the one who gave the idol any life or power of influence was one person who chose to worship it. You can idolize anything or anyone, including yourself.

What in your life have you allowed to take over the position of God? What have you been committed to entrusting your hope and faith on above God alone? There is a very high chance that you're facing some consequence because of it. Psalm 115:4-8 describes idols as the following:

> *"Their idols are silver and gold,*
> *the work of human hands.*
> *They have mouths, but do not speak;*
> *eyes, but do not see.*
> *They have ears, but do not hear;*
> *noses, but do not smell.*
> *They have hands, but do not feel;*

---

2   1981. Berean Strong's Lexicon 6459. Pesel. NAS Exhaustive Concordance of the Bible with Hebrew-Aramaic and Greek Dictionaries, Bible Hub. https://biblehub.com/hebrew/6459.htm.

> *feet, but do not walk;*
> *and they do not make a sound in their throat.*
> *Those who make them become like them;*
> *so do all who trust in them.*
> *- Psalm 115:4-8 ESV*

There is pact of a union that comes with idolatry.

Maria's mom was aware she placed her faith on a spirit of death to prevent her daughter's death, but may not have been aware of the pact she made when she handed her faith over to it. Like the pact a husband and wife make at a wedding ceremony, vows or an exchange of agreements, are completed when someone entrusts any area over to an idol. With Maria's mom, she came in agreement with the spirit of death, the spirit who was responsible to protect her daughter, she handed over her faith to that spirit. God doesn't share His glory with anyone. He is the only true God and doesn't make room for idolatry. Through the act of bestowing her faith upon that spirit, she inadvertently displaced God from His rightful place.

In the Mexican Catholic church, if the saint honors the person's prayer request, the person will dedicate one of their children to the saint or commit themselves and their families to the Catholic faith. El D.F., or Mexico City, is said to have thousands of street shrines to San Judas Tadeo. I've heard that people walk on their knees form their towns with bloodied legs as they arrive to the Catholic church where the saint's shrine resides.

Mayan mothers and their children - Guatemala

Church service. - Guatemala

I got to see one San Judas shrine in person on my visit to Zacatecas, México. There are many devoted followers of that idol everywhere in México and Latin communities in the U.S.

    I once threw away my mom's San Judas Tadeo jewelry and prayer card. She had a dresser area dedicated to prayer to La Virgen de Guadalupe, Jesus and any other saints she thought would listen. There were candles and flowers on her dedicated altar in her bedroom. I was a teenager. I grabbed the San Judas Tadeo jewelry beads and the prayer card to the saint and walked out to the street to throw it down the sewer.

    When she asked where it was I told her what I did and she got so mad at me. I have since learned to respect other people's belongings, however the good that came from it was that it started a really good conversation with my mom. "Mom, but that's an idol, you're summoning evil spirits, pray to God instead." She ignored me and in anger yelled, "Do you know how expensive that was!?" It was 24k gold, and my face went blank realizing that detail just then. "And I need you to respect my faith Arisbet, I've told you many times, respect my faith!!!" She had a point.

    "Mom, ok you tell me that the virgin you pray to is La Virgen Maria - Mary the Virgin who God chose to have Jesus as described in the Bible, correct?" She looked at me with an all of a sudden switch to full attention and eager to hear what I had to say. "Yes…" She listened attentively. "Ok then who is she!?" I asked pointing real fast and with dramatic effect to the photo of La Virgen de Guadalupe on her dresser, and not allowing her to respond I continued, "Because this lady appeared in the sky to some indio and she has a different name, her name is 'La Virgen de Guadalupe' mom and according to her name it could mean so many things but no one clearly knows if you research it", she gave me a blank stare in silence. I continued, "And Exodus chapter 4:20 says, *"You shall not make for yourselves an idol, nor any image of anything that is in the heavens above and you shall not bow yourself down to them, nor serve them, for I, Yahweh your God, am a jealous God',"* I didn't pause, I kept going, "Someone carved those images of the virgins distributed all over México mom, a man or woman carved those, and the Bible is clear in

The shrine to San Judas Tadeo I visited in Zacatecas. You can see that people leave clothing, photos, prayer notes, and other objects to the saint in hopes to get their prayer answered and see their miracle manifest. - Zacatecas, México

Exodus. God clearly instructed us do not carve for yourself any image male or female to worship them,"

It was hard for her to question anything the Catholic church taught but I continued, "- and not only Guadalupe, but then who is la Virgen de Zapopan, who is that lady mom? Or La Virgen de Ocotlán, o la Virgen de San Juan de los Lagos? There are many, not one of them is the Virgin Mary mother of Jesus from the Bible and the people in México who carved them have declared they are not Mary from the Bible."

I recognized how hard it was for her to let the idols go as she explained, "You don't understand, when I was left an orphan being cared for by Sra. Leonor, without my parents in the new rancho, all I had was La Virgen de Guadalupe. I prayed to her every night for protection." I understood even with hearing the truth, she would continue her faith on La Virgen de Guadalupe because this idol was so deeply rooted in her soul taking the form of a mother she never had. These pacts made with idols are strong. The deception is she was left chasing a hollow figure made of clay, leaving distance between her and God, our loving Father, who relentlessly and passionately pursues her to this day. I gently told her I was sorry for what she went through as a child and that I loved her. I left that conversation accepting that prayer was all I could offer at that point.

I've asked myself why is idolatry so appealing to us? Have you ever gone hungry? When you have an unmet need, you can't think straight. Your need is a distraction so the urgency to meet it becomes priority. Do you know what it's like to suffer from bitter cold for several hours on end in the peak of winter? There are dire needs we have and the condition we sit in wanting to fill those needs is so hard to bear we run to anything we can to meet the need. I think the bottom line is that idolatry is easier.

Idols are easy to run to because they don't have standards. This implies little to no consequence because there were no standards to break. Those who choose idolatry over God enter into loose commitment. There is little responsibility or accountability on you when you rely on idols.

Idols are only as powerful as humanity allows them to be.

Idolatry gives you the ability to comfortably sway any direction and to believe whatever you want. Idolatry gives you a pass from maintaining an actual relationship. An idol will not require of you what God is requiring of you. The trust, commitment, relationship and responsibility that comes with union with God in your spirit and soul surpass any requirements under idolatry. Idolatry plus God voids communion with God completely. Whenever I think of idolatry, scriptures that always comes to mind are Exodus 19 and 20.

In Exodus 19 we see the beginning of a re-introduction of a relationship between God and the Israelites. God offered the Isrealites the ability to speak with Him directly. We see the progression of God beginning to require things of the people before they even approach the mountain where God was to come down. Exodus 19:10 *"The Lord also said to Moses, "Go to the people and consecrate them today and tomorrow [that is, prepare them for My sacred purpose], and have them wash their clothes and be ready by the third day, because on the third day the Lord will come down on Mount Sinai [in the cloud] in the sight of all the people. Then Moses brought the people out of the camp to meet God, and they stood and presented themselves at the foot of the mountain."*

God expressed the requirement of preparation and warned of the consequence that would ensue if they did not complete the requirement. Exodus 19 verse 22 continues, *"Also have the priests who approach the Lord consecrate (sanctify, set apart) themselves [for My sacred purpose], or else the Lord will break forth [in judgment] against them [and destroy them]."*

People don't like that. Idolatry is easier.

We continue to read the reason God asked something of them and God expressed His intention to bring the fear of God over people so that they would take their relationship with God seriously. Exodus 20:20 says, *"for God has come in order to test you, and in order that the fear of Him [that is, a profound reverence for Him] will remain with you, so that you do not sin."* In Exodus chapter 20 God delivered the Ten Commandments. Notice the very first thing God tells them before even addressing their behavior requirements.

"You shall have no other gods before Me. You shall not make for yourself any idol, or any likeness (form, manifestation) of what is in heaven above or on the earth beneath or in the water under the earth [as an object to worship].

You shall not worship them nor serve them; for I, the Lord your God, am a jealous (impassioned) God [demanding what is rightfully and uniquely mine], visiting (avenging) the iniquity (sin, guilt) of the fathers on the children [that is, calling the children to account for the sins of their fathers], to the third and fourth generations of those who hate Me, but showing graciousness and steadfast lovingkindness to thousands [of generations] of those who love Me and keep My commandments."
- Exodus 20:3-6 AMP

Idolatry was God's first point to address on the Ten Commandments. He prohibited it and accompanied the command with a warning that the consequence through their idolatry would reach their future generations. Why do you think the first thing God addressed was idolatry? Above addressing the way we should behave? Before do not murder, before do not to lie, before saying do not desire your neighbor's goods and don't commit adultery, God put his number one on idolatry. I believe if we can get the idolatry issue out, then the rest of the commandments would not be a problem for us. If you serve an idol, the insufficiency of that worship will drive you to do any of the below commandments in your attempt to get your needs met. Why do you think the act of idolatry would include a consequence of a generational curse to the third and fourth generations? Even if it's an innocent act of hope and faith on the idol you chose, you are entering into an agreement within your spirit and it carries down to your children and their children and so forth. We can pass down idolatry like we pass down genetic disease.

One of the most chilling Bible verses I have ever read follows up after the commandments were delivered in Exodus 20.

"Now all the people witnessed the thunder and the flashes of lightning and the sound of the trumpet and the smoking mountain; and as they looked, the people were afraid, and they trembled

Me, the day of the wedding.
- Guatemala, Guatemala

[and moved backward] and stood at a [safe] distance. Then they said to Moses, "You speak to us and we will listen, but do not let God speak to us or we will die." Moses said to the people, "Do not be afraid; for God has come in order to test you, and in order that the fear of Him [that is, a profound reverence for Him] will remain with you, so that you do not sin." So the people stood at a [safe] distance, but Moses approached the thick cloud where God was.
- Exodus 20:18-21 AMP

    The Israelites had the invitation to go to God directly and instead they chose to keep going through Moses to reach God. The chilling detail of our human nature to place the responsibility of sustaining a relationship with God on someone else, goes way back. The unsettling reality that many leave the responsibility of maintaining our relationship with God onto others has deep roots in our history. God was willing to speak directly to them and they in turn declined that offer, even after everything God had already done on their behalf! I mean they saw first-hand an entire sea was parted, bread fell from the sky, and still as a collective they were like, *'Nope, we're good. You go Moses and tell us what God says.'* That sounds completely crazy! Yet, many people repeat this same response today.

    Jesus came removing the separation from us and God. The Holy Spirit is readily available to lead us as Moses did to the place where God will speak clearly and directly to us in our personal day to day lives and people still reject His offer. Many today prefer to go through a priest, a deacon, a pastor, a religious Bible reading friend, a spiritual mentor, a ministry leader, a praying grandmother…etc., to hear about God. This reality today is completely crazy to me. The Israelites already completed the tasks to be allowed to approach God, were given the opportunity they still stayed a far distance away. Today many people complete all the tasks their church requires of them, complete all the volunteer hours, put in time on Sundays to help and serve, and they still stay a far comfortable distance away from God. I believe this is the first step to idolatry. If you keep that safe distance away you will inevitably fill the place with someone or something else.

While we anticipate eternity, I want you to know that God intended this glory of union and to abide together here and now. Heaven will be glorious, but we are supposed to experience His glory through His presence here on Earth. You can live united with God as one, through Salvation in Christ, with all the blessings of heaven, right now. The Holy Spirit makes a home in us. In our faith commitment with Christ we take on a new spiritual position of victory over sin and death and we take on heirship in Christ (Romans 8). With our union in Christ, we accept a responsibility in this union to reconcile people to God through the ministry of reconciliation as described in 2 Corinthians 5:18, and the Great Commission as implored by Christ in Matthew 28:16-20. In return, on God's end of this pact are an innumerable amount of promises. I wish I could describe the list of promises God offers us under this pact of a union here but they are countless. God promises to never leave us nor forsake us, to remain within us (His Holy Spirit), to strengthen and sustain us in difficult times, to rescue us from destruction, to take vengeance on our behalf, to keep us in perfect peace, encouragement and joy in the face of trouble, deliverance from evil spirits who oppress us, to watch over us with His loving eyes, to instruct and teach

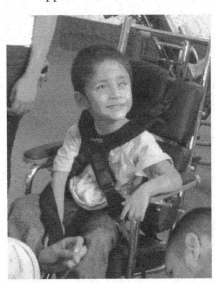 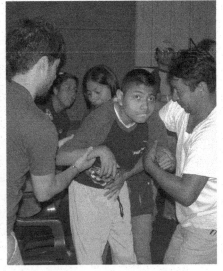

Wheelchair repair and distribution for people in the city. We were able to make adjustments to the fitting of their wheelchairs and spend time encouraging the families.
- Guatemala, Guatemala

THE PACT OF A UNION

Food and shoe distribution to families. - Guatemala

us, to give us guidance in what decisions to make in life, to give us power in times of weakness, to take on our burdens and worries, to heal our broken hearts, to bring healing to our bodies, to bear good fruit, to bless our children and our children's children…and many more vows on God's end.

Consider your needs and consider the idols you erected in your heart to meet them. Who or what have you placed all your faith in? When I think of people relying on idols I imagine the scene of a person crawling in the desert, in the middle of nowhere, in search for water and trying to stay alive. All of a sudden they see a great waterfall ahead and they use up all the energy they have left to get to that waterfall in hopes that they will live. But when they reach it and get closer, they realize it's an illusion. A mirage. Idols are exactly that. There is hope and there is a way of escape out of idolatry. In Deuteronomy 28, God reveals that the blessing can come to you and your future generations by repenting and turning away from idolatry. If you find that you have erected idols in your heart, the good news is God provided a way of escape.

You cancel out and destroy any idol by first acknowledging they are idols you set above God. You then renounce your allegiance and union

Lake Atitlan - Guatemala

to them and whole-heartedly repent to God. Repentance means not just feeling bad, but a regret with change of behavior, not to return back to them. We come into union with God through repentance and salvation in Christ. Surrender your heart to God completely and profess Jesus as Lord and Savior of your life. You no longer belong to any idols and you yourself are no longer placed in the position of God in your life. I would emphasize that the next important step is looking for God's character when you read the Bible. Learning who God is will be breakthrough for you to never return to idols again. You will grasp an awe and reverence towards God and experience God's sufficiency.

 Whatever you need, God has it for you. You need peace? Great news, Jesus is the Prince of Peace. Philippians 4:7 assures us, *"And the peace of God, which surpasses all understanding, will guard your hearts and your minds in Christ Jesus."* Are you heartbroken? *"God heals the brokenhearted and binds up their wounds [healing their pain and comforting their sorrow]"* (Psalm 147:3 AMP). You feel unloved? 1 John 4:8 says, *"God is love"*. 1 John 4:16 says, *"So we have come to know and to believe the love that God has for us. God is love, and whoever abides in love abides in God, and God abides in him."* Romans 8:38-39 affirms, *"neither death, nor life, nor angels, nor principalities, nor powers, nor things present, nor things to come, nor height, nor depth, nor any other creature, shall be able to separate us from the love of God, which is in Christ Jesus our Lord."*

 Are you unsure about what direction to go in life? Do you need advice, help, and an advocate as you face life every day? The Holy Spirit is ready as your personal guidance counselor as it is written in John 14:26, *"But the Comforter (Counselor, Helper, Intercessor, Advocate, Strengthener, Standby), the*

Holy Spirit, Whom the Father will send in My name [in My place, to represent Me and act on My behalf], He will teach you all things."

Pick your struggle, there's a scripture. God's word is constantly assuring you and I that God is the source for all of our needs.

On Monday May 19, 2008 we went to Lake Atitlan, one of the most beautiful lakes in the world. I loved being there and as I looked over the waters I was overcome with gratitude. The next day I would return to San Salvador, El Salvador.

Tsunami

DIALOGUE-DRIVEN VIGNETTE

Imagine the following event.

You arrive at an island in the Caribbean. A series of massive tsunami waves grew up to 30 m (100 ft) high once heading inland, after being created by the underwater seismic activity offshore. Communities along the surrounding coast suffered catastrophic destruction, which resulted in the loss of hundreds of thousands of lives. There were survivors.

The plight of the affected people and countries prompted a worldwide humanitarian response. One of the largest donations came from a multi-billionaire, the richest Man in the world among all nations. This Man sent over ambassadors to the affected areas. A primary goal was for trucks to post at specific areas to distribute the basic need for clean drinking water and other resources. Volunteers wore shirts branded with the Man's corporate name.

There is an overwhelming response of gratitude from the community. Imagine you are right there and witness a scene with rows of semi-trailers loaded with basic supplies to aid the survivors. You reach a trailer and witness a scene where a volunteer works sluggishly. Despite the urgency, he works with indifference and motivated to earn a wage.

A man walks up to receive a box from him and you hear the following conversation:

Volunteer X

Local: "Thank you so much, thank you, thank you, thank you…"

Volunteer X [handing out more cases as local grovels at his feet]:
"Well I am a good person."

Local: "You are our savior; you came to help us when we were in
desperate need,"

Volunteer X: "Yes, actually yes, I am a good person. Uniquely gifted."

Local: "You don't understand how much we needed this, my family.
We have nothing. I don't know how to repay you...
We would have died."

Volunteer X [realizes the local is giving a unique credit to him for what
he is distributing]: "Well, my boss especially chose me. He gave me a
special gift. Only I can get you more water.
But you have to do just as I say."

Local: "Yes, please. We suffered great loss, and we will need more
help...I will do whatever I have to in order for your boss to keep sending me help. I'm desperate. I have nothing."

Volunteer X: "Every time I give you a pack of water, I need you to
do the following things. If you don't do the following things, then
my boss will be very unhappy with you and he will cut you off from
receiving."

Local: "I will do exactly as you say, please. I will not disobey you,
whatever you say I will do."

Volunteer X: "I know you don't have much but since my boss requires
everything of us, you will have to bring a portion of what you do have.
If you fail to bring a portion then he will consider you ungrateful and
you will not have your next provision."

Local [now afraid of the Man the volunteer describes, he decides to
submit to the volunteer]: "Yes, I will bring my portion."

Volunteer X: "One last thing. This is very important. You cannot talk to
my boss, only I can talk to him. But don't worry, I will make sure I tell
you everything he says. Besides, I can tell you about him myself. He's a
good guy. Trustworthy. A generous boss, as you can see."

Local: "I understand... *I'm unworthy.* I believe you. I can communicate
to him through you if you can just make sure you tell him how
grateful I am."

***

Blindly, the local and his entire family continued to approach the trailer
fully committed to serve the volunteer. Enslaved, they met the volunteer's demands without question.

At the trailer a few feet away, another volunteer works hastily to hand out waters. This was the conversation between that volunteer and a different local.

Volunteer Y

Local: "Thank you, thank you so much I don't know how to repay you."

Volunteer Y: "Oh – well you don't. I didn't do anything. I'm just handing it out to you."

Local: "What can I do for you? How can I show my gratitude for your goodness towards us?"

Volunteer Y [now confused]: "What? No – I'm just an ambassador. You see I was sent here…by my boss. He sent me to hand these things to you so that you would live.

I didn't do anything. I didn't buy these things for you."

Local: "Ok but I want to follow you, serve you, something in return for your generosity and your kindness in giving this to me and my family."

Volunteer Y: "I didn't do anything. I get the privilege of working for my boss, I was just sent here. I love doing His work for Him and am grateful to Him myself."

Local: [falls to the ground at the volunteers feet]: "Please, what can I do for you, anything…"

Volunteer Y: "Don't do that! Get up! Listen! I'm only serving you what I was given.

I used to be in need just like you.

My boss came to my community and helped to rescue me years ago. I was receiving like you are receiving now. Then I joined His mission. Because my boss also provided for me, I left everything behind to travel across the world to give this to you. I work for Him now. Do you understand? I was only sent.

If you want to show gratitude, go see my boss yourself!"

Local: "I can? I can go see Him myself?"

Volunteer Y: "Of course! In fact He wants you to go see Him. I was ordered to tell everyone. He wants you to meet Him yourself. He asked me to make sure I connect you to Him. He is closer than you think. Here is the information you need to find Him.

Don't wait for tomorrow, go now."

The Local, speechless, and with overwhelming joy - ran to the Man himself and took his entire family.

Author's Note:
There are really only 2 types of believers in this world and Jesus describes both in scripture. They are the Wicked Servant and the Good and Faithful Servant.

This colloquy describes first The Wicked Servant, Volunteer X, who takes advantage of his or her position and the people they are sent to. The level they do this could be minimal where it's overlooked, all the way up to the highest extreme where it becomes news in the media and we hear about their great fall. "I am a good person." They believe they are good and live as though they don't need God. "Yes I am a quality person. Uniquely gifted." They credit themselves to be uniquely chosen by God and the gatekeeper of blessings to come to people. God will only bless others through them, only if they get the offering, only if they preach, only if they pray... They take advantage of the ignorance of people who are new to the faith or simply ignorant of scripture and desperate for God's love.

"I know you don't have much but since my boss requires everything of us, you will have to bring a portion of what you do have so the provision to me. If you fail to bring a portion then he will consider you ungrateful and you will not have your next provision." They take things from people who have nothing, using

scripture to force them to give in order to get something from God. They describe God as someone to be afraid of, a God who would easily cut them off if the person refuses to obey what they say.

They take scripture and twist it to make God sound like their own version of a god. "One last thing. This is very important. You cannot talk to my boss, only I can talk to him. But don't worry, I will make sure I tell you everything he says." They make sure people don't really connect to God on their own and stay in Biblical ignorance. They have to be the interpreter of what God says for each person's life – even though they have no clue what God is saying for their lives. This establishes their primal need for control. They place religious acts above loving people, mostly because they themselves refused God's love in order to give it to others.

The local saying, "I understand…besides, I'm worthless. I believe you." Is a reference to the reality that people who blindly follow wicked servants have a damaged self-identity. They don't know who they are in Christ, and see themselves as unworthy of connection with God.

This Local person, like the wicked volunteer, built their house on sand, without a solid foundation. Relying on their own abilities, they lack genuine faith and are unable to live out the fruit of the Spirit - even if they are familiar with the Bible verses.

> *"Not everyone who says to Me, 'Lord, Lord,' will enter the kingdom of heaven, but only he who does the will of My Father who is in heaven. Many will say to Me on that day [when I judge them], 'Lord, Lord, have we not prophesied in Your name, and driven out demons in Your name, and done many miracles in Your name?' And then I will declare to them publicly, 'I never knew you; depart from Me [you are banished from My presence], you who act wickedly [disregarding My commands].'*
> *– Matthew 7:21-23 AMP*

The other is the Good and Faithful Servant, Volunteer Y, who over-emphasize the fact that he or she is only sent and redirects others to access God for themselves. They use urgency and every means to make sure the person reaches God. They are the salt and light of the world. They have to keep expressing over and over to people the fact that they should not be regarded so highly, and redirect all attention to God. Some people may call them humble but it's not humility, it's constant submission and obedience to God.

This second volunteer built his or her faith in Christ and take credit for nothing. "I didn't do anything. I didn't buy these things for you...I'm just an ambassador..."

Because the second volunteer chose to act on what God instructed, he was able to not only sustain his relationship with God but also connected the local and his family to God successfully as he continued to serve the line of people in need. "Don't wait for tomorrow, go now," is a reference to their urgency due to the understanding of what the Bible says, salvation is for today. The Bible describes these people to be those who built their home or life on a solid foundation – built on a rock.

The Two Foundations in Matthew 7 as described by Jesus reads as follows:

> *"So everyone who hears these words of Mine and acts on them, will be like a wise man [a far-sighted, practical, and sensible man] who built his house on the rock. And the rain fell, and the floods and torrents came, and the winds blew and slammed against that house; yet it did not fall, because it had been founded on the rock.*
> *And everyone who hears these words of Mine and does not do them, will be like a foolish man who built his house on the sand. And the rain fell, and the floods and torrents came, and the winds blew and slammed against that house; and it fell —and great and complete was its fall."*
> *– Matthew 7:24-27 AMP*

El Salvador & Honduras

CHAPTER 10
The Time In Between

If you could be anyone in the Bible, I promise you would not want to be a prophet. Yet, the amount of people in the Christian community who claim to be a prophet or prophetess is incredible. Prophets in the Bible had a heavy responsibility and were especially selected by God to deliver a message to an entire generation. They did not have it easy and couldn't get away with what people today who claim to be prophets are getting away with. Prophets in the Bible were persecuted for warning and exhorting the people of Israel and leaders. They were not celebrated. Unlike today's prophets who receive honor wherever they go speak, prophets in the Old Testament spoke to God's children unpopular and uncompromising messages that were not sugar-coated. They spoke God's truth for the precise time, which people resisted to hear. Down to John Baptist and Jesus, prophets were chased by religious people to be killed for carrying out God's will through their calling and obedience of delivering a message on behalf of God. Trust me, you wouldn't sign up for that responsibility.

Despite the incredible pressure placed on the role of a prophet, many Christian leaders today add it to their titles. I think it's because the demand for one particular thing is so high. *Hope.* Believers seek out people who identify as prophetic with so much anticipation and desperation looking for a direct personal message from God to feed their hope.

In El Salvador at one of the churches we visited, the pastor's wife identified herself to be a "prophetess" and dedicated some of her preaching time to give prophetic word to people. While we were able to pray for people, I perceived that most of the people were really rushing to the altar hoping and expecting a prophetic word from her. We were getting ready to head out after time ministering to people and some of the women in our group gathered after the service where someone was doing this pastor's wifes' hair. She overheard me talking to my friend Erin, who was frustrated that she was getting older and still unmarried. The pastor's wife paused and prophesied that Erin would marry a man soon and he would be in the beauty industry, specifically, that he was going to be a make-up artist. I stood there translating the prophetic message in complete angst. It was difficult because it sounded like the pastor was guessing a prophetic message to make Erin feel better.

I translated it but said, "Hey, I don't know that you should believe all that, ask God for yourself. Don't worry so much Erin, your future husband will come soon." Erin's problem was that this woman was very well known in El Salvador among churches and regarded highly for her 'prophetic gifting'. My friend was a few years older than most of us on the team, so marriage was a sensitive topic for her. When marriage was brought up, we could all clearly see her sadness and frustration. It appeared to be easy for this "prophetess" to give her a 'divine word from God' about it. She was really trying in some way to keep her hope alive, even if it meant forcing a false message out for her.

Erin ended up marrying a guy who was a psychology major and no connection to the make-up industry.

In El Salvador, we stayed at Hotel Alamo, a villa style hotel with Spanish terra cotta roof. I roomed with ten other young adult women. Yes, you read that right, *ten,* and how they say in Dallas, "It ain't pretty". Our trip leader was incredibly organized. Looking back, I'm sure it was maybe impossible to allow us more rooms in a way that made the entire plan work. I really admired his commitment and dedication to making that trip the best experience for everyone. Every girl on that trip was nice but you can imagine there were falling outs among everyone. It's ten different personalities. On top of it all, when I say our schedules were full, believe me it was a full list. This was part of our schedule:

Saturday
6:00 a.m. – Wake up.
6:30 a.m. – Have breakfast.
7:00 a.m. – Have personal devotion time with God.
8:00 a.m. – Prepare to leave.
10:00 a.m. – Centro Comercial Plaza Merlot (mall).
1:30 p.m. – Women's Prison ministry.
5:00 p.m. – Shopping at a multiplaza.
7:30 p.m. – Special dinner with locals.

Sunday
8:00 a.m. – 1st Sunday Service ministry.
10:00 a.m. – 2nd Sunday Service ministry.
12:00 p.m. – Break for Lunch
2:00 p.m. – Free time and Shopping at Galerias (mall).
6:00 p.m. – Dinner as a group at Galerias.
5:30 p.m. – Leave for San Pedro Sula, Honduras.

Private School outreach. - San Salvador, El Salvador

Before I arrived to El Salvador we were told many neighborhoods were unsafe and we would need security to escort us everywhere we went. The cycle of extreme gang violence that oppressed so many of these neighborhoods was still a concern for many although by that year so much of it had subsided. I could be wrong, but I don't think I know of another Latin country, besides Cuba, that suffered this much violence and terror among it's own people where they fought each other in such a way that left families in constant terror. Despite attempts to get it under control, they struggled to get the country back to peace. The El Salvador I was in at that time was no longer the El Salvador of the 80's, but we still saw the results of a violent past. It was mostly quiet in the mornings and evenings. I didn't see kids playing outside in the neighborhood we are staying at. No one was outside riding bikes despite the beautiful summer weather. We could see it in the women of the community, who carried along with quietness and highly observing of their surroundings.

We visited a foster home for girls who were pulled out of broken homes. They called them "At-risk" girls and that title they put over them really bothered me. I mean they had already gone through harsh experiences, why label them that as a name over yet another temporary home. A better name would offer them some hope. "At-risk" evokes the perilous in-between state they were in, caught between a fractured past and an uncertain future. Will they make it after this or not? Not sure, you're "At-risk". The place was in a location called Antiguo and there is nothing antique about the place. We spoke to the girls in small groups and they taught me how to make a bag out of plastic and cardboard. They made these bags to make money to help pay the bills for the foster home.

Many of the girls had gloomy faces all the time. It was hard to get

Girls foster home - San Salvador, El Salvador

one to smile, and that really surprised me. Still, I could relate. The assumption is that the good work this organization is doing should be impacting them in such a positive way that they should be living in some type of hope or aspiration. I supposed we should have seen hope or probably some optimism, but it definitely shouldn't have been difficult to see a smile from girls of youthful ages. That was a time when life is usually filled with laughter, especially being Latinas. *'Why is it so hard for them to smile?'* I wondered and observed quietly as they showed us their manual crafts. I didn't want to get into the details of how long and how often they had to make things partly because I was afraid of the answer. Yes, afraid of the answer that would tell all of us that the ministry was mismanaging finances. An then also partly because I was more interested in hearing their stories. Two of them told me with tears in their eyes that they wish they could see their families. Each one was there under different circumstances and it was hard to get them to open up. I decided to then focus on talking about the crafts and encouraging them with the hope God offers us in relationship.

Friday May 23, 2008 we went to visit a women's prison. One of the girls from the team was going to give a message to the women and we were going to sit with them as they ate. The goal was to get to know them and pray for them. I was assigned to hand out a gift to them as they walked down a line. I wanted to be assigned to sit and talk to them, but in these trips, you do what you're asked to give everyone a chance to experience ministry in different areas. Plus, I didn't want to be difficult with the organizers as it's hard for them as it is to manage all the work they are leading for such large groups.

Being there and looking around, I thought it was strange. It didn't look like prisons in the U.S. with ultra high security entrances, background checks, etc. We were in a common space that was open, with a ceiling but no walls and rows of tables where the women sat and a stage where our team all stood together. I can't remember the message our team member gave because I was dazzed by the women. The look on their faces were grim. They were there but they weren't there, you know. They weren't listening, as if they couldn't listen because all of the problems within them resounded louder.

Although some looked towards us, their minds seemed distracted. Their clothes were worn, and their hair mostly undone. I looked at a woman who was notably zoned out and wondered what she did to be there. She must have had children and had to be near 30. I was shocked to see women my mothers' age and older in there, just aging. The message was over and we all walked off the stage to take position in the venue. I was assigned to hand gifts that were mostly toiletries. My friend pointed it out giggling that each lady would pause to hug me so they could sniff my hair. "No, they're just in need of hugs, they are after all moms on Mother's Day," I explplained. Very quickly I realized it was true when one woman specifically wouldn't let me go. I thought again she needed a hug but nope, she took a long exaggerated sniff of my hair.

Among each experience, with my friend Erin, the teen girls at the home and the women in the prison, I saw they all shared the same middle ground as they stood between hope and despair. Hope and despair are understandably points of wavering for all of us. We are consistently in and out of hope, quickly falling into despair depending on the situation and regardless of where we're at in life. Erin hoped for a future husband, the ministers in El Salvador hoped for a bright future for their country, the girls at the teen home hoped for a better future ahead of them and the women in the prison hoped to see freedom sooner than later.

Biblical hope is not mere wishful thinking, but a confident expectation on something to happen in the future. That confidence is based on a variety of factors which altogether led you to believe with certainty.

> *"Therefore, having been justified by faith, we have peace with God through our Lord Jesus Christ, through whom also we have access by faith into this grace in which we stand, and rejoice in hope of the glory of God.*
>
> *And not only that, but we also glory in tribulations, knowing that tribulation produces perseverance;*

> *and perseverance, character; and character, hope.*
>
> *Now hope does not disappoint,*
> *because the love of God has been poured out in our hearts by the*
> *Holy Spirit who was given to us." - Romans 5:1-5*

Hope is developed in tribulation and it does not disappoint because it is *sourced* in God and it's *based* on God. The scripture notes the source of hope as, *"being justified by faith, we have peace with God through Christ,"* and so *"we have access by faith into grace in which we stand and rejoice in hope,"*. The source of hope is not ourselves, our jobs, our assets, who we know, a minister, etc. Biblical hope is sourced directly from God. This hope provides assurance and motivation for you to live confidently. You are certain, without any doubt. It's the same way you step into the shower and have confident expectation the water will run through the pipes or step into your vehicle and have confidence the engine will run. Biblical hope is a state of living with confident expectation beyond any doubt. You don't turn your shower on with extreme worry and concern (unless you didn't pay your bills). Taking action to turn the knob is easy. You're so confident you do it half asleep in the mornings, at least I do. In the same way, living with Biblical hope feels that carefree. The time in-between, where you find yourself betwen hope and despair, is critical. I mean the time between whatever it is that you're hoping for and the moment when you get the answer.

I'll illustrate it for you with the growth of a seed. When a seed is planted, it's buried underground. From your above-ground persepective, you can't see anything anymore. Even the seed itself is surrounded by complete darkness. Both you and the seed enter into a position in time of the complete unknown. While scientists have been able to use technology to see the microscopic movement of cells as the seed breaks apart and grows, no one has been able to completely and fully see what occurs between the moment a seed is deposited into the soil and the moment it buds and sprouts. This time lapse is what I call the critical "time in-between".

Imagine you plant a garden. You have a seed you sewed on the ground. If you were to pluck it out the next day, you may not see anything different. The seed may look the exact same as when you deposited it. But it's not the same. The moment it entered the soil, something began to happen within the seed. Work has already begun to take place. In fact, visually nothing has changed from your perspective by observing it from above ground. If you base your behavior on what you cannot yet see, you will be disappointed. You could lose sight of where it was even planted. But

 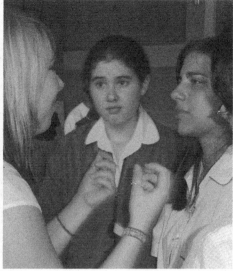

Private school outreach - San Salvador, El Salvador

becaue you have past experience, you trust within you that it will one day sprout. That's faith. Believing without seeing. Your faith affects your behavior differently than someone with no previous experience. You would show up every day to water it because you have that confidence of the result. No one has to beg you or ask you to go out there and water it. Since you planted it, *naturally* you continue to visit it daily to maintain it with an expectation of seeing results. Now, it's growth is not *based* on you. It's based on the sun being the sun, water being water and soil being soil. Each of those are critcal contributing factors, none of which you created. This is what I mean by hope is based on God. It's also true that you have to respond accordingly to the fact that God provided light, water and soil in order for your seed to grow. This crucial time in between is depending on you.

    Just as you would handle a seed you deposit in soil, you must handle the seed of faith you deposited in your heart when you contemplated the idea of a loving God who wants a relationship with you.

    Many people today show up to a moment in their hearts where they attempt to connect with God, and experience their faith die off during the time in between. What I mean is, as soon as you contemplate the idea of a genuine relationship with God, you will quickly enter into situations that will test your faith. Situations where you will be unsure if God even hears or sees you. For some these testing moments may come immediately and for others it may take a few years. I don't mean you had a bad day, I mean *testing* situations. Your loved one dies suddenly and shockingly.

Playing soccer with private school students. - El Salvador

Someone's diagnosed with a terminal disease. You lose everything you ever worked for, forced to start again. You experience the worst betrayal. You'll step into seasons of life where you will feel isolated and alone despite having many people around you. Your hope will waiver and you may start falling into despair. In order for you to maintain that confident trust in God has to be backed up within your soul. In respect to maintaining hope, if I could point to one key thing, it would be the grace of God. Recall how Romans 5:1-5 says, *"Therefore, having been justified by faith, we have peace with God through our Lord Jesus Christ, through whom also we have access by faith into this grace..."*

God's grace is the water to your faith.

It's effortless on your end except for the requirement that you must believe and receive it. The basis of your hope is God's complete grace and unmerited favor. It's a free gift to you from God because you are His and He is a loving Father who sees you and loves you. This grace is God's undeserved favor which cannot be earned and is freely given to you daily. A benefit you receive which was pre-paid through Christ.

The action of lights turning on in your home occurred because there was a pre-payment. The action of water running through the pipes in your home occurred because the means to provide was pre-paid. The action of your engine functioning properly in your vehicle, was an operation that was pre-paid. You didn't make any of it happen with your effort and each produced results on your behalf because each item was pre-paid.

In the same way, the ability to live in a position of hope for a good result is due to pre-payment. Jesus pre-paid the grace that gives you full confidence to live daily during the time in between *with unwavering hope.*

You can live with a feeling of effortless peace at the death of a loved one because Jesus overcame death.

You can overcome the bitter betrayal of a friend because Jesus forgave Judas and was able to still hand him bread at a dinner table.

You can continue to build after losing everything you ever worked for because Jesus was left with nothing on the cross *and still resurrected to new life* on the third day and if the same spirit that rose Jesus Christ from the grave now lives in you as a believer (Romans 8:11)...what can't you possibly overcome?

God's grace keeps your hope alive and waters your faith, sprouting deep roots in your soul and spirit. God's grace is not only His nature, but the powerful acting force of God that works in us to bring results. This is what Paul was talking about when he spoke on God's grace being his strength in difficulty.

> *"But He has said to me, "My grace is sufficient for you [My lovingkindness and My mercy are more than enough—always available—regardless of the situation]; for [My] power is being perfected [and is completed and shows itself most effectively] in [your] weakness." Therefore, I will all the more gladly boast in my weaknesses, so that the power of Christ [may completely enfold me and] may dwell in me."*
> *– 2nd Corinthians 12:9 AMP*

In weakness, the grace of God produced good results in the life of Paul as he suffered the most difficult circumstances of imprisonment and persecution. The action of a seed sprouting happens without your intervention and you simply wait daily with expectation to see something sprout. You can live life resting in the power of God's grace. You don't need to live anxiously or stressed daily about what you could do or who can help you get the result you're looking for. Erin didn't need to listen to a false prophetic word to get her hopes up about meeting her husband some day. She simply needed to be more secure in the grace of God. The unmerited favor of God over her life despite her past mistakes or time 'wasted' on past lovers. She could rest in hope with the assurance that God would give her a good husband in His time. The women in prison could have done without our visit if it meant they were sufficiently secure in God's grace which was not dependent on their past mistakes. The lack of understanding God's grace is why we were there to begin with, because it is by grace that anyone can be saved (Ephesians 2:8-9). The teen girls in the home could experience that situation in the home with joy if they knew the God of grace would see them through.

I have to emphasize this truth, that while you and I change our minds constantly about when we will extend grace to someone who does not deserve it, God is not this way and extends grace to the worst of us. He will not keep His grace from you at any given moment, regardless of how you fail and fail again in this lifetime. If you're hopeless, go to Him. Humble yourself. Ask for His grace and receive it by faith. God's grace is your assurance of overcoming. God's grace is your sufficiency to not give up. It's your million dollar bank account when you need to make a withdrawl. God's grace is your full coverage insurance, with $0 co-pay, to undergo life-saving surgery. It's not something you think twice about. You snatch it.

You must wake up each day convinced that grace is a primary quality in His heart and His nature, proven through the scriptures. You didn't deserve it, you didn't earn it. It's how God works. Nothing you ever do can change that about God. Once you become truly convinced of this, the time in between will be a different experience for you.

Your life is supposed to *produce* and *yield good things!* Jesus said in John 15:4-5, *"Abide in Me, and I in you. As the branch cannot bear fruit of itself, unless it abides in the vine, neither can you, unless you abide in Me. "I am the vine, you are the branches. He who abides in Me, and I in him, bears much fruit; for without Me you can do nothing."* You're meant to be a tree that bears much fruit. The fruit bearing is not just for you, but for those around you. If what is coming out of your life is not good, accept the grace of God.

Everyone watching will not only be in awe of the person you become, but your unwavering faith will inspire and encourage them during their time in between.

Consume

Mi deseo es estar aquí
     Contigo
          Ser inseparable
               Para siempre

Escuchar más de Ti
     Tu Voz
          Captivar mis sentidos
               Unidos

Entrar por Tus puertas
     Seguirte
          A donde te plazca llevarme
               Y Quedarme

Se derraman las lagrimas
     Me Ves
          Y en llanto servirte
               A Rajatabla

Al pasar momentos Contigo
     Resucitas
          Mis fuerzas, alma, y mi ser
               No Me Pesa

Llegar a Ti y dejar pasar el tiempo
     Rendir
          Mis rodillas a tus pies
               Indudable

Aquí - es el estado del saber: Tú lo eres todo
     Me consumes

Poem Translation:

My desire is to be here
　　　　Together
　　　　　To be close
　　　　　　Forever
To hear more from You
　　　　Your voice
　　　　　　Captivate my senses
　　　　　　　United
Walking into doors You open
　　　　In pursuit of You
　　　　　　　Wherever You lead
　　　　　　　　And stay
When tears flow
　　　You see me
　　　　　And in weeping I still serve
　　　　　　　Rigorously
Time with You
　　　I Resurrect
　　　　　My strength, my soul, my being
　　　　　　　No longer weigh
To come to You, give up my time and
　　　　　Yield
　　　　　　My knees at your feet
　　　　　　　Undoubtedly
Here - is the state of wisdom: You are everything
　　　　　You consume me

Author's Note:
This poem is expressing my desire to be "here". Here is any place where I seek personal time with God, a prayer room, a mountain, a beach shore, the plane, my balcony, cooking in my kitchen, having coffee at a café, working out at the gym...you get the picture, anywhere. I walk through the conversation with God saying I'm here.

First, I'm here because I want to – not because I'm forced to or because I 'should' be here as a professed Christian. I'm here to be close to God and hear what He has to say.

Sometimes, here, all I do is cry and hear nothing back, but I know God sees me and understands. And when I spend time with God He revives me internally and gives me new strength. It's not a burden, it's a joy.

*It's an act of yielding to God in my life,
because I recognize God is everything - and I am not.*

CHAPTER 11
Pura Vida

May 29th, 2008 I arrived in Costa Rica. On the plane I pulled open my Bible to study scripture and the woman sitting next to me stared surprised to see me read a Bible. She began a conversation with me out of curiosity. Back then I noticed frequently in every country, that adults thought it was shocking to see a young girl read a Bible willingly. My plane neighbor's name was Sara. She continued to tell me about how her husband died of an incurable disease and how she would take care of him before he died. She fed and bathed him on his last days. "Mi unico amor," she said, he was her only love. "I'm so sorry you lost him", I said, offering my condolences.

Whenever someone shares a loved one died, I do my best to just listen. I do this because I have never had anyone close to me die, so I would not come from a place of understanding. I listened to Sara for however long she was willing to speak of him and then I decided I'd move on to another topic. She openly shared with me the story of how they met and how she didn't really care for him at first, but he was persistent and pursued her. The first day they saw each other, he followed her home to ask her parents if he could date her, and she cried because she was scared. Creepy. I was expecting a sweet love story and this lady just straight up said 'oh I married my stalker'. She got in trouble with her parents because he kept calling her house and asking for her.

"How did he get your number though?" I asked, "I got him to leave me alone on one day by throwing it at him." she replied, "I wasn't thinking and it was a big mistake" she sighed. "Uff, I know what you mean, but you really had to be firm with guys like that, otherwise they don't stop." I said. I knew by experience. She nodded in agreement, "Yes but he wouldn't listen to me, fue una locura." she expressed with frustration as if she was back in her schoolgirl uniform and the guy was still chasing her. "Y luego mujer…" I asked attentively, porque estaba buena la novela (it was getting good). "And so then I gave up and he reached my house again and turned and yelled at him, '¡YA! Por favor ¡Déjame en paz! no quiero nada contigo! Que no entiendes!? Yo no te quiero Juan Manuel!!!' and I buried my face in my hands and wept in a way that no one could have comforted me. When he saw how I reacted, he turned away slowly and left. That day

Local girls after their dance performance at church - Costa Rica

he left me alone." *'This love story is a nightmare,'* I thought.

I felt so sad for her teenage self. "Y luego…", I asked, wondering how this nightmare led to an 'I do'. "And the next day he returned and followed me again, and every day after that." He returned every day after that until she finally agreed to date him. She ended up marrying him. This is one of the women I spoke to in my life where I obtained a passionate drive within myself to help other women. That young school girl within who couldn't get a guy off her and her parents were clueless to her problem. Experiences like these really pushed me to helping other women around me to not repeat a story like hers. She continued with a reassuring smile, "Well but later you know the years pass and you grow to love the person. Love begins to grow and that is what happened with me. Love grew inside me for him. We had kids y así fue."

Whether she grew to love him or not, on this day she didn't express herself of him with deep sorrow and endearment now that he was gone. You know, the *'half of me is gone'* sorrow I would imagine a lost love of your life may feel like. But what did I know? I placed my hand on her shoulder and said, "I'm sorry". She changed the subject. She told me she had a home in Costa Rica and her daughter lived in her back house. She told me she suffered damage to her ear. I asked her if I could pray for her and she agreed so I prayed healing for her ear and body, and I prayed blessing on her life and that God would restore and renew her. This is one of many stories I can point back to which helped fuel my passion for women's ministry. Although I wasn't sure how I could help other women from preventing things like that from happening to them. I thought in time God would lead me towards that effort.

Costa Ricans, or Ticos, are some of the chillest people I've ever met. 24/7 chill, and at every age – young or old. So many people had my last name, Sandoval. In just one day, I met three. Strangers greeted me with "pura vida" before they said anything. Respectfully, you should reply "pura vida" with a smile. The phrase means a lot. It means, hello, what's up? What's good? How are you? I'm well, life's good. Similar to pa'lante for Dominicans, it also means press on. You messed up? Pura vida! You lost your home? You wrecked your car? Pura vida! You lost your job? Your spouse left you? Pura vida! You lost a limb? Pura vida! Oh well, life goes on, look up, move forward. It means look at the bright side and live life! It is the chant of the nation. They refuse to stress over absolutely anything.

The level of gratitude for simply opening your eyelids and breathing was as wild as their jungle. I've never seen it anywhere. It should really be this way all around the world. Nothing should kill your optimism. They are open-minded people, with welcoming souls. They don't shy away from strangers but also don't overstep and try to engage you first. Their ability to take it one day at a time was truly unmatched. At that moment in my life, it was impossible for me to live without thinking of the next year or the next 5 years. Ticas lived out the benefits of not being consumed by worries, and not being concerned with the possibilities of *'what if'*.

Have you ever wondered how it is possible that any one person could live in such a point of calm, where they are not concerned about tomorrow? Jesus describes the process in Matthew 6. He explained the importance of living one day at a time in Matthew 6:34 where He said, *"So do not worry or be anxious about tomorrow, for tomorrow will have worries and anxieties of its own. Sufficient for each day is its own trouble."* Christ breaks it down and begins by addressing first the condition we are in which leads us to worry

CFNI students during morning prayer. - Costa Rica

and live in a state of anxiousness about tomorrow. The condition is found
in Matthew 6, verse 24.

> *"No one can serve two masters; for either he will hate the one
> and love the other, or he will be devoted to the one and despise the
> other. You cannot serve God and mammon [money, possessions,
> fame, status, or whatever is valued more than the Lord]."*
> *- Matthew 6:24 AMP*

Being overly worried and anxiously consumed about where our
lives will end up tomorrow is sourced in serving two masters. How is that
possible? Whenever I heard this verse preached, the preacher focused on
warning against making riches and wealth your God. But Jesus made this
statement before explaining that we are not to worry about tomorrow's
concerns. Christ emphasized us constantly pursuing God's plan for our
daily life and personal conformity to His standard of righteousness. We
can only do this completely convinced that He is the provider of all our
daily needs. By choosing to believe this as truth and adopting this into our
lifestyle then fear, worry, stress and anxiety about our tomorrow must go.
None of that has place in your life anymore if God is the master you serve.
The phrase "therefore..." in the scripture verse acts as a bridge, connecting
the idea of serving only one master, God, to the way we should live our
lives.

By living a life of service divided, attempting to juggle pleasing God and at the same time chase desires of this fleeting world, you'll
suddenly stop and realize you have already picked one. *"No one can serve two
masters; for either he will hate the one and love the other, or else he will be loyal to the
one and despise the other."* If you stopped right now to analyze the direction of
your life, would you identify it as a life lived seeking first the kingdom of
God or to meet all the desires of the world? A life lived consistently worried about tomorrows is an indication that God is not completely master.

A good way to help yourself when you are consumed with cares
of the world or stress and fear is to take time to do nothing and just sit in
prayer. During these trips we took breaks in the day to do devotional time
and pray either alone or together as a group. I will tell you that while corporate prayer is encouraging, the best prayer in my opinion is done alone. A
place and moment when it's just you and God. In Mark 1, Jesus is recorded
in verse 35 to have left everyone to go pray in the morning while it was still
dark. Now, prior to this Christ had done a lot. The Bible records He was
baptized, He was tempted by Satan in the wilderness, the angels ministered

to Him, He preached, called people to repent, He recruited His disciples, He taught in the Synagogue, He healed the sick, and finally, in the morning at Galilee He left to pray. We see in the life of Christ that prayer can help us to recalibrate and not allow whatever it is we have been through - good and bad - to deter our path. We will be able to see and focus in on fulfilling God's plan for us. Prayer is like a reset button to help us see what God sees and value what God values. *If you want to live a life free of anxiety, choose first God's kingdom.*

There's no way around it. We are not supposed to worry about basic needs, financial stability, or provision. That's not God's will. His will is for you to seek first His kingdom and the provision will come. So many people all over the world live on a day-to-day hustle and grind to make things happen and try to relieve the burdens they carry. The burden of acceptance, temporarily met by materialism… "If I can get that luxury car". The burden of finding purpose chasing a job title… "If I can earn the promotion to 'Partner', 'CEO', 'Founder'…". The burden of value met by net worth and status… "If I can get a larger return, If I can just reach six figures". Name your burden, there's a point when worry, fear and anxiety will lead you to chase and labor after 'mammon' on a daily basis. Stop and analyze the activity of your life and the needs you are working so hastily to meet. Seeking the kingdom of God meets those needs and beyond. You will reach contentment.

Nothing and no one should master over you, but God.

As you read this, consider all the things you carry on your shoulders and remember what Christ said in Matthew 11.

> *"Come to Me, all who are weary and heavily burdened [by religious rituals that provide no peace], and I will give you rest [refreshing your souls with salvation]. Take My yoke upon you and learn from Me [following Me as My disciple], for I am gentle and humble in heart, and you will find rest (renewal, blessed quiet) for your souls."*
> *- Matthew 11:28-29 AMP*

This is again, in a different place, Christ speaking on the importance of seeking first the kingdom of heaven! *"Take my yoke upon you and learn from Me…"* Christ explained placing priority in the kingdom of heaven and in return we will receive rest. He asks us to take on His service that He gave us to do, in other words, the service of the kingdom of God! We are to run after God in such a way that with God as number one in our daily activity, all other things will come.

What is that activity? The Holy Spirit will lead you. It looks like extending a helping hand, sharing a prayer, serving those in need, encouraging someone, sharing the gospel, you get the picture. It doesn't mean you become oblivious to your needs or ignore your needs. It also doesn't mean you mismanage your finances or neglect your responsibilities. It simply means your needs do not dominate or direct you as master, taking over your life purpose.

Think of it practically. If you pick up an object like a hammer and use it to prop a door open, but it is never used on a nail, then that hammer is not serving it's purpose. Use a microwave as a stepping stool, and I assure you, that microwave is not serving it's purpose. Use your time daily worrying about your life, worrying about tomorrow, what you will eat, what you will wear, I assure you you're not serving your purpose. The cure to anxiety is seeking first the kingdom of God. You find your purpose in putting on Christ and placing His yoke upon you. Today we can live a life that daily finds rest in Him.

By the time we reached Costa Rica we had done a lot. Many of us just really needed rest. What better place than this tropical paradise? I thought of how when people refer to missionaries doing the kingdom work, most people imagine it to look busy and always serving. It can be equally productive to rest. Through scripture we learn rest was part of Christ's ministry work. By contrast, I noticed the communities in Costa Rica fostered the need to rest. You have open parks and green spaces that invite you to sit, think or wait. Every major city in the U.S. I can think of was built preventing walkability or spaces that would invite residents to stop, pause and rest. I found this interesting.

Observing Ticas live day by day and not consumed in worry, was refreshing. Similar to the European way of living, it's a way of living that even if they were worried you couldn't tell because instead of sharing their worries with you, they'd just smile and say, *"Pura vida."*

CHAPTER 12

Tombs

As tired as we were, like all other trips, we had a list of assignments. We mostly served in a local church ministry and did teen outreach. One day, we went out to speak at the schools. I arrived with the team to an auditorium full of teens only a few years younger than me. I try to focus on a group of faces in each section of the crowd when I speak to a large group to feel like I'm talking on-on-one with someone. I find my message becomes more conversational. I saw them pay attention and it meant a lot because teens in general, but especially here, carry much indifference. My friend Angela was scheduled to share her story of abandonment with them. She has a powerful story. Her dad was a drug dealer and her mom was a prostitute and both were crack addicts. After brutally murdering her newborn younger sister, her parents left their other infant daughter abandoned in their home where she survived several days. The police took a crime scene photo upon entering the home after receiving a call from a neighbor. They found her, a tiny baby sitting alone in the living room of an abandoned house. That was my friend Angela. How did she survive? Why did they spare her life? She was taken into custody and was soon up for adoption. Even though every medical professional who evaluated her determined she would end up with mental problems, a speech delay and even end up following after her parents lifestyle, Angela became none of those things. She was about my age, a natural beauty with perfectly curled eyelashes, black full bodied hair and flawless brown skin. We met a few years ago at my church. My then pastor who worked with her at a school invited her to youth service. I was in charge of greeting visitors and obtained their information for follow up. After getting her info I invited her to grab coffee sometime and hang out. We've been friends since and we both ended up going to the same Bible school.

Before we were up to speak, Angela pulled me over and said, "Arisbet, I don't know what to say, I'm nervous." I firmly replied, "Yes, you do. What do you mean, you have an incredible story! Tell them how your parents abandoned you, drug addicts, left you as a tiny baby all alone in your house and how by God's grace the police found you, dirty, soiled and alive! Tell them how you were told by the system that you would end up a crack addict, a prostitute and have serious mental issues as an adult. How although the world declared all these things over your future as a tiny child, a great God exists who said NO, and you are none of those things today! And that same great God can do something radical for their lives too. In your own words, speak from your heart." Her story is still one of the most incredible testimonies of a life redeemed that I've ever heard. She stepped out, shoved her nerves aside and shared her incredible story to the audience of teens.

I was up after her to deliver "a call to salvation". It's not really a sermon but more the final stage of a sermon tied to the testimony and persuading the audience to make the decision of salvation. I wish they knew a lot of things that I couldn't communicate in such a short time. At their age, I needed so much the guidance of parents. I knew by looking at them that possibly 99.9% of them were just like me, with parents who were physically there but not presently involved in their lives. I knew most of them may have been raising themselves, each other and their siblings. I gave them a *'listen to me and wake up'* message. It was silent in there and I could see they were listening. I asked them to make the commitment in their heart. I knew by experience, that you don't have to walk up to an altar or stand up or raise your hand in order to genuinely mean the decision to give your life to God. I asked them to do it within themselves right where they sat that very moment, and afterwards, urgently continue to pursue God on their own. Then the pastor walked up to me to finish off with a closing statement, but it felt abrupt. One of my teammates agreed and expressed, "That was a missed opportunity. After Arisbet's message it looked like they were ready to give their lives to God and the pastor should have called us up to pray for people if anyone did want to come down." Instead the pastor just closed with a thank you for having us statement. It was ok, I thought. I knew God did what He had to beyond what the pastor chose to do.

We drove back to the church to wait on next instructions as a group. Outside the church, someone asked for some of us to get together and take a group photo. The pastor arranged himself between me and Angela. He quickly leaned his head slightly towards me as he faced forward and spoke in a soft voice to me, "I loved your message and the way you speak." Everything slowed down instantly as I turned my head towards him and saw a disgusting smirk on his face, "I'm really impressed," he continued. I froze in disgust as he got close to pose for the picture. I know exactly what that was. He was a predator and wanted to see if I'd welcome his advance. I froze as I realized, *'Did he just come on to me?'* That really good impression I had up to that moment was shattered. When we first arrived, he was a breath of fresh air for all of us. His words were welcoming and offered his church as a retreat from all the work we had just completed in other countries.

We all shared the same opinion of him because when he greeted us at the airport he said, "I've heard you guys have had quite the stressful time so far. I want you to know you can relax. This is a time for rest and for God to pour back into you after feeling drained." We were all relieved to see he was so kind and welcoming. Also, that he understood we were tired of running from assignment to assignment. He shared a scripture and prayed for us. When we stepped foot in his church, we all felt the same warm welcome from his members too. People from his church were the nicest people. The impression by what I saw was, *'Wow, this pastor is doing a really good job.'*

Posing for the picture, I felt angry. I felt so sick to my stomach realizing this was the hidden reality. Frozen and in shock I didn't say anything. Angela heard part of what he said to me and mistakenly thought he was addressing her. She politely smiled and said "Thank you", as he looked back at me for a response. I imagined the hood part of me, the part Jesus died to destroy, rise up back from the grave within me, shove him and fight. But that was the young and afraid Arisbet from South Oak Cliff who didn't have anyone to defend her when a disgusting old man or a perverted teen guy came after me. I was wiser and mentally stronger at that moment, and relied on the Holy Spirit. Still, in retrospect, it's surprising that with all boldness I stood before narcos fearlessly yet I froze at an encounter with a corrupt pastor. The narcos were at least honest about who they really were. They were surrounded by darkness and didn't yet know the true power of God. This pastor was surrounded by God's hand working in others, and he still chose darkness within. That level of slavery is the hardest to make sense of. I became mute. I probably turned pale and forced a fake smile for

Speaking to high school students. - Costa Rica

Street evangelism. - Costa Rica

the photo, then quickly got away from him. God knew the darkest pit of his life and I was confident God had this situation under control.

Let me back up a little bit. Years ago at a church in Dallas, one of my best friends made out with the pastor's daughter's husband. The man was at the time the Associate Pastor of the church. From her own explanation, she tried to tell me it was consensual, that they were alone in the church, satan took over the situation, they both fell into sin and made out. I was a teenager and she was in her early 20s. I remember asking her how she handled it and what did she do afterwards. She said she told him she was sorry, and he told her not to be. She did not realize at that time that she did not consent. She was lured and hunted, like prey. He was so much older, a grown married man with kids. She was groomed by him for who knows how long, to get him to that moment with her. I remember being surprised in his betrayal of his wife. He had a cool personality, nothing out of the ordinary. I had the wrong impression of him too. He came across as a well put together man, clean cut, solid faith, wonderful father and loving husband.

The main pastor found out what happened, and she said he put her in what he called, "Disciplinary Action". The disciplinary action involved her having to meet with him one-on-one for 'counseling', even though he was not a licensed counselor. The associate pastor who made out with her continued in his role. It didn't make sense, *at all*. I remember one day after Sunday service ended, I asked her where she wanted to go eat. She said, "I can't, I have to go into pastor's office." I watched as she walked into his office alone. His wife wasn't in there. I never asked her, but I do wonder if the main pastor was a predator also. I don't have evidence the main pastor was inapropriate with her behind closed doors, but no man his age should have met with a young adult in her twenties for "disciplinary action" alone without his wife, her parents or other people present. I felt sad for her.

One Sunday she saw me wear a light pink top to service and she noticed the associate pastor looked at me a certain way. She told me not to wear it again. "Why?" I asked, "Because he looked at you lustfully so you shouldn't dress like that". I rolled my eyes at her like you would at your mom when she tells you not to come home late. I wore that same shirt to work and there was nothing revealing about it. She still didn't get this man had a problem. It was *his* problem. I could wear a turtleneck and the cult hermana skirts and he'd still have a problem. In the end, she still believed she was in control in that situation and consented the entire time.

We as young women, weren't briefed for that. Discussing the possibility of encountering predators in church leadership *was never talked about* in Bible school or church. There was no one telling us what we needed to do if we ever faced a predator in church as young adults or teens. This has to be addressed in the church. Keeping it hidden or ignoring it will continue to allow space for anyone who may want to prey on young girls, or boys, in minisitries.

This situation with the pastor in Costa Rica was not a complete shock, but I was so thrown off by it. The shocking truth of this reality and not the glossed over image I had, was disheartening. That original impression of a wonderful minister who loved his wife and his church quickly disappeared. The reality of ministers who use their positions to prey on women is not isolated. It just didn't make sense to be true in *that* church. His wife was gorgeous. I mean a beautiful woman who looked like she really stepped back to let him 'shine'. She spoke very well of him and supported everything he did publicly. They looked financially well off. He had a prospering and large church ministry in this incredible paradise of a country. I mean they looked like they had a successful and comfortable missionary life. He had so many willing hands to help him run the ministry. The members praised the church and how much they loved it. I heard people express how much God did for them in their personal lives. From the outside, it looked like everything was great. This was any pastoral graduate's dream life. There I stood looking around and wondering how many of these grown adults knew about the pastor's problem.

Our missionary team went to have dinner and fellowship at an apartment and I tried to really see if his wife knew. I just observed her from afar, but then she walked close to me. She didn't say much but I saw it in her face. She wasn't just sad, she looked trapped inside. It looked like emptiness in her, even past the meager shy smile. She didn't have much to say to anyone. Despite what looked like a thriving church, she didn't look excited.

I prayed for her privately that God would give her strength and guide her. I couldn't imagine what she was going through. I stayed away from the pastor every day I was there, I wouldn't go near him. It was chilling to see someone look outwardly as though they were working for God and enslaved to that type of darkness within. How he could speak with so much knowledge of God and be personally enslaved. How he could lead so many people, I mean the church was busy! I didn't understand.

"*White-washed tombs,*" Jesus said in public condemnation and grief in Mathew 13. In conversation with the Pharisees and teachers of the law, Christ gave them seven woes condemning them and disclosed their condition.

> "*But woe to you, scribes and Pharisees, hypocrites! For you shut the kingdom of heaven in people's faces. For you neither enter yourselves nor allow those who would enter to go in. Woe to you, scribes and Pharisees, hypocrites! For you travel across sea and land to make a single proselyte, and when he becomes a proselyte, you make him twice as much a child of hell as yourselves.*"
> *- Matthew 23:14-15 ESV*
>
> "*Woe to you, scribes and Pharisees, hypocrites! For you clean the outside of the cup and the plate, but inside they are full of greed and self-indulgence. You blind Pharisee! First clean the inside of the cup and the plate, that the outside also may be clean. Woe to you, scribes and Pharisees, hypocrites! For you are like whitewashed tombs, which outwardly appear beautiful, but within are full of dead people's bones and all uncleanness. So you also outwardly appear righteous to others, but within you are full of hypocrisy and lawlessness.*"
> *- Matthew 23:25-28 ESV*

The word hypocrite here is referring as to one who is an actor. In the beginning of Matthew 23, Christ starts with saying *"Do what they say but not what they do…"* which reveals that they have knowledge and some correct information about scripture, yet they are unwilling to live by the truth. He said they are like white washed tombs who for show look like they thrive but are concealing that they are actually dead. Not in the natural, but spiritually dead. Of all the words Christ is recorded to have spoken, the harshest words were spoken to the religious leaders. Here, the consistent use of woe sounds like a lament, a loud cry against their lives for their internal condition as Christ could see what was in their hearts and minds. His constant repeated cry of 'woe' reads like a wail at the funeral of someone they once knew. How they could stand in a position of spiritual death while being responsible for leading the community in communion with God, is chilling. Many leaders today stand in this same position.

I've met other people in my time ministering abroad and at home in Dallas who have suffered distress because of a corrupt pastor or leader. Some of the darkest stories I've heard came from pastor's kids who, despite growing up in the church, still struggle to surrender their lives to God in personal relationship because of what they saw in their parents and the leaders at the church. Christ's words echo, *"You yourselves do not enter, nor will you let those enter who are trying to…"*

If you stand in a position where you have experienced in some way hurt and offense because of a pastor or leader, and struggle in trusting God with your life because of it, consider the following. Of all the men Jesus called to be a disciple, *none of them was a Pharisee.* None of the men Jesus chose as disciple was a leader in the synagogue. There's a reason for that. Even Matthew, the tax collector who extorted money from many people, secured a position at the table! How is that possible? Despite the Pharisees and Saducees maintaining their leadership position within a synagogue, Christ disclosed their position publicly as being spiritually dead.

A leadership position and a church ministry title does not mean the person is right with God. The Pharisees put on legal requirements over people which God did not place. They added onto God's requirements with their own personal agenda in mind. They harbored sin and presented themselves publicly as sinless. They loved the best seats and to be regarded with honor because of their projected life of holiness. They misled people and Christ referred to them as blind leaders. Harsh. So harsh were Christ's words, it can be surprising to discover that Christ did not speak in that way towards people which the Pharisees, and possibly the general public, saw as the lowest of the low. People like men who had leprosy in Luke 17, the woman with the issue of blood in Matthew 9, the adulterous woman in John 8, or the Samaritan woman at Jacob's well in John 4, the unbelieving man at the pool of Bethesda, or the demonized man in Luke 4. All were given words of redemption and love. The Samaritan woman at the well received even the revelation of Christ as Messiah! How amazing is that! Of all people, Christ declared to her, *"I am He."* (Luke 4). *"I am He"* was not said to a Pharisee or Sadducee, not even to disciples is it recorded that He spoke in this way. No other group of people received such a harsh condemnation than the Pharisees received from Christ for the sin of hypocrisy.

I say this because many people will stay away from God when they find out that pastors or religious people in churches harbor sin and then say things like, "That's why I don't go to church, because it's full of hypocrites." No, you don't go to church because you don't want to. Because there are hypocrites at your job and you still go to work. There are hypocrites in your family and you still show up for Thanksgiving. Some of your friends are hypocrites and you still hang out with them. Everyone will be caught at one point or another saying something and doing the complete opposite. We all sin and fall short of the glory of God, Romans 3:23. We all need the grace of God daily. Although grace abounds we are not given a free pass to keep sinning. What the Pharisees did went beyond the meaning of 'hypocrite' that we are so used to hearing, meaning doing opposite of what they said. The word hypocrite in the scripture and the anger spoken in Christ's harsh words indicates they reached another level. When we study the word, Christ acknowledged the Pharisees were guilty of the sin of hypocrisy to such degree and then placed burdens on people, keeping them away from God.

We read in Matthew 24, Christ addresses the disciples saying, *"Take heed that no one deceives you."* It's our responsibility not to leave the faith if you discover that leaders live bound to inner sin. That is not your cue to exit the faith. In fact, you are asked in advance to be vigilant and to prepare even more in order not to be deceived because they are out there. That demands you become solid in your faith.

The other thing I'd invite you to reflect on is in Christ's words to describe them, calling them *"white washed tombs"*. Tombs containing the deceased, symbolizing the absence of former life.

At one point, they were alive.

I've seen people who followed these kind of leaders leave the faith completely. As I write this and think of people I have seen drop off from the faith, many today would consider themselves atheists or agnostic. We can't drop off and leave God on the other side of witnessing leaders in white washed tombs. We don't serve leaders, we serve God. I wish I could understand *why* people choose to take on a pastoral role just to lead people far away from God. If I had this answer, I'd have a best selling book here, but I can't explain that to you. It's senseless. The complexity of their personal deception is real. Many people fall so deep in sin that it's darkness blinds them to the goodness of God who saves and redeems the worst condition of man. If all you know is darkness, you adapt to that darkness and learn to live with it so much, you forget what the light looks like. They were once alive but forgot the purpose of the light, and forgot the benefits of living in the light. They lost complete sight, and lost direction. They don't see anyone but themselves. I don't understand it. I grieve seeing the many people who suffered because of those who lacked fear of God and still took on leadership roles.

Christ knows what we have faced when we come across these leaders. We are supposed to strengthen our faith, not lose it. We are instructed to run to God with more perseverance and more clarity of the truth in order to not be deceived. If you have been hurt by church leaders, I encourage you to search he scripture for Christ's teaching on the issue and for comfort. Everything has a purpose and God will turn your pain around for good. Romans 8:28 assures us, *"And we know that all things work together for good to those who love God, to those who are the called according to His purpose."*

I didn't tell my group leader what I experienced during the trip and looking back, I regret so much not telling him. Years later in Dallas, I was walking to the parking lot after an evening class on campus while completing my undergrad at Dallas Baptist University. I bumped into a guy who was a local I met on that Costa Rica trip. He told me he had bad news about the pastor in Costa Rica and that's how I found out. The pastor was having romantic relationships with several of the girls in the youth group – and it was many. The church community was torn and everyone was shocked. He said parents were angry and many members left. Several parents urged some of the girls to confess to the abuse, but in their eyes they were never abused. He explained that to many of the girls who got involved with him, the majority felt they were in love and the pastor loved them back. I didn't want to hear any more details about it. My stomach sank. The regret came back fresh. I should have said something, maybe some girls would have avoided the trauma if I had said something back then.

He said the pastor and his wife fled to Mexico.

He didn't face any charges.

MEMOIRS OF A MEXICAN MISSIONARY

Pa' Curar

Flor de misterio cúrame las penas

Aaaaaaaahhhyyyy malditas mis penas…

¿'Onde se consigue esa hierba?

Dicen por ay, "La piel de culebra…

En aceite, 3 veces al día como crema."

Hierba seca, cúrame el dolor,

Dolor de cabeza…de recuerdo anterior…

Cuanto me aaaahhhhrrrrde el rencor.

Que una limpieza, una barrida,

Que un té de manzanilla.

Pa'l coraje, pa'l enojo…

Pa' perdonar a mi esposo,

Y el maltrato…horroroso…

En la vida se sufre - amarga injusticia,

De tanta gente, pura malicia.

La agonía arrrrrrraaaaaastra mi ser con otra mala noticia.

¿Comadre, que será bueno pa' la depresión?

El orgullo y mis penas, me encierran en una maldita prisión.

Échate un trago de alcohol…un tequila.

Pásame la sal y limón.

Regresando al cerro, al rancho,

Buscando por la milpa, por el plan, por la costa del mar,

Buscando por el campo,

Tomando siempre el viaje largo.

MEMOIRS OF A MEXICAN MISSIONARY

Al pasar los años…

Y después de miles consejos,

La encontré.

La cura viene del cielo.

Author's Note:

This poem is about how Mexican women and men suffer through problems in life looking everywhere for a "remedio" - an ailment or remedy - to help them feel better and recover. They ask each other and each others' comadres about remedios and try everything to get relief. Common remedios are the use of herbs made into food or teas. Many seek tarot readers, santeria, praying to saints, offering their children to a saint, or to la santa muerte.

Many book appointments with people they call curanderos who do non-medical treatments, giving massages with creams. Some curanderos practice witchcraft candidly, using dried plants and brushing the person's body with it while chanting over them.

People look everywhere and ask everyone in their community, what they have used for things like headaches, body pains or depression.

Many travel back to their home towns in Mexico hoping to reconnect and make peace somehow with their childhoods, trying to find peace in their place of origin.

'Tomando el viaje largo' meaning most live their lives looking for these healing shortcuts but it's actually taking the longer route to heal, as they search for things that won't actually heal them within.

In this poem, I imagine a good ending where these women and men, in their search for remedios, will reach a point in their lives when they find the cure and realize all this time it came from heaven. Even if it's at old age or their death bed.

God is our greatest source of healing if you will only go to Him for it.

CHAPTER 13
Tragos Amargos

If someone were to ask, "Who are you?" you would start with your name, but that is not who you are. That's simply your name. You could follow it up with your job title, which makes sense as many of us spend the majority of our time working, but that's the output of your skill and ability. If you're studying for a degree you may say "I'm a student at…" or maybe your degree, but that's really your current focus and discipline. A glimpse into a season of your life is not who you are. You can state your ethnic roots and your physical appearance…but those are physical attributes, and that's still not who you are. We describe our identities based on things that can be easily taken away, and the lack of a solid identity has many people going through routines in life that are trail paths into a variety of destinations. What you actually spend your time doing in life comes from a personal belief of who you are. *So shouldn't you know?*

When I was crossing the border to the U.S., I said I was the girl whose name was on a U.S. birth certificate. I was driven up to the border in my aunt's car. She had her daughter's birth certificate and all I had to do was tell the border patrol officer that the name on the certificate was me. My aunt told me this was the only way I'd get to see my mom and that my parents were waiting on the other side for us. My mom and dad were actually waiting in a motel on the U.S. side because they crossed ahead of us through the Rio Grande. My mom recounted the story to me and how fear-stricken she was. The Coyote assigned to her led her through the entire way. After they reached the other side, he rushed her out and held her arm as they snuck into the U.S. town, pretending he was her boyfriend. Walking her arm in arm, she was drenched in water and in tears walking with the guy to the motel to wait for us. She was unconsolable waiting for us as she realized the risk she took, knowing she may not see us again if border patrol detained us. I didn't speak English so I just had to nod yes and confirm I was the name on the birth certificate. My brother Darwin refused to comply with my aunt. We hardly knew her and we didn't trust her. When the patrol officer asked him if he was the name on his certificate, he said, "No." and gave him his real name. The patrol officer asked my aunt to drive back around and denied entry, but he didn't detain us. We tried again and the second time my brother complied. We didn't have a choice. We didn't know

Los Arcos, Acueducto de Morelia - Morelia, Michoacán

what was going on and we had no idea where we were being driven to. We just wanted to be united again with our parents.

    I come from a family of hard workers. As illegal immigrants, my life as a kid in the U.S. began with an overwhelming sense of fear. It's scary to hear people speaking a language you cannot understand. Also, as a child immigrant, you are raised on the side of caution against deportation so the police are not your friends. Seeing a police car pass by triggered anxiety. Even after we got our residency, we would still hid from police. Everyone was 'la migra' or immigration officers to us. We lived with the understanding that this was not our country so whatever we did, we had to do very minimum in order to avoid attention. You have to take what you're handed and be grateful. That was the mindset. My parents were living in this foreign country constantly afraid and fear transfers.

    I grew up in Oak Cliff in the 90s off Marsalis Ave., at a time when violence and crime was up in Dallas. It was a difficult place for any parent to raise kids. People would get robbed and some killed for their tire rims, car systems, or jewelry. Teen gang crime was bad, although I've heard that Oak Cliff crime was nothing compared to what was going on in some hoods in California. The public schools in Oak Cliff were bad, and at that time, there was also a lot of hate against Mexicans. My older siblings experienced more of the discrimination in schools than I did. I recall them getting hate from non-Spanish speaking teens who were the first or second generation of their Mexican families born in the U.S. Hate from your own people didn't make sense to me, even as a little kid.

    Our neighbors were drug dealers and as a second grader, I don't remember how I found this out. It was common to see working women coming off of a high, looking for work on street corners. We frequently saw people asking for bus fare on our way to and from school. Like other hoods, kids grow up fast. My parents were once robbed at gun point in a washateria. I remember being at the house we stayed in seeing my mom and dad enter in to the kitchen frantic, and my dad with his face completely busted and smeared in blood. No one protects hood kids from seeing things they shouldn't. For those of us who had parents on survival, often, we as kids disappeared in the background. After the washateria beating my dad took, we moved to rent at another house, but still in South Oak Cliff because we couldn't afford anything.

I went to a majority black elementary school with a few Mexicans and frequently witnessed fights break out. I was once walked into the cafeteria in 2nd grade when suddenly kids swarmed and screamed towards the food line. I turned and saw kids shoving each other and teachers running to stop them. It was chaos. This kid fell maybe 3 feet in front of me holding his head with blood pouring down his eye. Another kid near him held up a cafeteria chair and went after him swinging it to gash his face again with the chairs' metal leg. The teachers were not able to stop him in time. My teacher was a sweet white lady. She stayed visibly calm, but I saw fear in her eyes as she managed to gather our class together and asked us to get in a single-file line to move us back to our class. I got used to it. By the summer of my 5th grade year, we moved out of Marsalis to the Kiest and Polk area of Oak Cliff.

While the public school in Oak Cliff wasn't the best experience, the chaos at home wasn't much better. My dad was an absent husband and father, but he did work hard to bring money in, put food on the table and pay the bills. My mom took on the stress and responsibility of managing and raising our family alone. Like many immigrant kids, my childhood was not easy. I was left as the oldest child who would do the housework, cook and help my mom with my younger siblings. It was stressful, when I was a child myself, as early as 5 years old, and all I wanted to do was play and be a kid.

The oldest of our sisters was always running away with boyfriends. I never got to know her because she didn't live with us long enough. My parents once paid over $1,000.00 in the 90s to a Coyote to bring her back to the US after she ran away to Mexico. She dated a drug dealer for a while and my parents were always driving around Oak Cliff looking for her. One day we went to McDonalds with my mom and siblings while my dad attended an Alcoholics Anonymous meeting. It was the perfect day for any kid, to get to go to McDonalds and play with your siblings. I stood there happy, when suddenly I saw my oldest sister run for the door like someone was after her with a gun. She ran away on such a perfect day. Nothing was wrong, my mom was just sitting there with all her kids in a safe place waiting on my dad. I saw the fear and pain in my mom, realizing she ran away again and may not find her. She couldn't grab all of us in time to chase after her. My mom stood at the door crying seeing her run off and glancing back at all of us inside. My sister was gone. I stood there observing such a perfect day turned into a nightmare for my mom.

My second older sister was always angry and I avoided her completely. She once beat me with a broom for laughing and left the broomstick mark on my tiny leg. I was in 1st or 2nd grade. My mom scolded her but she was powerless against my two older sisters. I never found out why. My oldest brother would cuss me out for simple things like leaving something out of its place around the house. He couldn't communicate with basic regard like, "Hey can you place this where it belongs?" No little girl should get used to having an older guy cuss her out for basic requests. I got used to it and learned how to manage. I didn't want to get beat or cussed out, so I began to isolate myself. With our oldest sister always gone, my mom tried to make the remaining two oldest siblings responsible for me and my other siblings so they could both go to work in low paying jobs. I knew very quickly that I was better off taking care of myself.

I began to learn how to cook in elementary school. I was about 7 when I tried to make rice for the first time. I was so proud of myself and excited to show my mom when she got home from work. But when my mom arrived she yelled at me for wasting an entire pan of rice. She was just stressed out and making ends meet so we couldn't afford to even waste rice. But I had to keep trying because I had to eat.

In 4th grade the Mexican lady who lived next door babysat a boy from my class at school and she didn't feed them meals. His little brothers smelled pancakes and snuck over to our back door to peek in our kitchen. I was making breakfast for myself and my younger siblings. I was so embarrassed that my classmate would find out that I knew how to cook for myself. But my concern for his tiny siblings beat my embarrassment and I made them pancakes to take back, and then seconds.

Despite having older siblings, we were disconnected. For the most part they all ignored each other. I understood very quickly, despite having my parents and many siblings in one household, that I had to figure life out on my own. If I had problems, I had to resolve them myself. My mom did the best she could considering her circumstances. No one struggled the way my mom did. If you would have asked me who I was as a little girl, I would have said I was not worthy to be cared for. Forgotten. Invisible. Unimportant.

I was 9 or 10 when I found out my dad was cheating on my mom. I was singing with him in the Catholic church choir and saw him hit on a

Monument of José María Morelos. - Janitzio, Michoacán México

lady, ironically with the same name as my mom, Maria. I didn't trust him after that. He was deceiving, living a double life. He had a wife and family and did that so easily, as if he was single...as if none of us existed. As a tiny kid, I remember believing he was not a good dad in my eyes anymore and I wanted nothing to do with him. I never saw him give my mom a hug. His betrayal made me sad. Also, I was confused by how easily he could sing to God and try to mess with another lady from the same church choir, who also had a husband and a new baby. I was mean to the lady after I saw that exchange between them, but it was honestly not her fault. She put his advances down and was visibly uncomfortable by what my dad did. I finally understood why my mom was always crying. I stopped singing with my dad at church once that happened.

In essence, my dad showed me through his behavior that God is not someone you take seriously and church was not a place I'd find value or identity. I love my dad despite this past. I have made peace now as an adult, and have worked to try and restore my relationship with him.

When I was a teen, our oldest sister came to live with us after she got pregnant by a boyfriend. She would pull me out of school to babysit her babies, and my mom agreed. After school, I was in charge of watching her kids and my siblings while my parents worked. I should have failed school and dropped out early with my sister and mom doing that, but I didn't. I got into a Magnet High school and figured it out. While my mom knew it was irresponsible of her to pull me out of school and expect me to provide childcare, I think my mom did it because she felt a lot of guilt with

The island town of Janitzio. - Michoacán México

my older sister. I wondered if my mom believed she failed her as a mother since she always ran away. She probably also felt afraid for her because she got pregnant by a guy none of us knew and imagined she'd soon be a single mother. I hated getting asked by people if my baby nieces were my daughters, and the look of shock and pity on their faces to see a young girl holding a baby. I would reply, "No!! I'm only a kid, this is my sisters' baby." Every time my sister would run out the door on a date or just to get out of the house, she would leave her kids with me saying, "I will pay you, I promise." She never did. I thought I should get paid if I'm always working.

I begged my mom to let me get a job like my teenage siblings. I got a job when I turned 14 the same way I entered this country, illegally. I was paid cash at the end of each day. I worked at a Mexican restaurant off the corner of Tyler St. and Jefferson Blvd. in Oak Cliff. The owners were an elderly married couple. All the waitresses were teen girls older than me and I just started as a buss girl because they served alcohol. The wife did not like me and I never found out why. But her husband loved me and was so nice to me. He looked at his wife confused as to why she was so mean towards me. One day I showed up wearing a white shirt, as she asked all waitresses to wear, but she complained it had a Tommy Hilfiger logo on it and snapped at me to go home and change. He saw how she spoke to me and he started arguing with her in front of me, and I stepped back. I asked her husband if I could use the restaurant phone to call my mom. I told my mom I needed her to pick me up. My shift was barely starting. When my mom pulled up outside, I handed the wife my apron and said, "I quit".

My second job was at Sonic off Zang Blvd. The managers were two married white people in their 30s probably. On my first day working as a carhop, I cashed out and was told by the wife manager that I was about $10 short on my register. I was precise and I used a calculator. I knew she was wrong. I told her that there was no way I was short, I had calculated everything correctly on all my tickets, but I paid the difference. The next day she told me I was $20 short, and I argued that there was no way, but again I paid it. My third day at work was a Saturday and she claimed I was short $150. I felt a sinking feeling in the pit of my stomach.

"One hundred and fifty dollars!!!!??? No." I told her.

"Okay well I have tallied the tickets three times already and you're short $150." She looked down at paperwork on her desk. "No. This is a mistake, the last two nights were mistakes. I don't have $150 to give you."

"Okay Arisbet, well, we will look over everything again and let you know tomorrow." It was late at night, I was tired and my mom was already waiting for me outside. When I got in the car she knew there was something wrong with me. As she drove me home, which was not a far drive, I explained to her all that happened. We had just arrived inside the house as I told her, "And now she says I was short $150". My mom was furious.

"Ah que la chingada hijos de su pu*a madre! Rateros! Agarra tu uniforme y metete al carro." She told me to grab my uniform and get back in the car, in the tone where like somebody's about to die at the hands of a Mexican lady. She drove me back to the Sonic, speeding in her beat-up car. She got out of the car, walked me to the door, and head high demanded that they come outside.

"Dile a esa pin*he vieja que salga!!" She demanded I bring the manager outside, but in Spanish, she said it with *'drag her out'* energy. By that time, both the wife and husband managers were there and they saw us from inside because the Sonic building was mostly windows. I asked them to step outside because my mom wanted to speak to them. All hell broke loose as my mom began to yell in Spanish while I translated.

"Dile que tu no eres su pen**ja, y que deberian de tener vergüenza por robarle a una niña!"

"My mom says that I'm not your pen**ja, and you should be ashamed of yourselves and that you're stealing my tips." (I didn't know how to translate pen**ja to English.)

"Y diles que no les vas a pagar un pin*he centavo mas!"

"And she says that I'm not going to pay the $150."

They tried to interrupt to offer an explanation but my mom wouldn't allow them to speak.

"¡A mi me vale madre lo que tenga que decir, vieja ratera!!! ¡Y ya, entrégales su pin**e uniforme y diles que se queden con su pin**e trabajo! Viejos cu**ros, hijos de su pu*a madre!" As she stood fuming, they were at a loss for words, just completely caught off guard and stunned. I mean, I was scared too. The lady turned bright red and her husband looked nervous.

"Mmmm...my mom says I quit and that here is your uniform."

I handed over the uniform to the wife. She looked so fearful and began to ask me not to quit, and that it was a misunderstanding. Deep down I knew my mom was right, and they were probably doing that to other teenage workers. Once we got home, they called my house to tell me they somehow found the missing $150. I thought they were afraid my mom was going to file a police report or something. They asked me to take my job back and return to work the next day but I declined. Nothing seemed to come easy and even trying to get a basic job came with hardship. I was grateful for my mom's strength, though. I learned to stand up for myself and not to give up when I faced difficulty. My mom was the sweetest lady you could ever meet, but if you messed with one of her kids, she was vicious.

My other older brother was 1 year older than me. He got into a lot of trouble. It's hard for me to describe what that time was like. It was a lot. As a little girl, he was my best friend. He started smoking in 6th grade, then started doing heavier drugs later. As he was in and out of jail, I went everywhere translating for my mom from case workers, to attorneys, in order to try to get him help. When we reached high school, he got into cocaine. He picked up problems with some drug dealers. The addiction got strong, money was short and he picked up stealing. He began stealing from my mom's purse, then my sisters' jewelry, then breaking into affluent neighborhoods in Dallas with his friends. He once showed up to our house with gold cutlery as a gift to my mom. Another time, a very expensive miniature dog. Despite all that, my parents decided to make him my driver to and from high school and I fought my mom against it.

"Mom no please find me a ride, he's *crazy*! I don't want to go anywhere with him!"

"You're going to be fine Arisbet, we don't have money for a ride right now and you two need to get along. It's only for a short while."

I was so upset. He really was starting to lose his mind to drugs. One day, we were driving home from Sunset High School and he saw a guy walking home with nachos in his hand, turning a neighborhood corner into Oak Cliff Blvd. This kid was just walking home. My brother said to me, "Hold up," and pulled the car over, opened the trunk, pulled out a gray metal bat and went after the kid to beat him for his Jordans. I was horrified. I jumped out of the car without thought and yelled at him to stop but also yelled so the kid could get a head start to run. The guy was able to pull away and he ran like a pit bull was after him down the street. My brother walked back into the car unphased. Another time, Darwin said he needed to stop by the store. The way he said it was all I needed to know something bad was about to happen. I told him I'd wait in the car and gave him my *'don't do anything stupid'* look. He pulled up to the Kroger (at that time) in Wynnewood Village and took a while. I wondered what was happening when all of a sudden I saw police cars pull up, and then police walked him out in handcuffs and into a police car. I remember looking at him arrested with his head hung and thought I love my brother and my heart broke for him. The officers walked up to me in the car and quickly realized I had nothing to do with whatever he did. They let me go inside to call my parents to pick me up. I got a ride paid for after that.

He lost common sense, but I saw a glimpse of his true self here and there. Like the day my parents asked him to teach me how to drive.

"Alright, this is what you do alright, pay attention to the master,"

"Shut up."

"You see the road lines on the ground, just match them to the corner of the windshield wiper and you're good, that means the car is in the middle of the lane."

"That's the stupidest thing I've ever heard! Oh my God, I'm going to crash and wreck!"

"No trust me, just try it. You're smart, driving will be easy for you." He patiently taught me how to drive until I learned. I wanted to cry. It reminded me of when we lived in Farmers Branch and he had to teach me to skateboard. "Aris pay attention, you have to learn how to skateboard so the boys don't make fun of you." I learned and skateboarded better than some of them. He also taught me how to ride a bike. He didn't want me to just know how to, but to be good at it so I'd keep up with him and the boys. He's the brother who found a dead bird and at the age of 7 rallied all of us kids together to give the bird a proper funeral. Every kid got serious, did their part and he led the whole thing. He officiated the funeral and in his kid words, said a prayer for the bird before we lowered the shoe box in the ground and buried it. At the age of 13 he rescued a bird who was caught in a net when we were playing in the backyard. When I gave up on the bird, my brother Darwin wouldn't let him die. The bird survived and flew away. That was the real him. Deep down he was a good person. We all carry deep sadness rooted in a series of events and experiences we lived through in our lifetime. One of mine includes seeing my brother disappear. Then years later, my youngest brother too. Also, standing back and seeing my mom fall apart through the years. She used to sing, just because. Over time I saw my mom's light flicker dim. If you would have asked me who I was in my teens, I would have said independent. A low priority. A helper. A laborer. Alone.

Tequila. Sotol. El Mezcal.

Mezcal is a liquor of choice for my family from Michoacán. Mezcal is what you would use for tragos amargos. Among the types of Mezcal produced in Michoacán, there is production that comes from Tzitzio, the town where my parents began their life together. Tzitzio, which means "beautiful place", began a tradition to bury January production inside glass jars for nine months, a time in which its notes and aromas become more complex. Nearing October and just before the Day of the Dead, people gather to unearth the mezcal and enjoy it among family paired with a good meal. Many, drink it hot and fast to forget the past they wish to erase, heal the pain of a deceased loved one or numb a broken heart.

In my dad's family, drinking starts early in the morning, and the reasons are unknown. I've seen my dad's mother begin at 10:00 a.m. and go on her day eating bean soup, a few handmade corn tortillas, and feel just fine. Normalizing it possibly helps pretend as if there are no reasons to embrace liquor so early, like it's a commonality equal to starting your day with a cup of coffee. Taking down a shot of Mezcal can become easy to some who have done it for years. In the same way, the broken moments from our parents' past can become an easy pain to swallow with years of suppressing and avoiding. The harm done to our parents ultimately impacts us, their children, leading to misfortunes that can affect our lives profoundly. It's hard to swallow.

While many people in our Mexican culture glamourize the obsession with liquor to heal the pain of life's difficult experiences, forget a painful memory, or numb feelings we are unable to handle sober - it does absolutely nothing to resolve the complexity of our broken condition. If anything, it makes it worse. Yet generation after generation, many of our families struggle in substance and alcohol addictions, to no avail, and without reaching the goal of inner healing.

I come from a family of people who are tenacious in what they want to accomplish. My dad's story of buying one pig that turned into the purchase of his parent's first home is incredible. My aunt being a coyote, crossing several immigrants across the border as a female leader, is astounding. My dad's entire family surviving death in the desert from cacti poisoning after crossing the border, is unbelievable. They were a breath away from death. *They all refused to die.* My mom convincing a company that she knew how to sew commercial linens (when she had no idea how) and then teaching herself how to on the spot when they gave her the job, is inspiring. I don't know a stronger woman than my mom, and I've traveled to over 10 countries and met several mothers who fought hard to provide a good life for their families. My mom passed her U.S. Citizenship test by watching T.V. in English, not knowing the language well, in such a short period of time of study. Whenever I think I can't, I remember my mom sewing commercial linens and my dad buying one pig that turned into a new home purchase. My mom and dad, desperate to provide for her kids in a foreign country, made the impossible happen. My parents began to buy their first home from white people who didn't speak Spanish, by the time I was in 6th grade, and then bought a second home after that. I hold a lot of respect for my mom and dad.

My Mexican family, like many others, deal with the setback that while we work hard, we can't express or communicate the issues we struggle with in order to be a family and not just be related. Culturally, men are not allowed to cry or share their feelings because if they do, he would be "pior que una vieja". Translated, it means he would be worse than a woman. Yes that phrase is an actual insult in Mexican culture. Problems never ended and my mom somehow handled everything on her own with my dad mostly contributing financially. That's another type of structure in many Mexican families, where women handle the kids and the men focus on bringing in money. My mom didn't have someone to rely on or really talk to but maybe a comadre or the Catholic priest at confession. When they had physical pain with body aches, my mom and dad tried to manage in ways they knew how. They have *'remedios'* (remedies) that could address any ailment. If it was a headache (brought in by worry and fear), la pomade de Campana, or drinking hierba de limón, or eucalipto. If it was a stomach problem (because of the stress), el té de manzanilla or té de hierba buena. For digestion, la hierba de epazote....and the list goes on. But often, those remedies didn't heal the condition completely.

Other times, my parents would go to a curandero named Don Chivo. A curandero is a person who, without being a doctor, practices medicinal or ritual healing. Don Chivo worked out of his garage and gave herbal remedy consultations, gave body massages and much of what he did was sourced in dark magic or witchcraft. Some people don't practice witchcraft with herbalist remedies and massage therapy. Many come to this practice growing up in Mexico and learning from their family who used natural healing remedies for ages. But Don Chivo brushed people with branches over their bodies and had several idols and images of people next to Jesus on the cross and La Virgen de Guadalupe. He would recite what sounded like séance evoking spirits to heal people. I got to see it in person at the age of 14 when I went with my parents and thought, '*This is crazy, why do they do this?*' But this is very common in Mexican families. None of that stuff ever helped them, but in the culture, that's all many Mexicans know to run to. What I clearly know is that regardless of your cultural background, whatever the adults suppressed and didn't deal with, their children will have to face and deal with one day.

By the time a girl had invited me to church at the age of 15, I had already gone through a lot. I had no personal sense of identity and distracted myself with drawing and painting. When I wasn't making art, I was micro focused on the stress at home and trying to avoid conflict. You would think I was desperate to meet God in relationship, but I did not care for God whatsoever. I felt I already knew all I had to know because my parents took us to Catholic church every Sunday. To me, God was far off and distant. He was powerful enough to create the world but not powerful enough to help my mom with all her worries or to have protected me from things I experienced. The conclusion I had was that God must not care enough to have prevented bad things from happening. God was a mystic, mythical figure from ancient times, who stood far off in the sky somewhere. I did not doubt God's existence, but I saw Him as the being that only watches the world and judges. So, as long as you don't commit a serious crime in your life, you're good and get into heaven.

When I share my childhood with people, they are shocked to know I grew up in the *hood, hood.* They're shocked that I cooked for myself and siblings since the age of 7 and that I started working at the age of 14. I think it's because I'm not the stereotype they have of kids who grew up in hoods. Although I'm a Mexican immigrant, people are surprised when they find out I'm Mexican. They look shocked when I speak fluent Spanish and fluent English without an accent. I rallied in the protests we had in Dallas in the early 2000s wearing a "Do I look Illegal?" sticker on my shirt and a lady ran to me from the huge crowd and yelled in laughter, "No, you don't look illegal!!!" She wasn't drunk.

I want to talk to you about identity. The same way people get my identity wrong; you very well could *potentially have your identity completely wrong.*

Identity formation is something we run through life pursuing, picking up ideas from people, jobs, our environment, our experiences - but for many, true identity remains incomplete or undiscovered. If a Biblical foundational principle is that we find our true identity in Christ, I would have been incapable of knowing it simply because I didn't have a clear understanding of even who God was.

When I gave my life to God at 15, none of my family embraced it. I was not celebrated for pursuing God. *It didn't matter.* My siblings made fun of me. *It was irrelevant.* My mom told me to stop reading the Bible. *I registered for Bible College.* My dad disowned me as his daughter for not being Catholic, but the skies were blue and the birds were chirping because I finally identified as a daughter of God. When you finally surrender to God, you find your true self. Nobody could convince me to leave my commitment to living for Jesus as Lord and Savior. I handed my family over to God as I grew older and began to discover my identity in Christ.

While I look at México with profound joy and a longing to return to Morelia, my mother looks back at México with deep sorrow as a nightmare that should not be revisited. My dad reminisces about the food in México, especially mariscos from Zihuatanejo, but overall, he is ok if he doesn't get a chance to return. Some of our parents carry secrets heavily in their souls, deeply hidden, and many of our parents will carry them to the grave. The complexity of their chaotic childhoods will remain unknown to many of their children.

What I can tell you with complete certainty is that Bible scripture offers revelation of God's intention with us as creation and explains how God's depth of knowing us is intricate. He knew us even before we entered our mother's womb and knew our identity and purpose. *"Before I formed you in the womb I knew you, before you were born I set you apart; I appointed you as a prophet to the nations."* Jeremiah 1:5. While everyone does not share the same calling of 'prophet to the nations' like Jeremiah, this scripture leads us to the conclusion that we were all created thoughtfully and purposefully by God. He is not only the giver of life, He is the giver of identity and purpose. We can conclude that we were not born by chance or accident. We're not supposed to live aimlessly wondering what it is that we're here for. Whether your parents intentionally planned you or not, God intentionally planned you and knew the end of your life before your first day on earth.

We don't have the parents we have by chance or a draw. After you were born, there are actions your parents took in your life that molded your identity. There are things that occurred in your life as shocking accidents or events you had no ability to protect yourself from, which also impacted your identity. Then, as you grew up there were choices you made that further established your identity in your spirit and soul. If you take the time to look back, and if you could un-pack all the big events that shaped you, what is the identity you have accepted? What have you put on to cover up your true identity in childhood or adulthood – who is that person? For many, those experiences are difficult to face. Tragos amargos. This is maybe why people who don't know God in relationship are called, 'the lost.' What was lost is identity.

At 15, when God powerfully set me free, I immediately handed the conflict of identity over to Him. What I discovered was the first thing God does when you hand your life over to Him is that He begins to put things in order. All the chaos created by what you lived in your past begins to come into order within yourself. It's what He did in Genesis chapter 1, when the Bible describes the beginning when the earth was chaotic, formless, empty and full of darkness.

> *"In the beginning God (Elohim) created the heavens and earth. The earth was formless and void, or a waste and emptiness, and darkness was upon the face of the deep."*
> *- Genesis 1:1 AMP*

In the same way the world was in this condition before God entered it, so is the condition of our spirit before Christ is welcomed into our lives as Lord. Our spirit without God as Master and Lord is void, empty and full of darkness. Everything is confusing. There is no order within and we can't make sense of the chaos that led us to where we stand on a daily basis. While some people can face this reality, others are comfortably adapting to the condition with temporary ailments like addictions, distractions, their work, and anything in between.

Ok, so follow me here. Genesis 1 verse 2 explains the condition, and verse 3 reveals God's intention. Genesis 1:2 says, *"...the spirit of God was moving (hovering, brooding) over the face of the water."* Here, the Holy Spirit was analyzing the situation and chaotic condition. Genesis 1:3 reads, *"And God said, 'Let there be light"; and there was light. God saw the light was good (pleasing, and useful) and He affirmed and sustained it."* Here, we learn God called the light day and the darkness night…and so forth.

We learn something so important about God here. His action response to entering earth in all it's chaos and disorder was first to *analyze* the chaos. The Holy Spirit hovered over analyzing and his work brought clarity, and order. His final result was that the yield would be a clearly defined and well accomplished purpose to each aspect of creation. The wind we don't see serves a purpose, the waters became ocean, land mass became a precise boundary, animals and vegetation all with their clear purpose and provision for creation. It's the exact same work God begins when you decide to surrender your life to Him.

What was chaotic is now clearly defined.

You no longer stare back at the chaos of your family's past, the consequences of your bad choices, and the tragic moments you've lived. What was dark is now illuminated and takes meaning. You now look at yourself and your condition as complete and whole, with a specific and clear vision of why God created you and what your purpose is. Note how the scripture says the darkness became night and the light became day. Why didn't God just get rid of the darkness? Here we see darkness served a purpose and that purpose was night.

Your darkest moments accomplish a purpose.

The moment God enters in, just as your best moments accomplish a purpose, your darkest moments also accomplish a purpose. Psalm 139 states that to God, the darkness is as light! *"...even the darkness will not be dark to You; the night will shine like the day, for darkness is as light to You."* This is comforting in that darkness is non-existent to God. Whatever is the scariest thing you have lived through, God is greater, and you can rest knowing He's got your greatest fears covered. Compared to His power, your fears are disarmed, and you can find comfort in knowing He's shielding you from your greatest anxieties. Like the earth sprouted vegetation and trees yielded fruit, your life bears and produces a good result for the world to benefit as soon as Christ enters your life, and the Holy Spirit lives in you.

Consider the condition of your world within. What is the current state of your internal environment? Who are you really? You are not the sum of all your desires, appetites, needs and drives that pull from your broken past life experiences and circumstances. You may feel left with an unclear identity.

Many people waste their lifetime searching for the remedy to the chaos they feel within. People chase money, career, addictions, the acceptance of others, and every effort to remedy the emptiness and pain they live with personally. Even when they reach a place of accomplishment or personal fulfillment, many remain discontent. It's never enough. If this is you, consider facing God about it today. If up to this point in your life you have done everything in your power to avoid the pain of your past, today is a good day to yield to God about it. If you are reading this with messages from the past, recounting memories on constant replay without peace of mind, focusing on past failures that accuse you, old grief that pains you – consider yielding to God now and pray the simple prayer in the end of the book.

Despite how you were raised (or not), where you have been in your life, what you have or don't have, who is around or who was always missing – you can only find your authentic and true self in God. The creator determined the purpose of His creation. Many people I have had a chance to share the Gospel with stay stuck at their inner condition of chaos. However, if you stay stuck at chaos, you'll never get to the *'putting things in order'* part with God, which leads to the clearly defined purpose.

Your identity.

God is faithful and will reveal to you your complete and true identity. The you He has known since before you entered your mother's womb.

Reflect on the scripture below as a personal affirmation.

> *"I will give thanks and praise to You, for I am fearfully and wonderfully made;*
>
> *Wonderful are Your works,*
> *And my soul knows it very well."*
> *- Psalm 139:14 AMP*

I invite you to search the scriptures to understand who you are as a child of God. If you are willing, God can and will work in your life to put order to the chaos.

CHAPTER 14
Dios Te Salve, Maria

"You know that some of our family are drug people."

"Tio, all Mexicans have family that are drug people."

I was joking. Sort of. But my tio Julio looked at me and gave a half nod in partial agreement. "No pos allí si tienes toda la razón hija."' Him agreeing so quickly made it funnier. He continued, "The guy who was getting married was our cousin Rogelio. And there was another guy who wanted to be his best man, a man named Antonio, who is what you call the kind of people that are just matones (killers). For no reason at all, they just kill, if it's a drug problem or respect problem, you know, matones. He wanted to desquitarse (retaliate) without reason right, I mean your dad really did not do anything but accept to be the best man. He tried to take a jab at your dad, at least that's what some say."

They used to call my dad 'La Pistola' in México, which means 'The Gun'. His personality is very social, funny and blunt. He was a party guy and he had a lot of friends. Another thing I see in my dad is that despite priorities being out of wack, he has a caring heart for people. So putting all that together, I can see how his cousin chose him over others. I can also see how someone would come after him out of envy.

My uncle continued, "So word on the street is that day, the guy who wanted to be best man was heading to the church to kill your dad. But when he arrived to the church at the end of the wedding, that's when your parents had just heard your older brother fell in the well and there was so much chaos from your mom screaming, to bystanders yelling out for help, that he did not reach your dad in time to kill him. Your parents rushed to leave where your brother was found and then went home, "

I couldn't respond. I was shocked.

"You know that her children have always been everything to your mom. Your mom would never have left one of her kids with anyone," Sounded about right. I know this story well. My mom has shared it with me a couple times but she did not know this detail that my uncle knew regardign the guy who wanted to kill my dad. "And then?" I asked. "Well I was there hija, and if you can imagine, your mom was losing her mind. The girl (babysitter) ran to tell her the baby had drowned… by the time she reached him, she saw her little baby gone, it was too late. Back then it was going to take time to drive him into the city to get him to a doctor so they tried to resuscitate him but there was no hope, he was gone. People kept trying but he was lifeless for who knows how long already. She just cried and held him, and most of the people went back to the wedding while your mom and dad went back to their house."

"I know, that's devastating. I know my mom still deals with the heartbreak." I said as I reflected on all the years I've seen her cry about it."Well let me tell you something else that is key here…Was it by chance that he drowned? What are the odds that this incident distracted the man's plan. What can we conclude about that?"

We both paused in silence at my mom's dining table. His wife sat there uninterested. Her empty stare at the dining room wall was icy, like she could care less, or reservedly carried a world of problems on her own shoulders that outweighed my mom's tragic past. But my tio voiced the conclusion that I reached in my mind. He said, "I believe that was not a coincidence. It was God's plan."

I don't understand. The passing of my oldest brother is not the first tragedy I examine and tell God, *'God, how was this your plan…You could have done something different here…'* My oldest brother Pedro was 3 years old when he died and the memory of his death still haunts my mom. She still feels that deep pain, and loss of the love she had for her son even after having so many more sons after him. Nothing fills that void.

The Summer of 2013 I was back in Tzitzio, Michoacán with my mom. When we arrived at the airport, it had been over 15 years since my mom had seen her mother. They didn't exchange words, but I saw the most emotional reunion as I watched my grandmother run to my mom as if my mom was a child and she embraced her baby tightly and cried silently. Their similarity in personality was so exact. My mom is the type of Mexican lady that I would describe as 'una mujer fina'. In English it may translate as elegant or someone with high class. She's not disrespectful, she's proper and holds herself to strict morals. She doesn't speak harshly to others (unless you mess with her kids). She's humble, shy and has an incredible servant's heart. I got to see her childhood home in Paso Ancho. I saw the river she used to play in as a child. One of her favorite happy childhood memories is running as fast as she could and plunging into that river. "Corría, me aventaba al río y nadaba de esquina a esquina," she has said to me. I stopped by my dad's home in Queretanillo also but we didn't spend long there. I thought both of their homes were beautiful.

The scenic drive down is captivating. The Cerro is covered in lush green vegetation, and the dirt is shades of reds, like the color of terra cotta

Tzitzio, Michoacán, México
Photo Credit: H. Ayuntamiento Tzitzio, Michoacán

clay. I saw a woman and her child walk up to the side of the mountain with a 5 gallon water jug and observed as she collected water that poured out of the side of the mountain. I pointed it out to my mom, and the taxi driver interjected, "Oh it's the best you could get anywhere in the world. It's naturally purified and very cold."

We drove down to Tzitzio where my mom lived when my brother died. Walking those same roads with my mom over 25 years later was a beautiful experience I will never forget. She showed me where our house was and I imagined her being a young teenager raising her small family and dealing with issues a young teen shouldn't have to live through. The house was super tiny and is now just ruins. When we left to the U.S., all of our stuff was trashed so she doesn't have any photos.

We then walked to the church she was married in. It's the same church where my dad's cousin's wedding was held on the day my brother died. I wish I could see a photo of my mom on her wedding day and just imagined what it maybe would have been like. She walked inside with me and let out a deep sigh. "What mom?" She took a long pause. "So many painful memories here." I sensed she regretted marrying my dad. We then walked up to the city office to obtain a birth certificate my mom needed, the real reason why we were there. I didn't see any kind of happiness in my mom's face to be back there. She still gave me the tour and pointed out my dad's mothers' home and other family members' homes.

On the drive back to Morelia, we passed a winding road. My mom pointed out a cemetery and said, "There is my baby." She said with deep sorrow. "Ulyses is there?" I asked, followed by, "Sir stop the taxi, let's stop at this cemetery." My mom interrupted quickly and said, "No...for what. My poor baby. There's nothing left there." I cannot understand that level of love. To have it so deeply rooted in you and then have it taken from you so suddenly. Love so deep, when uprooted, destroys a piece of you which you can never recover.

When we introduce someone, we typically start with the key identifiers that quickly express who they are. With God, the word is love. *"Theos estin agapē"* is the original Greek in 1 John 4:8, which translates *"God is love"*. That's the foundation of where you begin to understand Him. God has the most beautiful character and at His core He is love. The word "estin" in this verse in Greek means "I am, I exist". The word "love" in that verse is "agapē" meaning the highest form of love, the love of God for man and of man for God". Within Christianity, agapē is considered to be the love originating from God and Christ for humankind. One commentary I liked explained it this way,

> "We must beware of watering down "God is Love" into "God is loving," or even "God of all beings is the most loving." Love is not a mere attribute of God; like light, it is His very nature. As "God is Light" sums up the Being of God intellectually considered, so "God is Love" sums up the same on the moral side. Only when this strong meaning is given to the statement does St. John's argument hold, that "he that loveth not knoweth not God."
>
> A man who has no idea of any one of the attributes of God, as order, or beauty, or power, or justice, has an imperfect knowledge of God. But he who has no idea of love has no knowledge of God, for love is himself. God alone loves in the fullest and highest sense of the word; for he alone loves with perfect disinterestedness.
>
> It is love which alone can explain creation. Why should a Being perfectly blessed in himself create other beings, but to bestow a blessing upon them?" [1]

Source: 2010, Pulpit Commentary, BibleHub.com

"Theos estin agapē", God is and constantly exists in a state of perfect love, the fullest and highest sense of the word. Unconditional. Unquestioning. Unending. Unlimited. It's not dependent on what we do or don't do. If we love to our greatest capacity it can be described as "whole-hearted" love.

---

1   2010. Pulpit Commentary, 1 John 4. Bible Hub. https://biblehub.com/commentaries/pulpit/1_john/4.htm.

Preparing caldo de pollo with my mom. - Morelia, Michoacán México

And even then, for all of us, love is a choice and our expression of love is often based on certain circumstances we choose. While we live in a way of making the choice of stepping in and out of a position of love, God exists *from* a position of love. The Bible says, we can *"put on love"* (Colossians 3:14-17) similar to how we put on clothing. I mean, think about it. We are not love, but as people living on this earth can choose to put on love each day or go without it. God is not this way. God embodies love in every moment, simply by being Himself and existing fully. His very nature radiates love.

My mom loved my brother whole-heartedly, with all she had in her ability as a mother and her response to that love lost almost took her soul. We all have been a witness to the incredible actions taken by people who deeply love someone else. Parents who put their lives in danger to save their children. Individuals who donate an organ to save their spouse. Think of the greatest act of love you have ever witnessed. God is that to the most unimagineable level. His love surpasses the love of anyone you will ever meet. God loves you and me consistently despite what we do or don't do – in His "whole-existence". He breathes love. He works through love. He sees love.

Christ was the manifestation of His love and showed up on earth completely wrapped in love. I'm repeating myself, I know but words fall so short to explain what His love is like. It's not described, it's experienced and felt within. The love of God is not meant to be explained to fit a specific definition. His love is not captured in visuals. Any form of expression is limiting. It's like when you take a photo to capture a beautiful beach sunrise. What you see on the photo does not precisely capture the awe of experiencing the sunrise in person. Many who read or hear about God only have done so in attempts to intellectually understand God and are left with an incomplete image. An image taken and not a personal experience lived leads to religion, it leads to emptiness. In this lifetime, you and I get the opportunity to experience His love in our entire being, spirit soul and body, in ways that are indescribable and overwhelming when we come to God in faith.

The experience of God's love that I had at the age of 15 was the reason I maintained a relationship with God despite any difficult circumstance or any offense I experienced afterwards by other people, including my own family. The understanding that God passionately loves us deep within our core and in response, living from that position of love, *is a game changer*. An experience beyond what any sermon could deliver, beyond what any person could attempt to exemplify for me, beyond anything I've ever heard or seen. The experience of God's love comes with His presence dwelling within us. Through salvation, we become the temple of the Holy Spirit ensuring that His love never leaves us.

If you opened the Bible to the book of Genesis, you would see God the Trinity declaring Himself supreme. *'I am the creator of Heaven and Earth, I put this in order with just my words.'* Think about that. Whatever you and I create, we have to use our hands. God creates with one breath. By the time you reach Exodus you will see God initiate a re-introduction of Himself using Moses to deliver Israelites at the hands of the Egyptians. God shared His name as "I Am who I Am..." and in all majesty and splendor God releases a series of plagues. They were a glimpse of His unmatched power. He flexed a portion of His power which could not be replicated by the most 'powerful' magicians and workers of dark magic of that time. Using the several plagues, God described bits and pieces of who He is as the Great I Am.

If you keep going and reach Leviticus, Numbers and Deuteronomy, God continues to unfold His character and remains consistent, proving to be an omnipotent God. The only true God, as generation to generation, idols fell. A bit further after Joshua, Judges, Ruth, the books of Samuel, the books of Kings, through Psalms, and the books of the prophets, you will come to an intellectual conclusion that each book revealed a repetition of His character. You will get a very clear picture of a God who is patient, faithful, victorious, and so much more. But if you take all the descriptions of His character, and ask - what was the point of Him exercising and putting so much of Himself into mankind? You will see that God is truly motivated by one thing, and that is the recovery of His children. The reason for all of it, was love.

God lost love in the book of Genesis.

He in some way, lost humanity. Every book following the first, we see God running fervently after His children. Generation after generation, God used prophets and appointed kings to gather them back to Himself. Generation after generation, whether they were rebellious or faithful, His desire toward them remained the same. In God's sight was reconciliation. Event after event, God demonstrates His grace unceasing and His patience for each generation in pursuit of them. By the time we reach the first prophetic book, God is saying, *'I have shown you much of who I Am so far, I'm*

Danza de los Viejitos - Janitzio, Michoacán México

the one true God. I *Am your full sufficiency. You need no one besides Me, I Am your provider, I give and take away, I Am a God who sees, I called you out of darkness, I am light, I restore you back from slavery, I will show you the way to go, I bless, and I curse,'* and so on. Chapter by chapter, book, by book, God is revealing a new facet of His consistent character, in new depths with each passing generation. Finally you will reach the book of the prophet Malachi. In chapter 4 we hit a hard pause. God declares through the prophet Malachi that the day is coming soon – a day of Judgement. This is God's last communication recorded in the Old Testament of the Bible as a final admonition. *'I Am a God of final judgement, those who fear me will remain with me forever.'* It reads as follows.

> *"For behold, the day is coming, burning like a furnace, and all the arrogant (proud, self-righteous, haughty), and every evildoer shall be stubble; and the day that is coming shall set them on fire,"* says the Lord of hosts, *"so that it will leave them neither root nor branch. But for you who fear My name [with awe-filled reverence] the sun of righteousness will rise with healing in its wings.*
>
> *And you will go forward and leap [joyfully] like calves [released] from the stall. You will trample the wicked, for they will be ashes under the soles of your feet on the day that I do this,"* says the Lord of hosts.

> *"Remember [with thoughtful concern] the Law of Moses My servant, the statutes and the ordinances which I commanded him on [Mount] Horeb [to give] to all Israel.*
>
> *"Behold, I am going to send you Elijah the prophet before the coming of the great and terrible day of the Lord. He will turn the hearts of the fathers to their children, and the hearts of the children to their fathers [a reconciliation produced by repentance], so that I will not come and strike the land with a curse [of complete destruction]."*
> *- Malachi 4 AMP*

God is saying here, *'You know a lot about me by now, and I really need you to listen - a day of Judgement is approaching'*. While there was separation and they knew God intellectually, culturally, and religiously, now the urgency to know God deeply and personally in relationship will be required. Also, that judgement would be involved.

We reach Matthew Chapter 1 and it begins *"All of this happened in order for…"* So, everything we just read in the Old Testament books prior to this event in Matthew Chapter 1 – all of that happened in order for us to get to this one moment in time.

> *"All this happened in order to fulfill what the Lord had spoken through the prophet [Isaiah]:*
> *"Behold, the virgin shall be with child and give birth to a Son, and they shall call His name Immanuel"—which, when translated, means, "God with us."*
> *- Matthew 1:22-23 AMP*

We reached the point where God finally just says:

> *'I Am now with you'.*

After all the chasing of the Old Testament, speaking through other people to reach His children, God, wrapped in swaddle cloth, was born. 'Immanuel' meaning God with Us. It was no longer a chosen prophet explaining God's character, it was now God speaking on His own behalf. His love led to *God with us*. What a prophet could not do to reconcile us to Him in perfect union, God took the form of Man to reconcile us back. Jesus, wrapped in His complete glory walked out God's love fully and perfectly. As spoken by the prophets, Christ arrived on a mission to reach the cross and die for the salvation of every man and woman in the world in all time. All the previous books of the Bible powerfully illustrate various character traits and aspects of God's nature, offering glimpses into His complexity. This culminates Matthew 1, recording the moment as God prepares to fully reveal Himself through Jesus Christ, where His true nature is fully unveiled. Jesus is literally described as the word of God made flesh. John 1:14 describes, *"And the Word was made flesh, and dwelt among us, (and we beheld His glory, the glory as of the only begotten of the Father,) full of grace and truth."* Jesus *is the walking Truth. Also known as "the Way", the only way to God the Father. And known as "The Light of the world."* God encapsulated in one individual, was carried out to the world. I think this is powerful. No other gods recorded in all the gods worshiped on this earth, historically none, have ever come close to what God has done just in Christ alone. Not one.

The plan unfolded by God's love of redemption through faith in Jesus surpasses all labors of love recorded in all history. The Bible describes in detail how that very long plan, the span of several decades, a lot of pieces falling precisely into place, a lot of perfect moments, many of which cannot be explained. There were miracles, a lot of imperfect people leading the way, and many generations saying a resounding yes to God and walking out their assignments in their time in history. All of that just to get you and I reconciled to God in our lifetime.

My mom's tragic story of a love lost in the passing of her son left her spiraling as she faced the next several years. Considering my mom's story, it struck me that she still carries incredible grief today, and since we are created in God's likeness, how much greater must God's suffering have been in losing his only son? Wrapped with the entire essence of God's love – all of it in one person – persecuted and nailed to a cross for the reconciliation of all His other children. All of the hope in the world finally arrived in one person just so He would be led to death on a cross. Its inconceivable. I imagine the greatest emptiness existed in the heart of God for the next three full days following Christ's death. The Bible describes the point of Christ's death in Matthew 27.

> *Now from the sixth hour (noon) there was darkness over all the land until the ninth hour (3:00 p.m.). About the ninth hour Jesus cried out with a loud [agonized] voice,*

> *"Eli, Eli, lama sabachthani?" that is,*
> *"My God, My God, why have You forsaken Me?"*
> *- Matthew 27:45-46 AMP*

That question Jesus asked always bothered me. *"My God, My God, why have you forsaken Me?"* It is clear here that in His darkest hour, God left Jesus alone. If you feel God has left you alone, Jesus understands. It was recorded as a bitter cry from Christ's soul, out to God in the heightened agony of a painful death. I wrote all that to get to this conclusion for you.

The darkest day in scripture occurred so that in my mother's darkest day, she could be covered with God's presence and perfect love.

Christ suffered the darkest day to allow for you and me to not have to live out our darkest days without God's love.

His love is immeasurable. The cross meant you would not go through *anything* alone. Pause to settle in on this truth. God will sustain you in your darkest moments. When Jesus could not rest in God's presence on His worst day, you and I get to rest in God, literally with the Holy Spirit of God living in us, on our worst days. All of this made possible because Jesus suffered the darkest day and overcame the sting of death with resurrection.

'Dios te salve Maria' means "God save you Maria" and it's the beginning of a Catholic prayer to the La Virgen de Guadalupe that my mother Maria always prayed to holding a rosary. Whenever she whispered this prayer, I desired God to hear her and come to her rescue. For God to rescue my mom, Maria, from this dark past so it would no longer be a torment in her life. I believe God sustained her then, and that the mourning process is a continual saving within. The darkness that follows a significant loss is a constant companion for those who have experienced grief; however, even in the darkest moments of our memories, moments unseen by those around us, our Heavenly Father's presence remains.

God will continually preserve us wrapped in His love, if we are willing. I believe the only thing that can save anyone from absolutely anything they will experience in this life on earth is found in just one characteristic of God:

"God is love..." John 4:16.

CHAPTER 15
Worship Service

"Los asaltaron…y se robaron todo, pero no los mataron." My friend Irene said to me after hanging up the phone with Juan, another outreach team member. His dad sent a guy out to México in advance with equipment we would use on the upcoming trip. It's the Summer of 2009 and I was heading to Zacatecas, México. The last time I was in México was when I visited Guadalajara. The drive to Guadalajara was long and with a continuous loop of one Sin Bandera album with my oldest sister and her baby's dad as they traveled to visit his mom. My sister took me to help her babysit her daughters, and I really enjoyed the trip for the opportunity to see México again.

This time, I visited Fresnillo, Zacatecas where my friend Irene is from. The trip was so well organized. Irene held meetings with us at CFNI ahead of time so that we would all be prepared. She was like a sister to me. When I talk to her, I feel like I'm talking with family. She was a sharp, intelligent and beautiful girl with big brown eyes and long black hair. She had a fierceness and boldness to her that I can identify with, and she never apologized for it. She would say things like, "El enemigo es astuto Arisbet. Nunca le des el privilegio de intimidarte. Tu rechaza todo temor en el nombre de Jesus." When I say a sharp and fierce woman, I mean *fierce*. She was also fun and adventurous, and often up for a last-minute fun run. I admired how she held high regard for herself and was not impressed by any guy who approached her. She had an incredible respect for her parents, especially her dad, who was a very successful businessman.

We were warned to be careful traveling as the cartel had control over certain areas and it would be dangerous for us to be there. We heard this all the time and still chose to go. We trusted God with our safety and were mindful of what we did and where we went. Zacatecas is beautiful with Spanish colonial architecture, perfect for a movie set. I arrived to Irene's family villa, a beautifully designed home with several rooms to accommodate family and guests. One room was my favorite, it was built to be dedicated for prayer and worship. This room looked like a Catholic chapel within a home. It was one of a kind and had a dome roof with celestial images painted on the roof. Irene's ex-boyfriend was a known artist in the town and he painted the meticulous designs in that room and throughout

Overlooking Fresnillo. - Zacatecas, México

the home.

    My prayer for Zacatecas was that God would use us to bring hope, for people to decide on a personal relationship with God and for peace from the organized crime and violence we were briefed on before arriving. We were not allowed to be out past a certain time unless accompanied by one of Irene's family members. We were told of political corruption and their inability to trust police, and other warnings in advance to help prepare especially those outreach members who were not Mexican. Now, would I let my daughter take that trip out there knowing all of this information? Absolutely not. But I did not tell my mom any of it, because to me at the time, none of those details were cause for fear. I was fearless. Nothing was impossible for God and I knew my life was in His hands.

    We served in church evening services throughout the time we were there. Irene had organized a revival conference for the community to teach them practical Biblical teaching for spiritual growth. I saw many healings and miracles there. The missions team was spread throughout the congregation praying for people. The pastor said he wanted the church to begin to pray for the sick that were in attendance and I spotted a lady who had her right leg in a cast. She was sitting down with her leg elevated and resting on a chair in front of her. I walked over and asked if I could pray for her and she said yes. I asked her what happened and she said she suffered an accident, was in pain and could not move her foot or even toes. I believed God for instant healing over her ankle and without doubt knew she would be healed and be able to move it. She began to cry as I prayed and when I was done, she said the pain was gone and she began to move her ankle joint

WORSHIP SERVICE

and then she was moving her feet then toes in the cast. There was another person who rolled in on a wheelchair and walked out of the church with incredible joy and gratitude. I didn't see that person, but my team members told me about it in complete shock on our drive back to the villa. The things I witnessed in Zacatecas were incredible. People were so hungry to know more about God and they ran up to us without us trying to evangelize. It reminded me of the scripture that says the harvest is plenty, but the workers are few. Every service we attended was packed. There was one night that really blew me away. A scene I thought I would never get to see.

A good European friend of mine named Jean Luke had joined us on this trip. We were given the opportunity by a priest and leaders of a local Catholic church to have a night of prayer. Jean Luke asked it to be just a night of simply prayer and worship to see what God would do in the lives of people. He expressed how he knew we would confront a lot of idolatry and many did not have an understanding of scripture. Besides prayer and worship, there was no real agenda. Jean Luke gave a brief welcome, then worship and prayer began. When I arrived I remember just being so shocked that the Catholic church even allowed us to do something like this in their church. *'This would never happen in Dallas',* I thought. They are anti-anything non-Catholic, from my personal experience. I seriously doubted we would be allowed to hold a worship service in the Catholic church. I imagined a nun storming through the doors and kicking us out. I pictured the member who invited us there getting the talk I got when I was 18. The Sunday School Director's voice echoed in my memory, "We don't believe that here…"

It was evening and the sun had gone down. We were in one of the classrooms of the church, the lights were dimmed and they were playing worship music. The room was packed with locals standing and waiting to get prayed for, praying themselves, or singing the worship songs with eyes closed. People were really connecting to God, forgiving people they held resentments towards, some experienced physical healing. One by one, people's lives were being touched by God and it was evident! There was no program, no guest speaker. There was no worship band, and no food to enjoy after service, yet the room was packed. So packed it got hot in there, and still no one left.

Jean Luke called me over to help him pray for this one guy. He was a young adult maybe just over 18 years old who was dragged there by his mom. I mean he had an attitude. His mom looked so worried about him like he probably gave her a lot of trouble and she brought him in there out of desperation. I recognized the worry on her face, it matched my mom's for my brother. By the time he called me over, everyone who was in the team had already prayed for him and he just stood there arms crossed, hostile and prideful looking down at everyone.

I imagine he thought, *'wow these people are so dumb'*. Similar to what I thought at the age of 15 when I went to my first Christian youth service the night I committed my life to God. Jean Luke led the prayer and shared the Gospel with Him and encouraged him to open up his heart to God. By the end of his prayer though, the guy remained unmoved. I observed him while Jean Luke prayed. I asked God, *'What do you want to tell him…'* and waited, then God showed me. He didn't believe in God's power and that people were just being religious and emotional. I saw deep-seeded pride. I saw hate and resentment towards God. He declined Jean Luke's offer to commit his life to Christ and Jean Luke shrugged his shoulders and told me we should move on to someone else. I interrupted and told the guy, "Hey I just want to tell you something. In your heart right now you've hardened it against God. You made the decision to close your heart against Him, but God wants to challenge you. If you want to know what everyone around you is experiencing, the move of His presence, He Himself will show you right now. Make the decision to say yes to Him and He will show you His power. If you want to make the decision right now, God will instantly transform your life. He will do it right this very moment tonight. So I'm only going to ask you once, and then we will all leave you alone. Would you like to open your heart up to God?"

He just looked at me in silence with eyes wide, in shock. He nodded his head yes and looked down at the floor with his eyes open. I said, "I'm going to pray for you, and you within yourself just say to God, here I am God, I allow you into my heart and in your own words speak to God." I began to pray without touching him or holding his hand, or anyone around him touching him so he would know without a doubt it was the power of God. I kept my eyes open as I prayed and saw him begin to start crying, then he was weeping so much he hunched over and then quickly fell. I gave glory to God and was so happy for his life. His mom was a wreck after that, in tears of joy.

That happened inside a Catholic church. It blew my mind. It was an eye-opening experience that led to personal revelation about how the Bible explains that the true church is not confined to a building. The Bible says there is only one church – one body of Christ and it's made up of people who truly and genuinely surrender to God through salvation in Christ. If you look closely you can see a division of two different groups of people in every church. People who are convinced about God in a way that they genuinely and passionately pursue God in their private life, and people who reject God and live in complacency or indifference. Both kinds of people greet visitors at the doors of a church. Both kinds of people serve in leadership roles, and both kinds of people stand up on pulpits on Sunday

WORSHIP SERVICE

Outdoor Outreach events - Fresnillo, Zacatecas, México

mornings to lead ministries. There is a confusion in the world outside as they consider the idea of taking God seriously. I've heard many people's reasons for hesitation circle around the corruption they see in ministers and leaders confused at the people who follow them. They are so turned off to the Gospel and satisfy their needs for spiritual connection through horoscopes, crystals, yoga, meditation, ayahuasca ceremonies, you name it, anything else outside of a Christian-based church structure. In my ministry and life experience, there are many more people who believe God is not supreme and has limited power. Despite the many denominations out there, and all the churches that crowd our neighborhoods, we can still see only one true body of Christ made up by people who truly pursue God privately. The trip to Zacatecas re-enforced visually for me what the church looks like.

One day, a large group of locals and missionaries came together to visit a landfill community like the one in Nicaragua. We brought clothes to distribute to the people and toys for the children. I'll never forget seeing this little boy, handing him a ball and looking at me then looking down. Until then, I had never seen a child receive a toy and maintain a look of despair, as though he carried the worry of an entire lifetime on his shoulders. He was maybe 10 years old. I looked around that entire day at my teammates, and despite what we all observed, everyone carried light on their face. They offered smiles here and there, praying for people and encouraging them as they handed out items. I saw them work together in complete unity as if they each shared the same heart.

Worship.

Another day we organized an outdoor outreach event to share the

Gospel and pray for people. Missionaries and church volunteers rallied together to pray, then each with an assigned area, we walked out to gather as many bystanders as we could. There was a stage set up for someone to preach a message and musicians to play. After the sermon was over, we all began to pray for people. I spotted a girl in a hot pink shirt. A guy who looked like he may have been her boyfriend later joined us, and I witnessed to him too. Another day we visited the men's prison and got to share with inmates on a day when their families visited. I met a guy and his two sisters who visited him that day. They were so worried about him and I spent time mostly encouraging them. The guy had a really good attitude considering the fact he was in prison. His sisters were overwhelmed with concern. Families arrived with children to visit their loved ones and much of what we offered was words of comfort and encouragement for a better future. We also set up at the entrance to make churros (a Mexican donut like dessert) to give away to families who visited as they entered in.

Every day we shared meals together, and spent time getting to know the locals, especially the families who served in my friend Irene's church. At one point I was in the kitchen separating frijoles, one-by-one assisting in the kitchen. The unity among the church and the sense of strong community was beautiful. There was no pressure in forcing people to believe, but it was more about spending meaningful time together, hearing them out, laughing together, and joining in on basic, daily activity. I believe that's the most meaningful way to share the love of God with others. Nothing about the trip felt like pressure or a worship service defined by a strict program.

Worship service to God has no start time and no end time.

God corrected my view. Worship will occur anywhere where He

 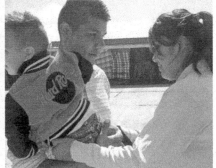

Ministering at the men's prison. - Fresnillo, Zacatecas, México
Left: These sisters were visiting their brother.
Right: A young mother arrives to visit, and hands her son to his dad in prison.

WORSHIP SERVICE

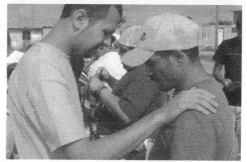

Ministering in the landfill community. - Zacatecas, Mexico

gets through to people and we as servants of Christ walk in obedience to reach the lost. I learned that whatever you do for God as part of the body of Christ, *is worship service*.

We are so used to thinking of worship in relation to music. Often you will hear people say things like, "I have a gift for worship." and what they mean is that they have musical talent. While you can worship God in singing and playing music, I would say that it's not the correct definition of true worship. There are many worship leaders and musicians who are very talented and gifted in playing an instrument or singing, yet they have never truly worshiped God. We see people get invited to church, sit through an entire worship service and still walk out unchanged and indifferent towards God. Romans 12 describes true worship.

> *"Therefore I urge you, brothers and sisters, by the mercies of God, to present your bodies [dedicating all of yourselves, set apart] as a living sacrifice, holy and well-pleasing to God, which is your rational (logical, intelligent) act of worship."*
> *– Romans 12:1 AMP*

The acceptable worship is not singing a song, it is a sacrifice where you offer your life yielded as an instrument in the hands of a master musician, Jesus Christ, walking as He did, in union with the Holy Spirit, and for the glory of God. You can sing a song in a worship service and never know what it's like to worship. It's a sacrifice in the sense that you are going beyond your feelings and die internally to all the world has to offer that appeals to your desires and appetites. Instead of pursuing the plans and ideas the world imposes, you decide to follow after God's instruction for your day-to-day living.

That's not the path the majority of people choose!

It's not convenient, it's not glamorous, it's not lavish, nor is it the easiest way to live. But Paul urges us to do so, and to commit to it daily. Worship is when we follow after His guidance and execute on what God has asked us to do. That doesn't always feel good and it's not always easy.

The process of presenting a sacrifice is a reference to the Levitical priests presenting their sacrifice to the altar. After the death and resurrection of Christ, we are now the priests and our bodies are the temple of the Holy Spirit. Your sacrifice of worship is daily and it's personal. Your pastor is incapable of making worship happen on your behalf. The lead musician in your church worship team is incapable of making worship happen within you. *You make it happen.* We do see people moved during worship songs in a service, where God is working in their hearts, yes, but we learn that it goes beyond that. While you live, worship involves your daily living.

How? The next verse in Romans 12:2 explains how.

> *"And do not be conformed to this world [any longer with its superficial values and customs], but be transformed and progressively changed [as you mature spiritually] by the renewing of your mind [focusing on godly values and ethical attitudes], so that you may prove [for yourselves] what the will of God is, that which is good and acceptable and perfect [in His plan and purpose for you]."*
> *- Romans 12:2 AMP*

You want to know the perfect will of God for your life? Take part in worship. Present your bodies as living sacrifice. It looks like forgiving someone you don't want to forgive. Worship looks like you waking up early to serve your community in some way, instead of sleeping in another weekend morning. It looks like encouraging someone in person instead of binging a Netflix series. Trust me, I get it. It would take Netflix posting the entire Oprah talk show from the 90s to take me out the streets for a good 2 - 3 weeks. I digress. It may be you spending time with your children instead of picking up another shift at work. God will impress upon you what that activity would look like in your personal life, and this is how to know God's perfect will daily.

Continue reading and Romans 12:4 describes that worship service we offer is us taking on our role as the body of Christ.

> *"For as in one body we have many members, and the members do not all have the same function, so we, though many, are one body in Christ, and individually members one of another. Having gifts that differ according to the grace given to us, let us use them..."*
> *- Romans 12:4-6 ESV*

We each have been uniquely gifted by God to serve together. It's time we no longer restrain worship service as a program within four walls of a building, led by one preacher, and a few leaders. We must see giving as more than just bringing in 10% of our income or a generous donation to a church ministry. We must recognize that we are held responsible for the gifts we are given by God, and the measure of faith we are given in order to fulfill worship service unto God every day we get to live.

When we step back to see where we stand in our faith as a nation, we can see the negative impact from the lack of understanding around what worship truly is. In their article, *"Modeling the Future of Religion in America: If recent trends in religious switching continue, Christians could make up less than half of the U.S. population within a few decades"*, Pew research reports that projections show Christians of all ages are shrinking from 64% to between a little more than half (54%) and just above one-third (35%) of all Americans by 2070.[1]

The decline of faith in America is happening quickly.

We cannot continue holding church services as perfectly organized programs, without teaching of the Bible which completely disregards God. We must stop looking at those who stand on pulpits to help us worship God, cheerlead us to serve, or usher in a spiritual revival. It's the work of each and every one of us to pursue God alone, and then together in community. It begins with presenting our individual lives before God daily in reasonable worship.

---

1   2022. Modeling the Future of Religion in America. Washington, DC: Pew Research Center. https://www.pewresearch.org/religion/2022/09/13/modeling-the-future-of-religion-in-america/.

CHAPTER 16

Cured

I entered into what looked to be a middle-class Mexican home. The woman we were going to pray for had been suffering with pain in her knee. We were invited to many homes to pray for people during this missionary trip. There were many sick people who hoped for physical healing. Jean Luke was leading the initiative for prayer visits. I met Jean Luke at another trip to Latin America. He was an older Spanish gentleman with white hair who grew up in France and the personality of a young college student. Even when he spoke Spanish you heard the French accent. Jean Luke was once married before and used to practice black magic. He was absolutely not looking for God when one day as he walked outside an alley, a man who was visiting France to preach met him. The man told him that God sent him to tell Jean Luke that he was going to get saved and preach the Gospel to many people. He was set free instantly, surrendered his life to God, and since then pursued God passionately. Jean Luke eventually enrolled into Bible School at CFNI in Dallas years later. His salvation is truly what many would call a radical 'Road to Damascus' type of salvation experience, like that of the Apostle Paul. The thing with Jean Luke is he knew too much about the powers of darkness already to live in a lukewarm faith. There was urgency in the way he ministered and he could not claim any ignorance of God's power and greatness having seen the other side through witchcraft.

His ministry was focused on healing and deliverance. The work is intense, but necessary for all of us. On this particular visit, the woman we approached in this small room sat down with stress in her facial appearance. I assumed the pain was unbearable. She said she needed prayer for healing in her knees. She was in constant pain and nothing would relieve her aches. As soon as we saw her, Jean Luke turned to me and explained the plan. "Ok so first we pray and ask the Holy Spirit to move and guide us as we minister. Whatever the Holy Spirit reveals is what we need to pray and do." We began praying just on our own for the Holy Spirit to do what He desired in her life. We didn't jump in and say God heal her. We asked first for understanding. Often people in their prayer begin to say things like, "I declare..." followed by a command. But God will not back anything up that doesn't align with His glory, no matter how fervently anyone wants to declare a result. Jesus only did what God had instructed Him to do and He spoke what God already declared and established.

Then Jean Luke stopped praying and asked her, "Hey did your father hit you when you were a little girl?" Her face was in complete shock and turned pale. "Yes" to which he continued, "Did he hit you on your back a lot?" He was precise and she began to tear up and responded, "Yes". There it was. I saw God begin to work inside her. I call it *'Spiritual Surgery'*. As a master surgeon, the Holy Spirit began opening a wound as if doing surgery no one could see, but we knew it was happening. Jean Luke looked at me and said, "Ok so now, we need to pray that she forgives her dad." She looked at him in complete shock. What does her dad have to do with the pain in her legs? But he spoke to her using scripture urging her to forgive him now, and she was willing.

He said, "The enemy has an opening to your life through the unforgiveness you harbor against your dad. Unforgiveness is an opening to bring pain and sickness into our bodies." She cried and said aloud, "I forgive my dad for beating me, I forgive my dad for hurting me…" and on and on in her own words and in tears. She also commited her life to Christ in Salvation. Then after she as done, Jean Luke and I prayed complete healing for her emotions, her memories and the pain in her body. After we finished, she was amazed and said aloud to us with excitement that the pain in her legs was completely gone. The shock that came over her was incredible.

Many people struggle to believe that God can heal them, but He will! Others doubt that a prayer to God would lead to their deliverance, but it does! I have witnessed it time and time again. One day during this trip,

Street evangelism. - Fresnillo, Zacatecas, México

CURED

Jean Luke and I got together in the church where I asked him a few questions, curious about how to put together the process that leads to spiritual bondage. With regards to deliverance, it seemed people we prayed for were still stuck in moments from childhood and there was a mix of experiences that kept them from pursuing God. I asked Jean Luke to explain from the top how we end up bound spiritually. Below is his description in what I call the 3 Access Areas and the visual I put together.

1. **Generational Curses (Deuteronomy 28, Romans 5:18, Romans 5:12, Exodus 34:7, Psalm 51:5)** - We are born into a lineage of generations of people and may carry generational curses. Whatever our parents did in their lifetimes, if they did not surrender their lives to God in relationship, then most likely they were carrying the generational curses from their parents, and so on.

2. **Trauma and Accidents** - Then as time passes, we experience emotional shocks, accidents and traumas. These are events that happened in your life which were completely out of your control, but greatly affected you. This includes physical and emotional abuse, fearful accidents, domestic violence, near-

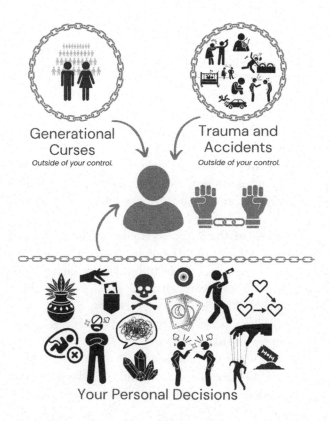

death experiences, the sudden death of a loved one, or being a witness to a crime. The Bible has stories which depict the results of recurring tragedies in each generation and how they were negatively affected.

3. **Your Personal Decisions (Galatians 5:19-21, James 4:17, Ephesians 4:26-27, Mark 7:20-23, John 8:34)** - 1 John 1:8 says if we claim to be without sin, we deceive ourselves. As you grew older and became independent, there were poor decisions you made which brought in more spiritual oppression over your life, like getting a tarot card reading, playing with a Ouija board, drug or alcohol abuse, pre-marital sex, abortions, etc. There are other things like unforgiveness, consistent lying, gossiping about others, speaking word curses over people's lives, seduction, lustful thoughts, anger episodes or manipulation. Those behaviors are less noticable to others, but access entries for spiritual oppression. These are open doors you yourself voluntarily took part in.

Today, you can take time to evaluate your personal life and generational history to identify things you need to renounce in order to see spiritual freedom in Christ. This is brief, but it will get you started.

- **Salvation in Christ -** You have to first surrender your life to Christ. Even if I or anyone in the faith were to pray for you, if you don't take this step, the enemy has rights to your life. Many people will be unwilling to even complete this first step and although my desire is to see them well, my prayer won't go anywhere because they refuse to surrender their life to God in salvation. If you haven't made this commitment I urge you to do this today. There's a prayer in the back of this book you can read to profess your faith in Christ as Savior. Connect to a good church to help you as you continue to grow in your faith.

- **Analysis of the 3 Access Areas -** Identify within each Access Area the things that may have given the enemy access. I've asked my mom and dad about their past and their parents' lives to learn what they got into. Of course they wouldn't tell me absolutely everything, but it gives me an idea. Also, God will open your eyes and bring things to your memory regarding areas of access. Consider objects you keep in your home that may have been dedicated to spirit dominance like the evil eye, idols, and any objects of witchcraft. Evaluate your personal life decisions and write out a list of

Church ministry - Fresnillo, Zacatecas, México

anything you did. Unforgiveness is usually the root to a lot of opression. Write a list of people you haven't forgiven, and be willing to forgive all.
- **Confess and Renounce (1 John 2:1, 1 John 1:9)** - 1 John 1:9 says that If we confess our sins, he is faithful and just and will forgive us our sins and purify us from all unrighteousness. Confessing means asking God to forgive you for the sin you took part in. You can do this on your own or with a trusted believer in the faith. To "renounce" means to sever any bond or pact that may exist. That is you are now going to remove any bondage or access point the enemy had on your life that keeps you under opression to any other spirit. The word "oppression" is used to explain what the afflicting spirits have done. They have taken power over you to bring you under submission and opress you, because of the access previously given to them. By renouncing, you remove access to their oppression and you experience true freedom only in Christ.
- **Redeem (Romans 6:23, James 4:7, Matthew 12:43-45)** - God's power is greater. Search the Bible for scriptures to address all those areas you identified. If substance abuse is prevalent in your family history, find scriptures that combat that and pray that scripture over your life and your future generations declaring they will not struggle in that area. Make time to study the Bible and apply the scripture in your daily life to combat any temptation to go back to your broken past or as you get tempted to hold unforgiveness again as memo-

ries return. Go down the list and find scriptures to pray over yourself and surrender each area to God. Be assured that you have victory in Christ!

There is a division among believers with varying levels of faith and theological debates concerning miraculous healings and complete deliverance. Many Christians even in the same church denomination disagree on this one topic. While we have all seen or heard of people being miraculously healed and delivered, it's still a difficult subject for many. Some will say it's impossible for us to be completely free here on earth as we live this life and we will only be fully free until we reach heaven. Some say your flaws are part of your testimony, and adopt their flaws. You'll hear some saying things like, "That's just the way I am," or "All of my family is this way," as a way of accepting their poor behavior or failings. That is complete deception, by the way. Others say we can absolutely experience complete freedom today, and we are created to live heaven on earth! That is, they believe you can be set free of everything and live in complete freedom in this lifetime. All sides use scripture to support their positions.

What I will tell you is that God is powerful and He can and will heal you, and He can and will set you free. I've witnessed it even in my own life. The Bible teaches us this. I don't know precisely why some people experience it and some don't. The Bible says consistently that the faith of people brought forth their miraculous healing. Jesus said in several occasions, *"Your faith has healed you"* (Mark 5:34, Mark 10:52, Luke 18:42). Faith is key to your healing and spiritual freedom. By declining to believe in God none of us would have a chance at freedom. The Bible also teaches us God's sovereignty and how He exercises His will. I've seen people who profess to have a serious faith in God never receive healing. While we see people's faces and hear their well intentioned words, only God sees the condition of our hearts. Without forgiveness, I believe many people remain opressed. Then, there are those who have full faith, forgave everyone with a sincere heart, and may never see healing. I wish I had an answer for why some receive healing and some don't or why some get saved and some don't. But without error, the Bible teaches that it's God's desire that all would believe and be reconciled in relationship back to Him. Christ came for the world, the Jew and Gentile alike. He is no respecter of persons and this freedom is available to you today.

> *"Opening his mouth, Peter said: "Most certainly I understand now that God is not one to show partiality [to people as though Gentiles were excluded from God's blessing], but in every nation*

Outdoor outreach events. - Fresnillo, Zacatecas, México

> *the person who fears God and does what is right [by seeking Him] is acceptable and welcomed by Him."*
> *- Acts 10:34-35*

Since God does not share His position with any other, nor does God share His glory, you cannot have a relationship with God and stay spiritually opressed. We have to look at scripture for the truth. The Bible says in John 8:36, *"So if the Son makes you free, then you are unquestionably free."*

From our experiences praying for people, I remember seeing those who had no knowledge of scripture suddenly overcome with joy and eager to know what the Bible says. Many people got saved in the events we held, from visiting the dump community, to the church events, and the local prison, that we couldn't keep count if we tried. People eagerly asked us so many questions about God and how to grow their faith. They asked us about scripture and if we could teach Bible studies.

The lady who was healed in her leg asked us to return another day to pray for one of her friends. Jean Luke responded and said, "But wait a minute, you're a believer now too! The same power of the Holy Spirit in me, is now in you. You go pray for your friend!" She was caught off guard with his response, as if God would really use her in the same way. He explained in detail that it's actually her responsibility to reach those around her. She believed him, laughed at his firm push towards reaching her friend, and agreed.

What he said was essentially,

'You're cured. Get up and walk in faith now.'

Famine

A NARRATIVE

There's a famine going around in the souls of man,
where God is dead in the hearts of those
who could not understand.

Many acknowledge God the Creator,
walking into churches without knowing God,
without knowing the Savior.

It's a form of merit, a participation recognition,
partaking in a presentation, properly orchestrated in visual perfection.
Glancing at each other to get a welcome, a smile, a nod.
Living for everyone's approval,
everyone but God.

The worship: a production. Singing beautifully written lyrics
with a perfect melody to arouse the emotions.
Arms stretched high with tears in their eyes singing,

"This is my desire, this is my devotion"…
And what God hears from the skies,
"Look how good I am, look how good I am"
is their heart's cry.

Famine…

There's soothsaying from many leaders in platforms who claim to speak in
His Name. Destorting God's image in exchange for followers,
in exchange for financial gain, in exchange for fame.
Soothsaying to reach the itching ears of the diseased.
Because the idols they erect have increased.

The idols increased in the land of the free and enslaved the deceived.
Many live chanting "God is dead."
Because they could no longer hear God in their head.

Where darkness is a dwelling place, with prisoners bound in misery.
Yet promote their position as desirable, especially in the fame and beauty
industries. They make it sound great, yet widespread discontentment
continues - along with fear, along with hate.

A dying of hunger on a daily basis, despite the surplus of accessibility to
the Bread of Life in many places. Where the word of God is set aside, and
discarded. From the Truth, their hearts and lives have departed.

Famine…

Famine is both an ending and a beginning.

It can be the path to spiritual death, but for those who survive,
famine can be the hope of new life instead.

Famine provides survivors a potential turning point, an opportunity to
transform. Where contradicting forces are disarmed and all have fled. With
the size of a mustard seed, obtaining a faith-filled tomorrow again.

A future where hunger and thirst subside, where all are no longer blinded
by the hustle and the daily grind. Where daily provision comes from Jireh,
the LORD who provides.

Where living worship springs from within, flowing from a contrite heart,
convicted of sin. Where idols are destroyed and empty chanting subside,
at the awakening realization that only God will suffice. Where every knee
bends to His Holy Name, and every tongue confesses His Lordship,
Jesus Christ.

Abiding in the new Eden within, the garden of life in the hearts of men and women. Deep within, as the temple of the Holy Spirit, and walking together again.

In complete closeness again, as Adam and Eve once did with Yahweh.

Author's Note:

This narrative is an illustration of churches in the United States of America and the spiritual condition outside of an authentic relationship with God. At best, it's an experience of famine. Further down I mention the silver lining, that famine can be a beginning. There's a point where those who are still able to recognize they have spiritual lack that they want something more than just religious activity or empty rituals and walk towards true connection with God.

"In complete closeness as Adam and Eve once did with Yahweh" is referencing the restored relationship we are given through Salvation in Christ.

CHAPTER 17

Religious

"I don't understand," I said, in complete shock. I sat in her office guest chair, starring at her in complete disbelief. "Yes, yes, I know, I know mija," she interrupted, "I'm sorry you cannot teach that here." My right arm naturally swung up in the air at that point - as my sass has been here since birth. "I can't teach (dramatic pause) *the Bible* here?? This is a church!" Her eyes widened as if she was shocked at my response.

It was my senior year in high school and I volunteered to teach Sunday school at the Catholic church in South Oak Cliff where my dad played the guitar. I invited one of my best friends who was Catholic to co-teach the class with me and she was the person who went to the teaching coordinator. She told her that I taught the class of students that they didn't have to go to the priest for the forgiveness of their sins. My friend didn't confront me about it after the class, but went straight to the coordinator.

My family and I had been members there for years. Mary was the coordinator in charge of overseeing the Sunday school classes and teachers. "Yes, well you have to teach only what the manual from the Catholic Diocese tells you to say. Just read it aloud and that's all…And, as Catholics, we believe that everyone must go to a priest in order for God to forgive their sins." She said that confidently, yet robotically, as if reciting a rule from a playbook. "That's not what the Bible says." I responded. Then, a moment of silence. Mary looked at me with regret and concern. "I'm sorry but you can't say that to the class and must follow what the manual says. You have to tell the kids they must go to a priest to be forgiven of their sins. This is our Catholic faith, you can only teach that." Immediately I responded, "Then I can't teach here. Jesus is our only mediator Mary, the Bible says it! Not a priest…the priest has no power to forgive sins, only Christ," I emphasized without hesitation. I stood up and walked out of her office frustrated and in complete disbelief. I left the responsibility to my friend to finish teaching Sunday class for that year. I couldn't really be upset with my friend. She was a devout Catholic and for many, that means obeying what the Catholic Diocese says without question, even if it's not Biblical.

That experience led me to wonder if other priests believed things that were not aligned with what the Bible taught. I desperately wanted to know that not every Catholic church functioned this way. I had never ques-

My Catholic Sunday School teacher badge.

tioned the Catholic faith before that moment. I just assumed Catholic priests and leaders read the Bible and taught based on what it said. This experience was completely shocking to me, as I grew up Catholic and held the priests in the highest position of spiritual leadership. So, I booked a meeting with the priest at another Catholic church where we sometimes would attend and my dad would also play there. My dad rotated playing in the worship teams at 3 different Catholic churches in Oak Cliff. This other church not too far from the one where I taught, was the one I trusted the Priest's judgement the most. He was a younger priest and his preaching style was, in my opinion, relevant and engaging. He spoke in words people could understand and didn't simply use the common Catholic phrases that sounded mechanical during a sermon. There was thoughtful delivery of the message and he shared his opinion too.

"Hi I have a meeting with Father Richie". The secretary looked up confirming my appointment and let me know he was not going to be available to meet with me due to a schedule conflict. "But, we do have Father Sam, and he would gladly meet with you now." *'Ugh. Not Father Sam'*, I thought. The guy had been a priest for ages, and most likely would have that old school 'obey the Diocese' mentality about everything. Hesitant, I accepted and she walked me into his office. The guy was maybe 70 years old, and looked like a nice man, nothing scary about his presence. He squinted his eyes when he smiled and ripples of wrinkles filled his face. He restated the amount of years he had served in the Diocese as a priest and how much he loved being a priest. "Well I had some questions for you I was hoping you could answer." At that point I was reaching 3 years into my relationship with God and had a good understanding of scripture. Although, I couldn't say I completely understood specific books like Numbers, the prophetic books and Revelation, I knew enough to understand and explain basic doctrine.

I began with salvation. The Bible teaches us "it is by grace you have been saved, through faith—and this is not from yourselves, it is the gift of God— not by works, so that no one can boast. Right?" He looked at me like he was done with me. "That's correct" with a half motivated grin and a slow blink. "So why does the Catholic church require people to do so many things as rules in order for them to be saved? Doesn't that confuse people to think they have to earn their salvation?" He responded in agreement,

RELIGIOUS

"Well yes, the Bible does say and we teach Jesus died for our sins and saved us through His sacrifice on the cross. As good Catholics, we must live by certain rules in devotion to the faith." "- As an example," I interrupted, "As Catholics, we can't even take the communion if we sinned that week. So, because someone committed a sin they can't walk up and take the communion that Sunday - and it doesn't make sense based on scripture why that rule is in place regarding communion." He replied, "That's the rule, you are correct, the person would be sinning even greater if they know they are living a life of sin and still take the communion." I responded, "But that's not what the Bible teaches about Communion." I began to recite scriptures to the priest, and question after question, scripture after scripture, he got intensely nervous.

It got to the point where he just interrupted me to say, "I'm not too familiar with the scripture." He didn't have words to explain because he didn't know the scriptures. He was at least honest. I disregarded the rest of the questions on my list after he said that, and got to the one. I asked, "Why does the Catholic Diocese teach that we must go to a priest to forgive our sins when the Bible clearly states the only one who can forgive sins is Christ and we only need to go directly to God through Christ in personal relationship for the forgiveness of sins? At confession, the priest tells us to pray certain amount of hail Mary's and Our Fathers, and so on, and finishes it with, 'My child, your sins are forgiven,' but neither the priest nor any other person on this earth has the power to forgive anyone's sins except Christ Jesus." He was really, *really* done. "That is our faith. And I'm sorry I have to go to my other meeting. I'm happy you have a desire to seek God at such a young age." He squinted his eyes when he said it, and looked as if he would have patted my head if I allowed it. He stood up and shooed me to the door.

That's the first time I recognized it. *Religion.*

In that moment, as a senior in high school, I decided I didn't want to be religious. God didn't create us for rituals that are empty. God didn't create us for routines incapable of bringing His glory, routines which He did not create, require nor accept. Rituals that God did not create, require nor accept give glory to man's ego or in Biblical terms, man's flesh. Following the rules set by people that are not supported in scripture will not lead us to closeness with God. This is how non-believers and religious people are the same, in that both satisfy their flesh above satisfying a commitment to God. God desires a relationship with us and we have the Bible to show us what that looks like. I walked to my car disappointed and even more discouraged than the state I was in when I arrived. This couldn't be the truth, but it was. "I am not familiar...I don't know that scripture," the priest admitted he didn't read the Bible and it echoed in my mind as I drove out of the long road ahead of me. The image of the Catholic church in all it's untouchable glory, suddenly dismantled in my mind as I drove away.

I finally understood why at fourteen years old, with my entire life going to these churches, I did not understand the actual reason Jesus hung on the cross. I never saw a Bible in the Catholic church pews growing up, only the book provided for that season by the Catholic Diocese. I remembered once opening the book in the back of the pew and realized there were only short verses of scriptures someone high up in the Diocese decided to include. It all made sense, and the issue of empty religious faith is not isolated to Catholicism. Religion has overtaken many in other Christian churches, Baptists, Non-Denominational, Assembly of God, Church of Christ...you name the denomination. Somehow we continue to fall in what the Pharisees fell into, *religion*.

Religious people don't realize God's love for them is equal to God's love for those who they perceive as lost or sinful. It's the exact same undying love they believe God has for them. They don't get a better version of God just because they don't struggle with the "horrible sins" others do. The people who they determine are "sinful" don't get scraps of God's love. Jesus said in Luke 5:30-32, *"And their scribes and the Pharisees complained against His disciples, saying, "Why do You eat and drink with tax collectors and sinners?" Jesus answered and said to them, "Those who are well have no need of a physician, but those who are sick. I have not come to call the righteous, but sinners, to repentance."*

Religious mindset keeps people from caring. Ideas of superiority keep them deceived when in reality, we all stand on the same ground. Under the right circumstances, we could all fail and be in the position we each perceive is inferior to where we currently are. Relationship with God will keep showing you how flawed you are and humbles you to constantly rely on God for everything. If you don't understand God, His nature and His essence, His desires, priorities, likes, dislikes, pleasure, pain, vision, will, standards, expectations, plans, etc., then you're living an empty religious life. Everything you do is missing purpose and direction, no matter how religious you may be. Spending time doing religious acts while not taking the time to understand and know God personally is a form of rejecting Him.

People who know God are amazed by the reality that we all deserve Hell, but are extended God's love and grace daily instead. This is God's saving grace and mercy over every person who will ever live. Despite deserving hell, we received God's perfect love and forgiveness. Christ brought heaven in His arms and in all His glory was crucified on our behalf, a ransom for our sin so we would be reconciled to God the father. The same power that rose Jesus Christ from the dead lives in every person who accepts Christ as Lord and Savior. We have the Holy Spirit with us, present in our lives every day. That understanding keeps you far away from empty religion. Not having that understanding personally keeps you in emptry religious cycles.

It's tragic.

It's tragic that on the other side of Christ's resurrection, many would live out this life of faith religiously. We can stay busy doing a lot of things that keep us distracted running the endless hamster wheel of church programs year after year. Religious. Believing we are meeting God's standard of piety meanwhile missing out on knowing God and missing the mark completely.

Religious people are not discovered to be religious in the long list of things they do to be regarded as a *'good Christian'*. You know, that long list of acts of compliance, looking, acting and sounding like a believer, the volunteer hours they clocked-in, Christian music they listen, dressing modestly, or even glancing in their Bible enough times through the week to demonstrate piety. The evidence is discovered by the long list of things *they fail to do.* There is a list of things they neglect doing because they either don't know God enough to understand what God requires nor how offensive their neglect is. Some may know what God has asked and still refuse, not recognizing the importance, and they don't fully understand the serious consequences of their inaction. The inability to understand what matters to God reveals the great distance between them. When you behave wreckless for example, if you don't understand how offensive your wrecklessness is or the consequence you will eventually face, you can very well be joyfully wreckless right now, completely settled and unbothered. If I could point to one reason our wrecklessness is offensive to Him, I'd say it's mainly because it separates us from Him.

People who maintain a relationship with God know how offensive the neglect of important things are and quickly repent, turn from their mistakes and align themsevles with the Holy Spirit. The only thing they did differently is that they got closer to God in order to discover this. Literally, *that's all they did differently.* They just got closer, and as a result, their closeness allowed them to face the harsh reality of how undeserving we are of God's presence, how unworthy we are of His perfect and unending love for us because our sin is exposed and in our face. You can't come to God acting like your sin wasn't that bad or like it happened so long ago that it no longer matters. Only those who recognize the severity of their sin will truly repent and reconcile with God. Religious people sugar coat their sin and it remains a boulder in front of them keeping God on the other side. They minimize the sin they grapple with, horde it, keep it hidden and in their private life they can't move a step closer to God because of it. As a result, religious people choose their pride, the guilt and the shame of sin over the presence of God.

You can't move forward with God without hating your sin so much, I mean you pointing it out a*nd hating your sin so much*, that you need it gone sin is an offense between you and God. The closer we get, we realize the urgency of cutting it out of our lives in order to stay close to Him. Once you take that step, you never want to know what life is like without Him *close*. You must face your sin head-on and desire God more. In closeness, you recognize your great dependency on God for absolutely everything. This is the life of sons and daughters of God who are Spirit-led. This is why Paul emphasized in Galatians 2:20, *"I have been crucified with Christ; it is no longer I who live, but Christ lives in me; and the life which I now live in the flesh I live by faith in the Son of God, who loved me and gave Himself for me."*

This is why religious people fall in and out of what outwardly looks like a life of faith. It looks like the pastor who was arrested for soliciting prostitution, or the evangelist who was abusive to his wife and neglected his children for years. It looks like the pastor's wife who uses her role to divide, mistreat and manipulate people in her church. It looks like the missionary who stole ministry money and struggled with a gambling problem, or the worship leader who hid his porn addiction and cheated on his wife for years. It's also like the father who pays the bills but never spends quality time with his wife and children, or the sister who treats strangers better than her own family. It looks like the mother who boasts growing up in the church, but neglected her pregnant teenage daughter. You get what I'm saying. All of them were religious.

Being religious is your easy step to atheism.

Religion involves no accountability and requires no urgency.

There's no urgency to teach a generation – *regardless of your denomination* - a Savior you never met, a Gospel you never personally experienced, a Bible you can't agree with, and scriptures you never read.

There's no urgency to speak to a God *you prefer to keep far away.*

CHAPTER 18

Like Him

I arrived early and stepped into the room with about 10 people of all ages sitting sparingly in the small room near the homeless ministry's kitchen. It was really early in the morning and the sunlight blanketed a golden glow throughout the entire room. It looked heavenly. Standing front and center was Mr. James, this incredibly nice and jolly man. I use the word "jolly" because he was like the image of Santa, mostly white hair, bright red cheeks and his shoulders shrugged as he laughed. He was always smiling, and whatever you were doing you could hear him laughing somewhere in the grounds throughout the day. He stood in front of the room and said to me, "Come on in, welcome!" as I made my way to a seat in the back. His wife Lina was passing out the grape juice and crackers for communion. Lina was also someone that carried a bright smile and a positive attitude. She was the type of person who opened her arms to everyone who walked through the ministry doors. They were the type of people you'd hope would lead a homeless ministry. They were down to earth, optimistic and loved the homeless community. Every volunteer who arrived early got to participate in communion and prayer before we took our positions in a serving area.

Anyone who drives through the city of Dallas will see homeless tents and stations under bridges, in public green spaces, and through the streets of downtown. The amount of homeless people have been a challenge for the city for years now, and the mission of this ministry was to meet their needs physically, spiritually and see if any were candidates for transitional housing. I mostly served in the distribution line and handing out a side item to place on guest plates, but one day I joined the kitchen staff and helped prepare lunch. On that day we prepared a chili recipe. It was pretty simple and the woman who was in charge was this very nice lady who was a really good cook. I admired her diligence and commitment to prepare a meal that was just as delicious as one she would have made to serve her own family. She worked fast, but I kept up with her. There was no time to waste as people would line up outside the gates early. They used their own personal recipes that they knew would stretch ingredients to feed many. After everyone of the guests ate, Mr. James and Mrs. Lina also offered meals to the volunteers who wanted to eat. Then, you'd see volunteers sitting and sharing a meal with the homeless or just sitting and spending time getting to

At the serving line for the homeless ministry - Dallas, Texas, U.S.A.

know them. You'd also see people praying for each other.

When I served in the homeless ministry I said my name was Lisa. It was easier for everyone to quickly say my name and bypass the long explanation on how to pronounce it and how I got my name. I got my name from some physician's daughter. His daughter ran into the delivery room after I was born. My mom didn't have a name for me and it was probably because my dad was an alcoholic, chasing other women and she was under a lot of stress. She was also probably depressed. My dad told her many times when she was pregnant with me that he wanted a boy. When her delivery doctor's daughter ran in to my mom's delivery room, he yelled at her, "Arisbet, get out of this room!" My mom asked him if she could name me Arisbet, without even knowing what the name meant. She just knew that was my name. My mom says when my dad saw I was born a girl, he never got close to me and that it wasn't until after I turned 1 year old that she noticed he showed me some type of affection. While I wasn't aware as a newborn what was going on, I understood rejection well. I believe we carry what our parents spoke over us deep within us even since conception, and it's one more thing Christ set me free from. Not only did He set me free from it, I can serve people from a place of understanding because of it. If you share this similar story in your life, know that God can set you free and use your experience to bless other people. God can turn even rejection into a gift. Genesis 50:20 and Romans 8:28 explain that even when loved ones act with evil intentions, God can turn it around for good, saving many lives. He works all things together for the good. Rejection can yield good, like empathy. Empathy is incredibly valuable when you serve others and many people lack empathy when serving those in need.

I really liked joining the team that walked around the Cedars area of Dallas to invite people to lunch. Walking around we would see the calm of whatever chaos occurred the night before. We welcomed anyone we saw walking the streets to make their way to the venue they called "Solomon's Porch" to take part in Saturday lunch. We walked in groups of at least 4 or more and there was team leader who had the most experience to guide us around a few streets and return back in time to serve meals. This was important because they knew how to navigate the group and kept us as safe as possible. We sometimes saw people walking around high on drugs or mentally unstable.

This ministry was like it's own church. Everyone I met had a heart for service. While I had many experiences that impacted me, there was one day that really stood out and marked me. I woke up early to go with my boyfriend at the time, Gerardo. We had just started dating and it was his first time volunteering to serve the homeless. He showed up wearing the cleanest Pumas I had ever seen, and of all colors, they were pure white. I looked down at his shoes and said, "Uh no. You're going to ruin those shoes, but ok." It seemed like a regular day, as we stood in the serving line and we were wrapping up as the last few people had been served. Then, this guy walked up to the line. He was really nice and there was nothing in particular different about him from anyone else. Until we started talking to him.

I stood out of the line with Gerardo and two other friends to talk to him. We asked him if there was anything he needed prayer for and just had small talk overall. I asked him how he enjoyed the meal. He was carrying his backpack and shuffled it around as he began to emphasize how blessed he was. He started to share scripture with us with words of encouragement. I was surprised he knew so much of the Bible. Eventually he unzipped his backpack and pulled out a brand new iPad. Those of us who stood there talking to him suddenly all looked at each other in amazement. I asked him "Wait why do you have a brand new iPad!?" He proceeded to explain he wasn't homeless, and that he uses it for ministry. He said he was called to minister to the homeless. Confused I asked him, "Why are you dressed like that though?" He explained, "Why do I dress like a homeless person? Well…Jesus was a king and took on the form of a man to save the world. I am only taking on the image to reach the lost." We all looked at each other speechless. It was an interesting perspective. This man took on image-bearing seriously. It had me reflect on how we enter the faith as belivers with the intention to become like Christ. We will have the greatest impact in anything we do when we take on the image of Christ as we live and serve.

"But whoever keeps His word, truly the love of God is perfected in Him.

> *By this we know that we are in Him. He who says he abides in Him ought himself also to walk just as He walked."*
> *- 1 John 2:5-6 NKJV*

The scripture in 1 John 2:5-6 explains that if we truly say we're believers in Christ, we would not only express it with our words, but also walk as Christ walked. The greatest accomplishment for us in this lifetime would be to look the most like Christ. A primal characteristic we saw in the life of Christ was servanthood. Specifically, Christ served those who had nothing to give Him in return.

> *"...but whoever desires to become great among you shall be your servant. And whoever of you desires to be first shall be slave of all. For even the Son of Man did not come to be served, but to serve, and to give His life a ransom for many."*
> *- Mark 10:43-45 NKJV*

I noticed a few things anytime I spent serving people who had nothing to give back in return. There were the volunteers who showed up alongside us and served with absolutely no faith in God or any professed belief in Christ as savior. The people who arrived and did not identify as Christians were there because they were passionate about community service and humanitarian efforts to be part of helping the "needy". Some looked at this service as a form of self-fulfillment, to find meaning and feel good about completing a good deed. I completely understand. You do feel purposeful in helping others. I saw clearly while working in this ministry that while completing good acts of service is commendable and something to be encouraged in anyone, acts of service without the shared love of God through the Gospel is lacking in impact. There's something extra that happens when we prayed for them aside from serving a plate.

I determined that acts of service, without the Gospel and love of Christ, *is not ministry.* Jesus didn't just heal someone completely and move on. He made a point to say, *"Your faith has made you whole, go and sin no more."* His focus was not simply meeting a material or natural need, His focus was their spiritual condition. Seeing God work in people goes beyond handing a meal, giving away clothes, or even teaching them a new life skill. When the Holy Spirit was free to work through our hands and hearts, the depth of the impact reached their core inner spirit. They went from "I'm worthless," to

"If that scripture is true, then my life does has value and purpose." Building relationships with them was important and the consistency of the ministry was important. It was good for them to arrive each Saturday and see familiar faces as they felt part of a loving community. Both the volunteer and the receiver experience transformation in the serving experience.

I learned many of the homeless had been mistreated as children. Some of their parents were irresponsible and they didn't have a safe home, so the streets were safer. Then, there were also immigrants who just arrived to Dallas with no place to go. They surely would find a job at some point and get on their feet. They didn't approach us the same way. They approached us with gratitude and talked about what job they were going to get with a guy they heard hired workers. You would also find many women high on drugs. Often, they would travel with a male. I wondered if it was for protection or if they were working girls. Then others had experienced a situation where they felt they were a complete failure. One man in particular had the story that he had a family and had lost his job. His failure of providing overtook him. I sensed there were other problems he was either unwilling to share or completely afraid to share. He explained how he had no motivation to work and couldn't keep a job despite trying many times. It was a slow progression into homelessness until he finally just stayed on the streets permanently and never went back home. He wasn't a drug addict or mentally incapacitated. Despite the many conversations and encouragement from many people, he couln't get back out there to work. He was one example I saw where I realized, *'wow, anyone can become homeless under the right circumstances.'*

Often, I saw how people approached volunteer work as a task to complete quickly. It was something to check off a list and then we walk away feeling really good about what they did for someone else. Some CEOs approached it as a cause they would show up for to help their businesses grow. It was a way to show they gave back to the community and were not all about profit, when in reality, it was a profit-driven motive to boost their brand and attract partnerships. Sometimes we only volunteer when it fits our schedules or when it's convenient, like during Thanksgiving and Christmas time. I hope you consider making volunteer time in your home town a regular and frequent part of your schedule. You will see your life change. When the Holy Spirit uses you in that work, you walk away with a greater realization of who God is. God will transform you as you approach service with the intention of being a reflection of Christ.

I am convinced part of becoming like Christ involves us serving the people no one wants to serve. This has to be part of your life if you want to experience the fullness of God. You and I are saved by grace and the purpose of our Christian faith is to become like Christ. From the very beginning, God's plan has been that in salvation we follow after the example of His Son.

Regardless of what you do for a living, or whatever life season you find yourself in, the goal of every believer is to be like Christ.

You reached the point of life success when God looks over at you, in whatever you find yourself to do, and He sees the image of His Son.

CHAPTER 19
Bible Study

I started hosting Bible Studies sometime in the summer of 2006. Since I was really looking for spiritual growth for myself, I didn't mind when I hosted a women's Bible Study group and I was the only one to show up. I sat and read and studied and read some more and journaled and captured summaries on summaries of what I understood. Then other times, I had a full table with a guest speaker at a local venue. The speaker was usually an older woman, sharing her wisdom with all of us. Later, around 2011 I did more of a book club. Together with my friend Mona, we selected a book, incorporated career growth and personal growth along with scripture study and called it 'Brunch and Learn Book Club'.

I limited the book club groups of women to under 10 and we met somewhere in the Bishop Arts area of Oak Cliff. As I write this book, I'm still hosting Bible Study groups and book club in the Bishop Arts area. I've seen women break down in tears at these meetings and no one cares that we're in public. I've seen women desire more of God and take what we learned to their personal lives and apply it. I had an atheist show up one day and at the start of the meeting she said, "Wait, is this a Christian thing? I'm atheist," to which I replied, "Oh girl you're good, stay!" I was shocked to see her smile, sit back down and listen to the entire teaching. I did say 'stay', but I really didn't think she was actually going to do it. I give the women gifts and create my own guided handouts to bring the message home with them after the book club is over. I put extra details in the experience so they feel special. I've witnessed God work in the hearts and lives of women in such an incredible way that it gave me so much fuel to keep going for myself and for other people. At one birthday dinner, one of my friends told me she took what she learned from book club and shared it with her husband, which led him to quit his job and find work that made him genuinely fulfilled. So many impact stories fueled me to persevere in my faith and I grew stronger in Christ.

I've hosted Bible Study groups where we got together sharing a meal, studied scripture then ended in prayer for everyone in the group. I've seen people get healed miraculously from physical injuries. Then there were times I prayed for people and even though they got healed miraculously and instantly, they still turned away from God. I've seen people in the same

247

room hear the exact same scripture and some accept God while others rejected Him.

In 2011 my friend Priscilla invited me to join her at a local community center in Oak Cliff to speak to teen girls. They were between 14 and 17 years old and I worked with her to teach the teen girls scripture along with practical life skills and personal growth using a book and study guide by Nancy Leigh DeMoss. Some of the stories I heard from the girls were so heartbreaking. One of my girls had been raped by more than 5 guys at a house party. Another girl, one of my youngest ones, told me one day in tears that she had the worst night. Her mom woke her up late at night and put her in her truck, then drove her to the strip club. Once they arrived, she pulled her out of the car, and walked her to see her dad, who was inside. She saw her dad walk out of the club and then stood at the parking lot as her mom and dad yelled and argued in front of her. I was careful in how I spoke to them to mostly comfort them with scripture and encouraged them to pursue a relationship with God. They were teenagers and that time in their lives was critical to make a decision to trust God. You could see the sadness they carried, mentally in and out of a dark place. Some rarely genuinely smiled.

Most of them were daughters of immigrant families whose parents were illegal so they had few resources and the community center was focused on helping those families. Because of my encounter with God at fifteen, I was so excited to teach them what I knew about God in hopes that they would know Him in personal relationship too. I wanted them to know they were worth everything, and their value surpassed any words I could use to describe. I wanted them to know the love of God deeply in their spirit. One day the lesson was on how they were princesses of God. With no budget, we did a backdrop, got a crown and took pictures. I told them their princess gown would be made out of toilet paper. I wanted to make them laugh. We took pictures as they held an affirmation scripture. The teaching was a focus on their true identity despite what they had experienced at home. Pregnancy rates were high in the local high school and some of the lessons were around them knowing their value and waiting until marriage.

I promoted the Bible Study handing out flyers at the local jr. high and high school. I recall being completely shocked when I handed a flyer to a middle school girl and her boyfriend snatched the flyer, read it and tore it up telling her, "Don't be listening to that trash!" I grew up in this same hood, so I guess it shouldn't have shocked me. When I was in jr. high my best friend was sleeping with 20 year olds and partying at the club on the weekends. That was normal in our junior high. Other friends had house parties and some of them had parents who let them drink at home. Another best friend of mine got pregnant the summer of our 8th grade year.

Teen Girls Bible Study, princess lesson.
- Oak Cliff in Dallas, Texas

I remember asking my mom to take me to visit her after she got pregnant. I left out the part about her being pregnant so my mom wouldn't freak out on me. We were fourteen. I remember sitting in her teen bedroom seeing her big baby bump, completely unsure how to talk to her. I just wanted her to know it was going to be ok. So, when that guy tore up my flyer in front of his girlfriend, I became fuel to reach more teens. My hope was to tell the teens all the things I would not have known about God unless someone invited me to church at fifteen.

    I was really cheering those girls on and did everything I could to be there for them for the season I was in their lives. I saw God do incredible things with those girls. One asked me to stay after class to share that her mom practiced witchcraft and she wanted to understand how bad it was and what it meant in relation to having a relationship with God. I shared scripture with her and she decided she did not want to be a part of that. She looked relieved! I was happy for her desire to serve God. While I was there to help and teach them, those teens taught me so much. They taught me how to see hope even in the worst situations, just by seeing how they responded to problems. They reminded me what it's like to have undeniable faith, as if I heard scriptures for the first time again, going back to foundational basics. They brought so much joy to my life.

    Eventually the class for teens came to a complete end. It happened after I proposed an event to reach their mothers. I encouraged my friend Priscilla's mom to lead the talk and share her testimony of what God had

Brunch & Learn Book Club - Oak Cliff in Dallas, Texas

done for her up to that point. It wasn't anything formal, just her sharing a word of encouragement to them and offer a call to salvation. I had prayed with her a few times by that point together with my friend Jean Luke and had seen a transformation of freedom from her dark past. She appeared excited and motivated to share with the group of moms, and so she agreed.

The plan was that after she spoke, Priscilla and I would then be ready to pray for the mothers who made the commitment to give their lives to Christ and then connect them to a local church. Both of them were eagerly on board and reserved the date with the owner of the community center, who was also Priscilla's father-in-law. I never spoke to him, but Priscilla told me that he was offended that we were holding a Christian event for the mothers because he was Catholic and only the Catholic faith was welcome there. Priscilla emphasized he was very angry. Also, after the event her mom got upset saying I forced her to get up there to give a testimony and that she regretted doing it. It was clearly not true that I forced her mom to do any of it. I forgave her mom for attacking me about it, realizing that her mom maybe felt it was easier to come against me, knowing I wouldn't attack her back. I wondered if others maybe criticized her and she cared a lot about the opinions of the other women. She taught all those mothers Zumba and most, if not all, were Catholic. Maybe she was humiliated hoping for acceptance and she felt rejected by them after sharing her conversion story. Rejection is a difficult thing to overcome for many women. These are all reasons I wondered may have been what led her to come against me.

It was not right or an excuse for what she did, but I was good. I let it go easily. I recognized she was still weak in her faith. We are all human after all, and will fail others at one point or another. I took time to think about what happened, and ended the girls Bible Study to avoid problems with Priscilla's father-in-law.

It was hard to leave that commitment because I saw so much growth in the girls. Even though I had to stop teaching after that, I knew we had taught enough where they would be ok. I stayed in touch with most of them on social media seeing them grow up and have kids. I continued teaching Bible Studies to college age girls – usually my friends and friends' friends, or whatever woman I came across in life. As time passed, my passion grew. It was a passion because learning and studying the Bible for myself solidified my relationship with God and got me through the worst moments in my life. I knew it would do the same for others.

Another Bible Study started after I met another friend, Delilah, one night. She was married and told me heartbroken how her husband was struggling with an addiction. He would preach as a guest speaker in different churches and he had a powerful testimony of how God rescued him out of many things, including a serious drug addiction. Although I didn't know him too well, I saw him as a genuinely nice guy who sincerely wanted to pursue a relationship with God. He knew a lot of scripture and it showed in his sermons when he preached. While I was not completely surprised at the news, I knew God could set him free. I heard a statistic by then about the high percentage of pastors who struggled with addictions, and I wondered why men's ministries and accountability was lacking in the church. She continued to tell me how the pastor of the church had him as leadership staff but was not helping him or keeping him accountable. She was going to leave the church, whether her husband left with her or not.

I told Delilah we could do a co-ed Bible Study at their home if she was open to it and maybe the Christian guys that showed up would help him. She was excited about it and agreed. I then mentioned my other friend Priscilla who had shared that she was struggling with her husband also, and he consistently rejected God or the idea of salvation. She felt sorry for Priscilla because her husband wasn't even saved, so Delilah said, "We can keep it at her house so hopefully her husband one day will get saved." We called it "Prayer Night Bible Study". It was open to men and women of all ages, not necessarily just young adults like me. After presenting the idea to Priscilla, she agreed, and it was great while it lasted. I invited as many people as I knew and put together basic Christian doctrine lessons, leaving time for open discussion and ended each meeting with prayer. Great things happened as people got saved, re-committed their lives to God and we saw miraculous healings. At one point we celebrated 23 salvations through that group alone.

One night, we prayed for a woman who was released from witchcraft and we saw an instant transformation in her appearance. She looked visibly different. I felt God ask me to pray for her ovaries and healing over her abdomen area for complete healing and she expressed she had an abortion. When she got home an hour later she had an urge to pee and released clots of tissue and blood. She freaked out and text me right away. Her abortion happened several years before this moment and she wasn't on her menstrual cycle. She was in complete shock and said, "God healed me from the abortion I had!" She was stunned at what she had experienced and couldn't believe the work of God inside her was so instant and evident. She invited her sister to Bible Study another day because her sister was dealing with depression and going through several problems.

Her sister arrived with a sling on her arm and told us she had an injury, but she didn't even think of asking for healing from that pain. Whatever she was suffering with internally surpassed it. We began to share the gospel message with her and opened up the Bible to read scriptures aloud to her. I felt to ask her if she believed it. She said no. She never really felt a connection to faith like that despite identifying as Catholic, but I stressed, "I get that. I believe you have never felt any connection, but you have to make a choice today. God is ready to change your life if you will only say yes to Him now. You can pray, 'God I choose to believe you, I believe what the Bible says is true. Help my unbelief" and she agreed. She prayed that aloud and said, "I choose to believe you God" and instantly she began crying as we all prayed for her. As she hunched over crying, I prayed healing over her arm in her sling, along with complete healing over her emotions and memories. She forgave people and said names aloud.

After we finished prayer, she was a new person. Her face lit up and she was instantly healed! Her entire side was no longer immobile and in pain and by the end of the night with tears in her eyes her arms were both raised and she was praising God saying "You don't understand, God healed me!!!" But I did understand. What she was saying was God healed what a surgeon couldn't reach with an instrument. God healed her internally, although we all could clearly see God healed her physical body as well. There were many people who came and were set free.

In my time of ministry in Dallas, I organized an outreach event with one of my best friends, Angela, called Shift 180. She went on the missionary trip to the Dominican Republic and Central America with me. This was the event we did in Higüey. We had decided one night after missionary work in Higüey that we would do the same event when we returned to Dallas, and we did! We collected over 80 forms, estimating over 100 attendees. We executed the event in under 3 months, with sponsors including

BIBLE STUDY

Shift 180 Outreach - Duncanville, Texas, U.S.A.
Top Right: Me and my friend Angela hosting the event.
Bottom Left: The gang violence skit which was part of the program. It addressed the dangers of gang violence and drug overdosing for the youth in the community of Oak Cliff.
Bottom Right: The young dad who was shot and killed not too long after the event.

Chic-Fil-A. The Dallas Morning News covered us in the paper and we were amazed. I got a call from the newspaper asking if they could place the event on the paper and then they called me back asking if they could interview the DJs I hired for the event as a feature article. I was glad the DJs got exposure because they did the event as volunteer time. I knew one of them as he went to my youth group in the church I got saved in. Angela and I organized the agenda to include a rap contest with the winner receiving money and studio time to record a song with the DJ. The program also included a skit from a local church that addressed gang violence and drug addictions among the youth in the Oak Cliff community. I was impressed with the skit myself, and as I looked around at the audience, I could see they were impacted by the message. It was not only awareness for the youth, but also the adults who were present. Not long after the event, one attendee who was a young dad and new to the Christian faith, was shot and killed. At hearing the news, I was devastated for his passing and that he left his son fatherless.

I also remember feeling convinced that God used Shift 180 to get his attention and I believe he is in heaven.

We were exercising our faith in ways we read in the Bible and whenever that happens, there is spiritual warfare you will face. None of the work I did came without opposition. If you begin to move in your calling and serve God by using your talents to reconcile others to Him, you can expect attacks to come against you. The Christian life comes with spiritual warfare and the word of God is the sword we need to use daily. The Bible says in Ephesians 6, *"Put on the full armor of God to withstand the fiery darts of the devil."* I did everything I could to prepare against personal attacks against my life, knowing how much God was doing in the lives of people.

I was running in my faith. *Fast.* I was doing a lot of good, and looking back I am so proud of myself having gone through everything I went through and still running after God with full commitment and passion. My faith remained strong despite many things happening that made others drop their faith and walk away from God. I was grateful to God for preserving my life, but what was around the corner would be some of the most difficult experiences I would face.

CHAPTER 20

October

She slammed the car door and said, "Ugh, my stupid brother." I leaned in from the back seat and asked her, "What happened?" She rolled her eyes responding, "He wouldn't leave me alone and kept asking me to give him your number." I was about seventeen years old, and that night we were headed to one of Priscilla and her dj boyfriend Stan's rap concert gigs. I ran in her house with her to get something that she forgot. Her brother Gerardo was laying on the couch watching a movie in the dark. That was the first time we crossed paths, and I never saw him again. My friend Priscilla had a lot of brothers, but the only one I knew was the one who went to my arts magnet high school. The brother who wanted my number was her older brother who I never saw because he was always out partying. Years later as I co-hosted Prayer Night Bible Study group at Priscilla's house, Gerardo lived next door to her, in the home they grew up in. I was in my 20s at that point and again she told me annoyed that he wanted my number. She said Gerardo and her mom wanted me to give him a chance and neither of them would leave her alone about it. Because he was her brother, I said we could hang out as friends and I invited him to the Bible Study. She gave him my number and he called me before I flew out to Quintana Roo, México that summer.

He was just another guy who thought I was pretty so I planned my 'friend-zone' routine. I had it down by then. First, you mostly hang out in groups. You go watch a game together, at a bar with a lot of big screens, because generally guys would associate you as a friend in that setting. At some point locate a pretty girl and then mention how she is *really pretty*. If he agreed another girl is pretty in front of you, you're near the friend zone finish line. At some point, I'd invite him to a prayer service (a sure turn off for even church guys). There's more in my routine, but you get what I'm saying. I'm very social and I had a lot of guy friends that were not romantic. Also growing up, my closest friend was my brother, the one who eventually lost it to drugs. I didn't meet every guy thinking romance.

We agreed to hang out one day, and because I didn't want him to get the wrong idea of a date, I made it a convenient stop at an Argentinian café. It was one of my favorite spots near my job at the time in Irving. Any given day you'd see Argentinos rush in and out, while some men would stay huddled in the tiny round tables talking really fast in Argenitian Spanish where all I understood was "che". My plan was to get a sandwich and check out the clearance books section on my lunch break. It would be casual hanging out during my break, like I would any friend. He showed up in a suit. I thought, *'Oh great, here we go.'* It seemed disingenuous, like he was pretending to be someone he was not and trying too hard to impress me. We sat and had an average getting to know you conversation. Then, we walked over to Half Price. I asked him, "Who's your favorite author? What books do you like?" and after a long "ummmm" and a long pause he said, "I like Encyclopedia Brown". "...uhhh... like the children's book Encyclopedia Brown? Like from elementary school?" He replied, "Yea..." I didn't shame him. I was like, "Ok for that we have to go to the far back children's section." He actually picked out two books from the Encyclopedia Brown collection and bought them. Hey, reading is reading, A for effort. After this event, I didn't see him again until one tragic night.

Everything shifted in my relationship with God on this one night. Priscilla called me non-stop one Saturday afternoon and none of the calls were coming through except for her last attempt. That was weird. It was like something was trying to keep me from being there, but I was meant to be there. She asked me to stop by her place to meet with this girl who was in town from Cali and worked in the film industry. She wanted me to go pray for her as she had a tough life and had started tapping into spiritual rituals, evoking spirits, using dark magic practice, etc. I hesitated because I had to go to bed early to pick up my other friend to take her to my church's early service. This other friend Val was thinking about divorcing her husband who was emotionally abusive to her. They were both military and I wondered if he was physically abusive and she just wouldn't tell me. I felt worried for her. We went to gradeschool together and she was my age. She told me she had been in touch with an ex of hers and was contemplating cheating on her husband and leaving. They had a son, and despite not being married or having children, I knew this was deception creeping into her life. We had just reconnected and I invited her to church so that Sunday was the first time she'd try to go to church again. I learned that she grew up in the church, but her family got hurt by people in the church so her parents stopped going. I was motivated in that if I could just get her in my church she would get back up again in her life.

"Please, please Aris, just stop by and pray for her. She really needs it." She urged me over the phone, so I agreed to go and said I could only stay for 30 minutes. I pulled up to Priscilla's house to see her brother's front yard full of cars and mostly guys for an outdoor Rangers watch party. He had a big screen set up playing the Rangers game. We made it to the World Series that year. I walked into Priscilla's house and met the girls she told me about, Lydia. She was very chill, and down to earth with that save-the-earth Cali vibe. She shared stories of her tragic past, including struggles in childhood and her story of being a teen mom. 30 minutes turned into about 2 to 3 hours as I mostly listened. Once I realized the time, I excused myself and planned to stop by again before Lydia flew back to Cali. I quickly rushed out and as I was walking out, an ambulance pulled up. Sirens greeted me as I stepped out like perfect timing. Priscilla and Lydia paced behind me as I walked over to Gerardo's front lawn to see who the ambulance was for. I jumped on the open concrete front porch of Gerardo's house and saw one of the guys from the party laying on the ground unconscious. Every guy appeared suddenly sober. I asked someone what happened and they said he just collapsed. The paramedics began to work on him as I held and consoled Lydia. I later found out they had been friends for a long time. That was the moment when internally something in my walk with God changed drastically.

You know how the Bible talks about *the fear of the Lord*? This doesn't mean to be afraid of God. It means to revere God, to regard God, understanding His supremacy, His character, His power above our own. What can we do when God has made up His mind? Can we change His mind? Before this moment, I thought confidently that God would answer every prayer with the outcome I believed to be the best. I confidently stood in the truth that God would heal anyone and God would redeem anyone. Nothing was impossible and my expectation was to never see a day where God didn't respond with what I thought was a 'good' result. Abraham prayed and God decided to spare a city. Mary asked Jesus and He decided to turn water into wine when it was not yet His time to reveal His power. Generations of Israelites cried out to God and God had mercy when they didn't deserve it. While Lydia was falling apart, I was pleading God in prayer.

I didn't even know this guy. Instantly, upon seeing him, I began begging God for his life. I stood frozen, and I begged God in prayer. He was young. He looked to be my age. *'God please let him get up…God I pray and declare healing over his body…If he took anything, drugs or alcohol, if this is an overdose, clean up his system…'* With my eyes open, I prayed in my mind as the paramedics worked on him. This is where everything changed for me. *I heard God tell me no.* The paramedics were still working on him…and I fell apart inside. I don't know what was happening inside me when I understood he wouldn't come back, but I fell apart. I began to feel like I couldn't breathe. I felt instant pain in my chest. I felt mourning type of sorrow. It was a heavy feeling I never felt before. I didn't even know this guy. *'No God, no please, why….why… God…he's young he can serve You the rest of his life…he can win many people for Jesus…he can have an incredible testimony…'*

I experienced a new side of God I had never experienced before.

The graffiti memorial wall for Minus. - Dallas, Texas

I didn't understand. I desperately wanted to know why and I didn't hear an answer back from God. I understood a hard concrete reality that when God says that's it, *that's it*. I understood a new level of God being supreme and God's ways not matching up to what we would expect from a good, loving God. The paramedics were still working on him with urgency. *'Why not...'* I asked inside my mind as I stared at him laying there, unconscious. I heard nothing back. I didn't understand. They kept trying to resuscitate him. He didn't stand up. Then I saw paramedics rush him onto the gurney, put him in the ambulance and speed off to the hospital. *'God you are good...please... give him another chance...give him more time...'*

I just couldn't understand. Because at this time, I was holding 3 Bible studies a week, I had traveled several countries, and I had seen God do miracle after miracle and answer a lot of prayer requests. I had seen miracles and people recover from sickness and disease instantly in Latin America and at home. I had heard several testimonies of people recovering from poor health conditions. People much older than him that should have died, didn't. Somewhere deep within myself, this was the first time in my life that I felt what it was like – deep within my spirit I grasped another side of God's supremacy. When God says no, *it's a chilling no*. All I can say to describe that feeling was that the fear of God fell on me solid.

I never made it home that night. I stayed at Priscilla's home as all the people in the party left and his closest friends all followed the ambulance to the hospital. I sat at Priscilla's dining table with Priscilla and her husband Juan. She served us coffee as we talked about what just happened. I learned he was a well known graffiti artist in Dallas who went by the name Minus. Up to that night, Juan rarely spoke, despite being at our Prayer Night Bible Study. He was a man of few words so standing in their kitchen that night and having a long conversation for hours with both of them together was a very rare event. He was visibly shaken and talking more than I had ever heard him talk. "I had just hi-fived him…then I looked back and he fell," he said as he stood by the dining table. He was looking for answers too. A few hours later, we received the news that Minus didn't make it.

I felt an urgency to ask Priscilla's husband if he'd like to finally make the decision to surrender his life to Christ. "You saw it today, tomorrow is not promised to you. God knows why He does things the way He does, but for some reason, you are still standing here, and he's not." I began to ask Juan questions about his life and he was an open book. I shared the message of salvation with him and he responded with "Yes, I'm ready to give my life to God." We prayed the prayer of salvation. Priscilla responded upset that he didn't make that decision a long time ago, and kept asking him, "I've told you many times before to give your life to Christ! I told you many times before that I would pray with you!! Why now!??" I was confused by her response as she finally got her prayer answered. He stepped back and tried to explain to her that he felt he had to now. I recognized that her anger was rooted in marital issues that I couldn't fully comprehend since I wasn't married. However, I felt a strong sense of happiness for both of them, knowing that their lives would undoubtedly improve! That night he entered into a new life, and I saw Juan change. I saw God reach his soul. One man left us, and another entered a new life in Christ. I understood none of it.

Four months later in February 2012, a girl in one of my friends groups was murdered. Her name was Linda. She met the guy at her church singles group, but I didn't know him. He became obsessed with her and after she kept turning him down romantically, he showed up to her apartments, approached her car in the parking lot and shot her in the head. I sat in her funeral hearing the song *I can only Imagine* by Mercy Me playing as people walked up to say their goodbyes. I was stunned. How does that happen to a girl like her? No one deserves this but definitely not a girl like her. She went to church, didn't get into trouble, was a good daughter, worked hard and pursued God sincerely. A *good* person. She was only 22. I stood at her memorial service numb staring at her photo slideshow projected above her casket. I saw her mom fall apart. Her world was gone. The song blasted, "Surrounded by Your glory, what will my heart feel?…Will I dance for you Jesus?…" and I remember asking God, *'Are you there?'* None of it made sense.

Have you faced shocking events, where you prayed and the result was tragic? Maybe you had one of your parents die. Maybe you've suffered the death of a child. Maybe you prayed healing for a relative and their sickness never left. Have you prayed several prayers to God filled with ques-

Linda's funeral. - Arlington, Texas

tions and heard nothing back? The indescribable feelings you feel towards God, your frustration, doubt, anger, bitterness, all of them are valid.

The time after Minus and Linda's deaths I recalled every unanswered prayer I had. *'God, why are my parents still not saved? Why is my family still divided? Why did my two of my brothers have to lose their mind? Why did I have to go through everything I went through as a kid? Why did I have to end up an abusive church? Why haven't I gotten married? Will I ever have kids?'* Like there was just this big magnifying glass on all the unanswered prayers in my life and a lot of questions on why this God, and why that God. That was the time I needed a solid church family the most and I didn't have one. While I did go to what I considered to be a good church in Midlothian, I didn't have the support of community in that church.

When you show up to God with complaints and questions of doubt, He sees your broken heart and begins to bind up your wounds as you complain. I've experienced it personally. I learned we can experience peace during tragedy resting in the reality that God is sovereign. The word *sovereign* means absolute and complete power. God, in His sovereignty, executes His will according to His plan and at the perfect, opportune time. This means that all power, rulership and authority belong to God, for our lives and the entire universe. Colossians 1:17 says, *"He existed before anything else and He holds all creation together."* God's sovereign choice considers everything you and I are incapable of ever seeing. Things like the heart of man, or the future events yet to take place. 2 Chronicles 20:6 reads, *"You rule over all the kingdoms of the nations. In your hand are power and might, so that none is able to withstand you".*

Revelation 8:1 reveals God as ever present, beginning and the end. *"I am the Alpha and the Omega," says the Lord God, who is and was and is to come— the Almighty."* This statement is beyond our full comprehension. His knowledge of events surpass our ability to recognize proper execution.

OCTOBER

Even if we could see the big picture of all the events in our lives, we would still be incapable to execute the best plan for us and everyone around us in the way God can. Because of this, we can trust in God to handle every area of our lives and trust that there is a good purpose despite the tragic events that don't make sense. Isaiah 55:8-9 really helped me in difficult times of questioning unfortunate events.

> *"For My thoughts are not your thoughts,*
> *Nor are your ways My ways," says the Lord.*
> *"For as the heavens are higher than the earth,*
> *So are My ways higher than your ways,*
> *And My thoughts than your thoughts." - Isaiah 55:8-9 NKJV*

Regardless of what may come I can trust that God's ways are higher and I can rest in His ability to see me through tragedy. You don't receive peace after you understand what happened. *You receive peace even if you never understand.* This is how: by trusting in God's sovereignty.

Without the answers, I urge you to follow God fully committed.

At receiving the news of Minus passing, I text Gerardo my condolences. I messaged him something like, "I'm sorry for your loss. I know this doesn't make sense, but God's plans are perfect and there is a purpose behind this." I invited him to church that Sunday and he agreed. With little to no sleep, I woke up on Priscilla's couch in time to go take my friend Val and her son to church. I told Val what happened the night before. After service was over she told me, "Hey I'm trying to be obedient to what God is asking me to do the moment He asks me. I heard God tell me to tell you not to worry about your brothers, and that you'll see all your brothers come to God before they die." I fell apart crying at the church entrance on our way out of service as she said that to me and I embraced her. It was so wierd that she said that. I was not thinking about any of my brothers at all, but as soon as she said it, it was like God dug deep in my being and pointed to something that was there. I was reminded even when I don't understand, and things look dark, nothing changes Him. He is a loving Father.

For second service, Gerardo arrived wearing shades. He was not the same guy I met at the Argentinian café. He was a broken person. He didn't say much and when we got to my church, he looked unsure about how to act. It was just like me that first time I went to a Christian church at fifteen. After the service was over, he asked if I'd join him at Glorias for lunch. I agreed to offer him company at that difficult moment. During lunch he started talking a lot, sharing memories of his childhood, memories he had with Minus and other friends. They knew each other since childhood and Minus was like another brother for Gerardo. He told me Minus was supposed to move in with him within a few days. I said hardly anything and mostly listened. Up to this point I had never witnessed anyone in this state of mourning a loved one and my heart went out to him. It was interesting to observe as he went from sadness to laughter. The memories were scattered as he jumped form Minus to his childhood, to his parents, to his friends and then comments about the future. I didn't share scripture, I didn't offer advice or encouragement. I just offered my presence. I literally said nothing. I wanted the best for that guy.

He got a text from someone as we finished lunch and then asked if I'd go with him to a graffiti memorial wall. A few people were reuniting at in Minus' memory. I said sure, but with hesitation. Then he asked me to join him for dinner. It was too much. I realized I was agreeing to spend the whole day with the guy.

Then, we fell in love, and I ended up agreeing to spend the rest of my life with him.

Gerardo and I on our wedding day. - Oak Cliff in Dallas, Texas

CHAPTER 21

Thieves

One of the biggest problems with religious people is that they are more desperate to see God in other people than they are desperate to see God in themselves. That is, they have a greater desire to see others exemplify God's character than they desire to personally exemplify God in their own private life. If I could point to one key difference between religious people and those in a genuine relationship with God, I would say that is a key differentiator. Taking this position of religiosity forces people to set the highest expectations on others according to their standard of Godliness, and cast judgment on them when they don't meet the standard. Also, what God presents in scripture as His standard is not a structure that religious leaders can benefit from. We see this template in the Pharisees and how Jesus pointed out they added on top of what was required, with their own laws. If they actually prioritized knowing God for themselves above their drive to dominate people, they would have known God and recognized Christ as Messiah. In personal relationship, a believer runs with their gifts and puts them to use, reconciling the world around them to God in whatever means God has provided for them. Your vision, priorities, thoughts and heart all align to His. This is why scripture says that those who love God will see their prayers answered. In relationship, you align your desire to God's desire. This is what it means to be in Christ, as this is exactly what Christ's mission was – to reconcile the world to the Father. The entire point of faith is relationship.

Religious people fail to pursue God privately and therefore can't resemble God publicly. I learned this very early on as I served in ministries and volunteered at different churches. Even attending Bible school I saw people stuck in religion. Many have head knowledge of what the Bible says yet remain in a position spiritual of depravity, no different than those who profess to not know God. Religious acts above pursuing God in relationship excuse people from things like, taking Christ's yoke upon you (Matthew 11:29), bearing much fruit and being a disciple (John 15: 8), taking on the ministry of reconciliation (2 Corinthians 5:18), the great commission (Matthew 28), putting on the full armor of God (Ephesians 6:10-18), loving one another (John 13:35), and so on. To accept the forgiveness of God and be saved by grace is just the beginning, but many people stop there. Being religious is easy. Living in relationship with God is dying to your flesh daily and being transformed into the image of Christ. It's not easy and it's why Paul stresses that the church body persevere and finish running the race of faith in Hebrews 12:1-3, *"And let us run with perseverance the race marked out for us, fixing our eyes on Jesus, the pioneer and perfecter of faith."* Religious people risk not finishing the race.

When I was in youth group at the Assembly of God church where I got saved, the youth pastor's wife Karmen came to me in tears asking me to pray for her and her husband because teens who had left the youth group, turned young adults, were blasting them on a website blog online. According to her, she said they were slandering their names and spreading hateful messages about them as pastors. I now realize those young adults were likely coming from a place of honesty.

I was about to start my first year at CFNI when Karmen's younger sister Casey had taken over the youth and young adults. I attended this church without my parents since my family was Catholic. One day, Casey the youth pastor called a youth girls meeting to introduce a new Bible Study we would start, and I attended. She began with saying, "Nothing that we discuss in this meeting should be spoken of outside this room." First of all, as an adult, now I know that statement by itself addressed to underage teens is wrong. Casey was addressing young underage girls and it was a way for her to protect herself from doing something wrong before she did it. The oldest youth girl in the room was in her early twenties, engaged to be married, and maybe one other twenty-year-old, but all other girls were underage. I was eighteen. The engaged girl, Daisy, asked what types of sexual positions were okay for a Christian woman to do when married. I made a confused facial expression at her question. The meeting was about the next Discipleship Bible Study we were going to begin, and there were kids younger than me in the room, under 17.

I'd like to pause here and address parents. Don't assume that youth pastors are mature and responsible adults and doing the right thing because of their position. Get involved, ask your kids what is going on, attend the meetings and even raise your hand to volunteer and be part of the activities planned. It's so important and you could save your kids from possible abuse. Casey sitting in front of me saw my facial expression and quickly addressed me with aggressive correction. She said, "Not everything has to be about God, Arisbet! When we are home, my dad who is the pastor of this church, will sit us down for dinner and we do not talk about church or God. He wants us to just talk about regular things. We are going to talk about sex here! And if you don't want to talk about sex you can just leave this church!" She swung her hand up and pointed me to the door. I was beyond shocked. Everyone in the room was shocked and silent. We could feel the tension. We were all just kids. Even the two young adults were early in their 20s and didn't seem to know what was the right thing to do. There was too much in her aggression for me to understand what was going on with her. What youth pastor's wife has ever kicked a youth kid out of a church for that? I kept my cool and sat through the rest of the meeting in silence.

Early that next week I was at CFNI's lobby outside of registration and called my friend Priscilla. I told her what happened with pastor Casey. She got upset and said she had enough of her attacking girls in the youth. I had no idea what other girls she attacked, as I had just recently started attending that church on Sundays and getting more involved. She said we needed to call a meeting with Casey and her older sister Karmen – the associate pastor who used to be our youth pastor. She continued to tell me things that Casey used to do to the youth girls in the years before I attended the church. Casey would harass them and insult them for wearing certain clothes. She'd blow up on the girls and embarrass them in front of other people. I was upset Priscilla didn't tell me that information to warn me prior to the meeting. She said she didn't warn me because she didn't want to ruin an opportunity for me to have a good relationship with Casey.

Priscilla set up the meeting with Karmen and Casey for after Wednesday night service that week. I was so ready to address the issue, but as Karmen walked into the office to begin, Casey found every reason to not go into the meeting room. She said she did not have time, she had to answer work calls and walked in and out of the church lobby with an attitude, snapping, "Ok well I have to work!" I should have left, but I waited in the meeting room with Karmen and Priscilla. Priscilla was getting frustrated with Casey for avoiding to meet and as minutes passed, Priscilla lost her patience, and she left abruptly. Finally Karmen pulled her sister in the room. She asked each of us to re-state what happened in the meeting. Casey said that I was disobedient by telling Priscilla what happened in the meeting after she told all of us that we were to not speak of what we discussed beyond the room. She accused me of rebellion.

I stated exactly what happened and continued, "Then Casey yelled, "If you don't want to talk about sex, you can leave this church!" Casey responded with, "I never said that." My stomach sank at seeing how easy it was for her to lie with a straight face. "What!? Yes you did, and you pointed me to the door." Karmen asked her sister, "Casey, did you say that?" Casey responded, "No I did not. I never told her that if she did not want to talk about sex that she can leave the church."

I was newly integrating myself to the Christian faith. I only had 3 years of being saved at that point and thought pastors took their role as sacredly as the priests presented themselves to. I couldn't believe a leader in a pastoral position, entrusted with teens would do that. I scanned her face and saw a very broken, deceiving, manipulative and immature woman. The last thing she needed to do was lead youth ministry. And it got worse. "Karmen, she's lying…" I interjected as I began to cry and Casey quickly added, "No I did not say that and Priscilla was not there! I said very clearly whatever is said in this meeting does not go out of this room. Arisbet went out and told Priscilla what was said in the meeting and that's rebellion."

Karmen calmly turned to me and said, "Arisbet, Casey asked you to not speak to anyone outside of that meeting about what was said, and you did tell Priscilla. That is rebellion and the Bible says that rebellion is witchcraft."

"What?…I'm not rebellious…" I responded. It was too much. I couldn't stop crying. None of it made sense. I cried out to God in my mind. I asked God to speak to Karmen in that moment and show her that her sister was lying. I asked God to help me in that moment. Karmen continued, "What we are going to do is pray, so Casey you will pray for Arisbet and Arisbet you will then pray for Casey and you both forgive each other."

By this time I had already read the Bible front to back twice. I knew enough of the scripture to know they were using it out of context. 1st Samuel 15:23 says rebellion is just as bad as witchcraft, and that word specifically is defined as the act of divination. The scripture verse in context also explains that "rebellion" or conscious disobedience was in regards to the express commands of God, not a manipulative youth pastor. The word explains specifically Saul's disobedience to God's instruction was nothing less than the sin of witchcraft, by definition soothsaying or divination. Me telling my friend how the youth pastor threatened me in a meeting to talk about sex or get out, was not rebellion. How could I explain that on the spot as I realized the whole situation was beyond crazy as it unfolded…I was past the state of shocked and left speechless. I was disappointed and hurt.

Casey said a short "God I forgive Arisbet." Meanwhile, tears and all, I prayed for her sincerely, *a long prayer*, that both were shocked by. The way I saw it, I was responsible to God to forgive her and hand her off to Him. I took God seriously and the word in Matthew 5:44, "…*love your enemies, bless those who curse you, do good to those who hate you, and pray for those who spitefully use you and persecute you,*" and in that prayer I blessed Casey and her family. I could not hold any wrong feelings against anyone – based on His standards, no matter how badly she treated me. They both looked shocked when I was done. Karmen then proceeded, "Okay, now Arisbet since you were rebellious and the Bible says that rebellion is witchcraft, I need you to go to the altar and spend time praying by yourself and asking God to forgive you for telling Priscilla what happened in the meeting and forgiveness of witchcraft." She said it with a look of concern.

"I'm not rebellious. She's lying." I responded. "I'm sorry mija but the word is very clear, rebellion is witchcraft." Karmen emphasized. It was unreal. I walked up to the altar, but I did not pray for forgiveness of rebellion or witchcraft. I asked God to defend me and I felt overwhelming peace come over me. In my prayer, I heard God say to me clearly, *'You don't have to do anything, I will defend you.'* After finding out about the problem, their dad, our church pastor, started preaching from the pulpit and saying things like, "Don't let people fool you. Witches are not ugly, they're very beautiful young girls." Priscilla and I were crushed. Even though he only knew the story his daughters gave him, I lost respect for the pastor, at that point. Despite his theology degree and his leadership in the AG denomination, I saw his behavior as shameful. He was in error by speaking that way of two young girls from the pulpit. It was wrong and there was no excuse for him doing that. All the youth knew he was talking about me and Priscilla. Priscilla was upset about the entire experience and cried a lot about it for several days. I encouraged her, because I felt fine knowing God would defend us.

Months later, a missionary visited the church and whispered something to Casey that no one could hear because he put his mic away. I don't know what he told her but she fell on the altar crying, then quickly ran to me, pulled me aside begging me in tears to forgive her. I replied, "Casey, I forgave you that night." She wouldn't stop begging and crying uncontrollably. She looked tormented. A few years later, her life started falling apart. Her husband, the youth pastor, cheated on her and they divorced. Then, she experienced health problems and one day after Sunday morning service, she had a stroke and the side of her face drooped down. I felt so sorry for her and prayed God would have mercy on her life.

You would think I would have left, but I didn't. I remember thinking I'm serving God not man. In retrospect, I realize I was conditioned to spiritual abuse and was unaware of it at that time. Still, I was in Bible School and ministering inside and outside the church, without it having discouraged me from pursuing God.

Years later, Karmen and her husband felt God calling them to start their own church apart from her dad's Spanish church. I helped them launch their new church and was so faithful. I went to their house for planning meetings, and one day I finally learned the truth behind what happened that night with Casey. I arrived at Karmen's home for a planning meeting and she opened the front door in tears.

I began, "Oh my God, Karmen what's wrong, what happened!?"

"It's my sister Casey. Please help me pray for her!"

"Why, what happened?" I asked. She proceeded to tell me that Casey had been living with them since she got a divorce and she walked up to the computer and saw Casey's social media page had porn on it. She explained that their mom sometimes walked into their home unannounced and she had no idea their mom was behind her and saw it too. Her mom called her dad and they were all falling apart. Stunned I responded, "It's okay, don't worry, we'll pray right now and -" Then Karmen interrupted me and said, "No – that's not all, I have to apologize to you, I'm so sorry Arisbet!"

"What - why?" She took a moment to cry as I stood there staring completely confused. "That day in the meeting, when you told me my sister yelled at you that you can leave the church if you did not want to talk about sex, I knew she was lying. I knew you were telling me the truth and my sister was lying....but I had to protect my sisters' image in front of my dad and the congregation, because if people knew she did that, she'd be removed from being the youth pastor. I told you that you were guilty of rebellion and witchcraft to protect my sister and our family image. I'm so sorry! Please forgive me!" I was...not expecting that. I told her, "Yes, I forgive you." and I joined her in prayer for her sister.

From the time I experienced that traumatic episode as a teen, to the time I learned this truth behind what Karmen did, was the span of several years. I was already near my mid twenties. I knew no one was perfect, but I was disappointed to say the least. She put her dad and the image of her family as priority over truly honoring God as a pastor's wife and protecting the youth she should have been pastoring over several years' time. The damage was done. So many of the youth had split up because of that one event with her sister. Casey lied to people about what happened and her dad speaking from the pulpit saying the most damaging things was irreversible. Not long after, I approached Karmen in her church office to let her know I was leaving. She threatened me that she would tell the members she didn't know why I left, and that I left without the pastor's blessing. She threatened they would assume I was no longer serving God. Another harsh let down. I forgave Karmen and left their church to join a ministry in Midlothian, TX.

Thieves.

The worst place to find bullies and abusers is on the pulpit of churches. There are many cases of spiritual church abuse everywhere in the world. If you find yourself relating to my story please be encouraged and consider the following. Nothing is ever left out of God's sight. If you have ever been mistreated by ministers of the faith, God sees you. There are common characteristics found in abusive leaders and as of now, I don't

THIEVES

know one ministry or organization which is helping to combat this problem. Religion is led by thieves. In John 10:1-18 Jesus explained this.

"I assure you and most solemnly say to you, he who does not enter by the door into the sheepfold, but climbs up from some other place [on the stone wall], that one is a thief and a robber. But he who enters by the door is the shepherd of the sheep [the protector and provider]...

Therefore Jesus said again, "Very truly I tell you, I am the gate for the sheep. All who have come before me are thieves and robbers, but the sheep have not listened to them. I am the gate; whoever enters through me will be saved... The thief comes only to steal and kill and destroy; I have come that they may have life, and have it to the full.

"I am the good shepherd. The good shepherd lays down his life for the sheep. The hired hand is not the shepherd and does not own the sheep. So when he sees the wolf coming, he abandons the sheep and runs away. Then the wolf attacks the flock and scatters it. The man runs away because he is a hired hand and cares nothing for the sheep.

"I am the good shepherd; I know my sheep and my sheep know me— just as the Father knows me and I know the Father—and I lay down my life for the sheep..."
– John 10:1-15 AMP

I've heard this scripture preached in sermons and it's preached out of context when they say the *thief* in this scripture is Satan, saying *'Satan comes to steal kill and destroy'.* The thief here is not Satan. Notice verse one where Jesus begins by saying the thief is someone who gets access to the sheepfold, that is the kingdom of God, by another way besides entering *'the door'.* Entering by the door signifies entering by God-ordained means. The Bible teaches that God ordained people for specific offices to help the rest of the Body of Christ. We learn this in Ephesians 4:11 *"...He Himself appointed some as apostles [special messengers, representatives], some as prophets [who speak a new message from God to the people], some as evangelists [who spread the good news of salvation], and some as pastors and teachers [to shepherd and guide and instruct].* The people who receive these gifts are God ordained. So in John 10, Jesus states here that He is the gate – the way into heaven, clearly identifying Himself as diety. He then also declares Himself as the good shepherd and that the depth of our relationship with Him is the same way He knows God and God knows Him. That statement by itself is so overlooked when people preach this scripture. Imagine what that means. It's incredible to think we share the same closeness in relationship with Christ through salvation, as He shares with God!

Jesus also explains that He lays down His life for His sheep, referencing His perfect sacrifice on the cross. The thief signifies people who God did not ordain, who enter into the Christian community to steal, kill and cause destruction in the lives of believers. Jesus emphasizes that their actions are driven by a desire for profit and gain. They care nothing for the sheep. Ultimately they lead them to spiritual death. The thief comes with an appearance of good intention, but they are hired servants working for wages and are only there to benefit from the role of leading believers. If you take time to study it, the message is alarming. Ezekiel addressed this in Ezekiel 34.

> *"... Thus says the Lord GOD to the shepherds: 'Woe to the shepherds of Israel who feed themselves! Should not the shepherds feed the flocks? You eat the fat and clothe yourselves with the wool; you slaughter the fatlings, but you do not feed the flock. The weak you have not strengthened, nor have you healed those who were sick, nor bound up the broken, nor brought back what was driven away, nor sought what was lost; but with force and cruelty you have ruled them. So they were scattered because there was no shepherd; and they became food for all the beasts of the field when they were scattered."*
> *- Ezekiel 34:2-5 NKJV*

Thieves come to steal, kill and destroy your life.

Consider the amount of people in your life who you allow to influence you including pastors, leaders, mentors, teachers, your parents, your siblings, influencers online, and even celebrities you've never met. Those who you allowed into your life to make life decisions based on their guidance. Maybe they are not gaining money financially, but it could be they get to control you. Maybe you feed their ego. Jesus says when the wolf comes, they flee. Satan is the wolf. When Satan comes to devour the sheep, that thief leaves the sheep to die. While you see leaders physically present in their churches, spiritually, they don't defend the sheep against Satan's attacks and the results are people leaving and division among the church body. The thief abandons the responsibility, abandons their post. They got the prophecy wrong. They blame other people for their mistreatment. They deny hurting you or deny doing it intentionally. They don't apologize and refuse to take ownership for their actions. They say they can't pray with you or don't know how to pray. They avoid and ignore your pain. They twist the truth of what the Bible says and teach false doctrine. So often we see this in churches, but also, we see this in business deals gone wrong among believers. We see this in personal problems within Christian marriages and among Christian families.

By the time I was doing Prayer Night Bible Study on Fridays, I was attending church in Midlothian and looking for a new home church closer to my home. Priscilla was struggling in her own faith and I didn't blame her considering what she went through in her past. She ended up joining a church led by a woman named Nancy who visited one of our Prayer Nights.

Nancy led a small congregation made up of mostly women and their husbands. A few years ago I tried to help her find a place to host her women's Bible Study group and she expressed a desire to start a church. I connected her with a Christian business owner friend I knew who owned a property on Tyler St. in the Oak Cliff area of Dallas. I didn't know Nancy well at all, but I wanted to support anyone who was doing outreach for women. We went together to tour the building, but she decided not to lease it. Fast forward to the day she visited our Bible Study a few years later, she told me she found a location and it was walking distance of Priscilla's house. When Priscilla told me she decided to join her church, I cautioned her to seriously re-consider it. I didn't trust Nancy was equipped for pastoring a church based on comments she made which didn't align with scripture. Also, Nancy expressed that her husband wasn't involved in her new church. She explained that he cheated on her with her best friend and Nancy sounded like she hadn't healed from that yet. Priscilla's husband would need a solid men's ministry since he had just committed his life to God, and so they knew right away that he wouldn't have support there. There was no vision cast for the ministry and it was still truly a women's Bible study group gathering.

I sometimes attended Nancy's services to support Priscilla and her family's pursuit of God. I began to realize over time that the women who attended wouldn't talk to me, and I didn't know why. I thought they were anti-social. It was a very small group of maybe 20 women and their kids and spouses. The men wouldn't take leadership and were the shadows of their wives, standing behind them silent agreement. The women held all the leadership roles and led all the initiatives. I noticed spiritual abuse in the times I visited. One Sunday service, Nancy shamed people from the pulpit because they didn't give their tithe. She made certificates and had each person stand on the stage after she called the family names. She left only two families sitting on the chairs and the rest of the families stood on the stage looking down at the 2 families. She said from the stage, "Everyone I called out is a faithful giver and has always given their tithe." As the families on the stage held their certificates and looked down at the two families left, I scanned their faces to see if they realized what was going, on but they really didn't. It was shameful. Priscilla and I both went to Bible School and we knew too much for her to have stayed there. They focused a lot on "deliverance" ministry but people would keep coming to Nancy for the same problem over and over again. She called herself a "prophetess" and would give people false prophecies and they wouldn't correct her. At another service, she 'prophesied' to a Hispanic pastor who sometimes preached at her church. She said he had been praying for a house and God was getting ready to give it to him. After service concluded, I said, "How awesome, you've been praying for a new house!?" He responded, "I don't know why she said that, I don't want a house. I have never prayed to God for a new house and I'm happy where I live." I urged him, "You need to tell her that. Go tell her." He shyly declined, and said it's ok. He really didn't see any issue with it, and continued to preach at her church whenever she gave him the platform. I could see every red flag but to Priscilla and other people, they were green lights, and they still stayed in her church.

I later found out that in a leaders meeting Priscilla and Nancy told all the women that I had a spirit of Jezebel and I shouldn't be with Priscilla's brother Gerardo, who I was dating at the time. It was the worst betrayal I ever experienced by anyone. This was the friend I spent so many years helping, down to praying her husband to Christ, praying for her mother and family. I stood in her Catholic wedding when she decided to go back to Catholicism and our entire church turned on her. I helped her when others rejected her. For several years I was a support to her and her mom over several years. Priscilla's cousin who served as one of the women in Nancy's leadership, was the one who confessed and apologized to me. Her cousin left Nancy's church and started visiting my church. Out of guilt, she apologized and said, "Hey I have to apologize to you about something...When I was going to Nancy's church, in a meeting Priscilla and Nancy told the women not to associate with you because you had a spirit of Jezebel. I'm so sorry for joining them in rejecting you. I love my cousin, but I don't know why she did that. But now that I know you, I know it's not true." I felt sick to my stomach.

Her cousin continued, "Remember one time you prayed for a girl

in one of Nancy's church services? And then you invited her for coffee…"
There was no way she would have known that because no one knew I invited the girl to coffee except the girl herself. "Yes! How did you know that?"
She responded, "Nancy found out about it and told her not to go anywhere with you because you had the spirit of Jezebel and the demon would could come on to her. She told her never to talk to you." It was sick. Her cousin explained that Nancy and Priscilla then held a meeting with the women after I got engaged to Gerardo. She said both Priscilla and Nancy announced that Gerardo couldn't marry me because I had a spirit of Jezebel and Priscilla said, "She has a spirit of Jezebel and she's going to control my brother." I didn't want to know anymore. It was so sick. All the memories of how harshly Nancy and Priscilla treated me during those previous years, for absolutely no reason, all came back fresh.

The worst time was when Gerardo proposed to me. Gerardo told me that at a church service when I was not present, Nancy prophesied to him that he needed to break off his engagement with me because I was not the wife God had for him. I heard about it from him a day or two after it happened. I went to Priscilla and asked her what was going on, and in tears, I asked her to pray with me. She responded, "You need to let him go. You've already done enough for me and my family, just let him go and move on." I looked at her with shock and completely confused, but little did I know she was the one who orchestrated the fake prophecy with Nancy. I had no clue what was going on and I innocently went to Priscilla thinking she had good intentions for me and her brother. I would have never imagined that from anyone, much less someone I once considered to be as close as a sister. Memory after memory, it finally all made sense. I was completely unaware at the time, and I asked Priscilla to be my maid of honor. She accepted, without it bothering her conscience, she stood up there on my wedding day. I felt sick.

When Gerardo didn't immediately break off the engagement after Nancy's false prophecy, she offered to pray over his house. She brought the other women with her, including Priscilla. I was there and made dinner for everyone for what I thought was a kind gesture. I was shocked as Nancy and the women went through the entire home praying as if Gerardo was going to live there alone. She didn't consider me in any of the praying and didn't bless our future home together. She then asked me if she could use the restroom and took Priscilla and another lady with her. I saw them whispering to each other and when they saw me approach, they quickly became silent. Before leaving, Nancy gave Gerardo a journal as a gift. When she left I read the front page, where she wrote, "You need to make a difficult decision but God has already told you and you have to be obedient." What should have been the happiest moment in any girl's life, felt like a nightmare. Priscilla's mom knew what they said about me and didn't stand up to defend me. Instead,she joined them, while I was completely unaware about much of what was going on at the time.

We got married in three months. After Gerardo married me, I went to church with him the first Sunday after we returned from our honeymoon. Nancy said in her sermon that she made a mistake and got the prophecy wrong, but that God is merciful. I was upset. Gerardo wanted to stay in her church, and being newlywed, I wanted to follow after his leadership as my husband. However, I prayed privately that God would show him we needed to leave. At one point Nancy's worship leader, Jessie, who was a girl I met at Karmen's church, told me I couldn't help with clicking 'next' on a PowerPoint slide. She came to our house as newlyweds and literally said to me, "I don't feel you're called to work the PowerPoint slide." The reason I did it was to serve next to my new husband at church. I told her, "I'm glad you're doing this to me and not a new convert because I can tell you to your face what you're doing is wrong, but a new convert would leave God."

A few Sundays into our marriage, Nancy tried to be nice to me and prophesied to me that I was called and gifted in prophecy and that God was going to use me in her church. I was ready to leave her church whether Gerardo followed me or not. It was too much and there was no fear of God in her. By that point, Nancy and Priscilla were nightmares. Priscilla went the extra mile to trash my character to anyone who would listen to her, even after we were married. There was no excuse for her behavior. After Priscilla's cousin told me this, other people told me the exact same thing.

Memory after memory, it all made sense finally. Nancy called herself a prophetess and her ministry focused on deliverance, yet she couldn't reach out to minister to me if she truly believed what Priscilla told her was true? Instead she asked everyone to stay away from me? And they listened to her? All the women carrying Bibles in and out of her church thought that was normal? All of them believed that was the Christian thing to do? I wasn't the only woman who was mistreated by Nancy. When we left, Gerardo sat with Nancy's husband to tell him why we were leaving. By that point, the women started rejecting Gerardo also and he couldn't pretend it wasn't happening. Nancy's husband said he always wondered why other women would just disappear from her ministry, and thanked Gerardo for talking to him and not just disappearing.

When Priscilla's cousin confessed to me, I decided I had to confront Priscilla with Gerardo present. When Gerardo's mom found out, she threatened me that if I said anything to Priscilla she would lie to Gerardo and tell him I cheated on him with another man. I was four months pregnant with our first daughter, Arixeny. I sat in front of his mom at the local diner, pregnant, in complete shock at his mom's words. She threatened me not to confront Priscilla and said, "I'll tell him the lady at the salon told me she saw you with another man, that I showed her your picture on my phone and she said yes that's her and confirmed it. You don't know what I'm capable of doing." Despite her threats, I was respectful to her and I stood up for myself, pregnant with her son's baby. "You can't threaten me, he will know you're lying. What your daughter did was wrong and sick. She went as far as trying to stop us from getting married. There is something seriously wrong with her. I'm going to stand up for myself, and she can't keep attacking me like this." It took everything in me not to fall apart, but I didn't and walked out of that diner with my head high. Psalm 118:7 says, *"The Lord is with me; He is my helper. I look in triumph on my enemies."* When Gerardo and I confronted Priscilla at her home with her husband Juan present, she denied everything. She said what her cousin told me was not true and she never said that about me in any meeting.

Priscilla's mistreatment continued years after that confrontation. She attacked me at a family party pregnant with my second daughter, Xaeli. Gerardo stood up to her as other family members watched, including her kids. Then, when I delivered my baby Xaeli at the hospital, my newborn was rushed to the NICU. I called Gerardo's mom and she put me on speaker as I layed on the hospital bed. She told me Priscilla was with her. I began telling his mom what happened, then I said, "Please pray for my baby," and Priscilla refused to pray for my newborn as his mom sounded confused over the phone. I had enough. I recalled how for several years of friendship, I was there after all of Priscilla's miscarriages. I showed up to her door with flowers when she couldn't get out of bed after a miscarriage. I was always there. Years later, there I was on a hospital bed in tears and she refused to pray for my newborn baby who was rushed to NICU. I can't write everything I have gone through in this book, it's dark and it's a lot, but this day marked me. Those years after marriage having to keep dealing with his mom and sister, were some of the hardest for me. I never wanted to see Priscilla again, especially after that moment.

I held on to God stronger than ever. Scriptures flooded my soul, *"Our battle is not against flesh and blood, but principalities and powers...You anoint my head with oil, surely goodness and mercy will follow me all the days of my life...You prepare a table before me in the presence of my enemies...You are my beloved...I have loved you with an everlasting love...no height, no depth could ever separate you from the love of God... 'Vengeance is Mine, I will repay,' says the Lord..."* and scripture after scripture, in isolation and in prayer, I prayed my way through the years. God sustained and restored me. I trusted God to rebuild me stronger than ever. Even before Gerardo showed up into my life I had already been through a lot. You will never know how strong you truly are until you survive any and every experience that what was supposed to completely destroy you.

It took me over five years of hard work with God to truly forgive Nancy, Priscilla and her mom who together continued gossiping about me. I went through several phases, including anger, disappointment, discouragement, sadness. I mourned the years of what I mistakenly thought was a friendship. I mourned the idea of ever having a good relationship with my husband's mother or joining a 'good' family. In Spanish, you'd say something like, *'lo liberé y lo enterré'* which translates to, *'I set it free and then I buried it'*. Then I got to a point where I felt sorry for Priscilla, her mom, and Nancy, the same way I felt sorry for Casey and Karmen. More time passed and I then got to the point where I started praying for them, their families and that God would bless them. Then finally, one day, after praying with my friend Jean Luke, I felt God remove everything. All the damage I felt about what they did. It was gone. I felt free. I knew I reached complete forgiveness because I got to a point where I said deep within my heart, *"They owe me nothing."* I was able to call Priscilla and her mom and tell them I forgave all of them. I didn't speak to Nancy, but I didn't have to, I truly forgave her.

It's critical that you recognize that the mistreatment of others does not absolve you from your responsibility to forgive, *completely*. Unforgiveness keeps us from closeness to God. This is why forgiveness is not an option, it's a requirement God placed on us, and it's something you can do today without their apology. Study and pray about complete forgiveness. If you feel you can't today, try again tomorrow. It took me way to long to get to that point. By the grace of God I'm here and grateful to have healed from those experiences and now I get to help others with my story. There are many resources out there, primarily the Bible, for you to reach the point of complete freedom in forgiveness, whether you get to tell your offenders or not.

If you have been on the other side of the damage caused by church abuse or mistreatment, I'm so sorry. It is not easy to recover, but it's not impossible. Please find comfort in this one thing: *God saw all of it*. God understands the condition of your heart and any hesitation you may have from integrating yourself again into a church or a ministry. As long as you place the entire situation in the hands of God, you will be ok. Christ emphasized the solution in John 10. He is the Good Shepherd. While the Bible says the Holy Spirit has gifted specific people, not everyone who claims to be called to lead is actually ordained by God. When Christ says, *"My sheep hear my voice,"* we know that we can recognize Christ in people who He called to lead. Ultimately, we are to only follow after Christ and His voice. This is the solution to not facing the damaging results that occur at the hands of thieves.

If you were mistreated by church leaders, and you are still pursuing God today, you're doing a great job! Your life is complete. You lost nothing, because you still have God. He is everything. Many people completely leave their walk with God after experiencing church abuse. *Your spirit is still alive in Him!* Your faith is still kindled, while others search for faith in anything and everything outside of God. If you find yourself at the other side of damage caused by leaders in church, I urge you to find a good supportive community and keep going through the process of complete healing with the Holy Spirit.

The negative experiences you had with church people have a purpose. God will use all those bad experiences to shape and mold your character, if you let Him. You will become more like Christ, which is the end goal. You will bear more fruit, and your experience can help other people in the future. Because of what I've been through, I can empathize and understand others with worse experiences than mine. Get stronger in your faith, don't lose it. Many lives will be saved because you made the choice to keep walking after Christ, our Good Shepherd.

Remember Joseph, and his words in response to the moment he finally faced his family. You know, the brothers who out of jealousy, instead of loving him, left him for dead. When those brotheres faced Joseph again, they were there to receive food during a famine. It's so symbolic. Joseph blessed them and Genesis 50:20 records a life-changing statement to all parties involved.

> *"You intended to harm me, but God intended it for good to accomplish what is now being done, the saving of many lives."*
> *- Genesis 50:20 NIV*

La Novia

Se asomó el Futuro para preguntar,

"Ayyyyyyy mija, ¿¡Cuándo vas a cazar!?"

"¡¡¡No sé!!!" le grité,

Corrí al Tiempo para investigar.

"Cuando Dios diga, calmadita muchachita, la hora va llegar."

"Pero dice mi mamá que ya se me pasó el tren...y no regresará."

El Tiempo mantuvo su silencio.

Voltie al Pasado y me regaño,

"¡Ya no mires pa'tras! ¡Mil veces he dicho, tu boda no esta aca!"

"Pero es que no entiendo..." le reclame, y lloré.

Volteé al Destino, y me dio un consejo.

*"Pero mujer, sigue en tu camino. Los planes de Dios son perfectos.
¡Tu historia está en Sus manos, confía en eso!"*

Mire hacia el cielo y le llore a mi Padre Celestial.
Dios me escuchó, y por Su mano me mandó:

La Sabiduría,

*"Mantiene el temor de Dios. Estás en el camino correcto,
eso te lo confirmo yo."*

Y me mando la Paciencia,

*"Tranquila, no es bueno estar de prisa. Lo más bello se formará
dentro de tí...tu transformación está en vista, mira."*

Y vino el Entendimiento,

*"No será la idea de la cual te aferras... La visión de Dios es más grande,
te lo ha dicho el Pasado, y te lo muestra hoy el Presente."*

Luego, paso el Agradecimiento,

*"¡Feliz cumpleaños! ¡30 años de favor mujer, mira a tu alrededor!
...y hay mas bendiciónes por llegar. Adelante viene lo mejor."*

Después, llegó la Paz.

Sin palabras,

Sin hablar.

Me puse a bailar,

y deje de llorar.

En Barcelona, allí por el mar.

Di la vuelta,

y Me abrazo La Felicidad.

Reí a carcajadas,

y deje de preguntar.

Dí gloria a Dios, y pude descanzar.

Tome a Jesus de la mano,

paso a paso.

Enamorada, arrodille al altar.

Soy La Novia.

LA NOVIA

English translation:

The Bride

The future poked it's head to ask,

"Oh no young girl, when are you going to get married!?"

"I don't know!!!" I yelled,

I ran to Time to investigate,

"When God indicates, calm down young lady, the hour will come."

"But my mom says the train passed..and it won't return."

Time maintained it's silence.

I turned to the Past, who scolded me,

"Stop looking back! I've told you a million times, your wedding is not here!!"

"But I don't understand..." I demanded.

I turned to Destiny, who said,

"Woman, stay on course. God's plans are perfect. Your story is in His hands, trust in that fact."

I looked to the sky and cried to my Heavenly Father. God heard me and from His hand He sent me:

Wisdom,

"Maintain the fear of God. You're in the right path, that I can confirm to you."

And He sent Patience,

"Calm down, it's not good to rush. The most beautiful things will form inside you...your transformation is in sight, look."

And Understanding,

"It will not be the idea you hold on to so firmly...God's vision is greater, the past has shown you that and the Present affirms it today."

Then Gratitude,

"Happy birthday! 30 years of favor woman, look around you! ...and there are more blessings to come. The best is approaching ahead."

Later, Peace arrived.

without words,

without speech.

I began to dance,

and I stopped crying.

In Barcelona, there, by the sea,

I made a turn,

and Happiness embraced me.

I laughed aloud,

and stopped asking.

I gave glory to God and rested.

I took Jesus by the hand,

step by step,

In love, I knelt on the altar.

I am the Bride.

Author's Note:
This poem captures the pressure I felt at this moment in my life to be married. I personified the Future, poking it's head to ask me when I'm going to get married.

But my mom said the train left and it will not return!" The train leaving is a saying in Mexico expressing that you're time for marriage has passed.

I personified the gifts God gave me. Gratitude wished me a Happy 30th Birthday, and asked me to look at my surroundings, and notice all the blessings I already had and that the best ones were ahead. Finally, Peace arrived in silence. I describe how it led me to Barcelona where I finally embraced happiness with God in regards to marriage and my future. I began to dance is a reference to finally accepting my position with joy. I gave glory to God and was able to rest about it.

The end references a point where I re-ignited my love with God in Christ during that season. I found I was already in love and accepted my position by His side, as according to the Bible, we are the body and the bride of Christ. Reaching the altar and kneeling references to making a renewed, personal commitment to God.

CHAPTER 22
Lavished

When I was a child, there were so many things I wanted that were not good for me. Almost everything I desired was insignificant, for temporary pleasure and in short time, became useless. Aren't we all that way as kids? We couldn't clearly identify what was valuable and even if it was presented in front of us, we would not choose the valuable option. Cheap plastic toys that would break at first use were incredibly valuable to me. Candy. Shiny objects. And then once we were handed those cherished items, we so easily forgot about them. Many so neglected they broke or got lost and we couldn't recall when or where we lost them. We think as adults that we are no longer at this level of immaturity, capable of recognizing and pursuing what is truly meaningful and valuable. However, if we really take the time to evaluate our lives, we discover that there may be areas in which we still struggle with this issue of value.

Friday October 23, 2015, I finally made it to Barcelona. My friend Nia decided to join me last minute, although I was ready to go alone. On the flight out of Dallas, I sat there thinking about how I wanted the trip to be a fresh start for me personally. We got to the airport early and our flight to NYC was cancelled. We rushed to find another flight that would take us to Spain from DFW. People who were peaceful and calm, suddenly quickly turned ruthless. *'Savages,'* I thought, as I witnessed how little it takes for us as humanity to lose it. We found a connection to Amsterdam. All of our plans were quickly tossed up in the air. The hostess came to ask if I could turn my light off because most people were sleeping. I couldn't sleep and I was writing in my journal. When I turned the light off I saw a rainbow appear on my fold out tray. Literally impossible. This was God showing me He was with me. I see rainbows everywhere, even when it's literally impossible for them to show up, like at that moment in a dark airplane flying in the darkness of night. I took a picture.

When I arrived to Amsterdam, my walk through their airport made me realize that this was the beginning of God showing up to teach me what this reset truly meant. The scripture Proverbs 16:9 came to mind, *"A man's mind plans his way [as he journeys through life], But the LORD directs his steps and establishes them."* My plans at the time were to grow and advance in my career, settle down and start a family, continue ministry work with women and

The view of Barcelona from the Port Olympic district - Barcelona, Spain

take more missionary trips. I had so many ideas on what type of businesses I could open, to finally open a women's clothing store was one. I wanted to pick up painting again and have an art show. I planned to travel more. My time spent in thought of what I would focus on after this trip ended had me creating several mental bucket lists as I navigated through airports.

    Amsterdam was another world just within the airport. I stopped at Starbucks and they only served simple coffees, just coffee or shots but no long list of flavors or drinks. I bought my signature drink, the mocha with caramel drizzle. On the flight to Amsterdam, an old couple who looked to be Indian or from Thailand were on the flight. The man had a heart attack on the plane and almost died. We were crossing the ocean and I began to pray for his life. His wife had a red dot and powder on her forehead along with a lovely colorful wrap dress. The people who went to help him were able to resuscitate him and he walked out of the plane.

    We arrived to BCN around 1:00 p.m. on October 24th, a day before my birthday. I've dreamed of going to Barcelona for a few years now and was so excited to see the city. Four years after that tragic night in October, I continued to do ministry work at my jobs and through Bible Study groups. Gerardo and I split up a couple months prior, and I wanted so much to move on, settle down and start a family. Barcelona was a reset. I created an itinerary to see my three favorite countries, Spain, France, and Italy. I booked the flights and the hotels for one solo trip to Barcelona, Tarragona, Paris, and Rome. I looked down on the sidewalk ahead and envisioned a green arrow that said *'START'*, leading to a wonderful future and leaving the past behind.

    I jumped into the taxi expectant, and handed the address to the driver. "Princess Hotel," I said and started a conversation with him. I asked him where to visit and then transitioned to his life and family. He began sharing his frustration with the Catalans and the political issues including his problem with young adults in Barcelona. "They do not want to commit to marriage! These kids!" He sounded like the older generation who thinks we are just so irresponsible and immature. "How crazy is our government that they allow these kids to give up so quickly after they get married, they can cancel the entire thing easily in very few days! It's crazy!" They had something called Divorce Express, to help the government keep up with people filing for divorces shortly after they got married. I mentioned to him how in my travels to Quintana Roo, I learned much of the Mexican resorts are owned by the Spanish. He became frustrated again and told me, "Yes but do we bring that money back to Spain!? No! You know where they live? In Italy, in France, the UK, everywhere else in Europe except our native land. The economy here is so bad. This is a serious problem here." He also shared with me how the elderly were forgotten. Many lived in these tall apartment buildings they called "pisos" in areas called "distritos" and their kids didn't visit them. Because they can't walk down without assistance, they stayed locked up all day and were left neglected. He wanted to end the conversation with a positive note though, and as he pulled up to the hotel, he told me where to go for the best Iberian meat.

    I stayed in the Princess hotel which did not look at all like the photos. The bed was so hard which made me want to check out and book the Hilton down the road, but I stuck it out. I unpacked my bags and slammed my suitcase on the hard mattress. Yes, even harder than the twin beds in Nicaragua's missions trip, except this was a four-star hotel in Spain. The balcony view made me feel better about it. I booked a room by the coast so I could be close to one of the places that captures my heart – the ocean. I could see the city, and we had a nice shopping center next to us. We went

Performers playing for an audience. - Barcelona, Spain

Flamenco performance finale in Las Ramblas district. - Barcelona, Spain

to the mall and had tapas on a rooftop. The city was incredibly stunning at nightfall.

The next day, our plans were to explore and go to the FC Barcelona game, then tapas for dinner. We went to church first. I actually made it to my friend Earnesto's church. It was very old school and evangelical. I knew Earnesto from back in Dallas and was very happy for him in establishing himself as a missionary in Barcelona. We talked about me going back to do a missionary trip there and serve in his church in the future. I took a taxi back to the hotel and learned more about the unrest in Spain. The taxi driver, like the previous one, shared his frustration with Catalans wanting independence from the rest of Spain. All of the taxi drivers I asked said they do not want to have Catalan separate. Catalan people, although their communities were smaller and bring more money to Spain (the reason they want the independence), felt their separation will help them prosper as a cultural group. At least that's what the media reported in the news.

The taxi drivers said most of Spain is against it. They said when Franco died (the Spanish dictator who brought industrialism to work for many) there was a vote among politicians to decide if Catalan should stay separated and all signed and agreed that what was best for Spain was for them to stay united. They told me that the bottom line was that the disunity they currently faced would bring the country down. Unemployment was high and they explained that the Spaniards who had money left and took their wealth outside of Spain. There were a lot of Asians running the corner stores and cafes and they spoke perfect Spanish. The Catalan people speak in what sounds like Castellano Spanish, French and Italian all mixed together. Instead of "Ciudad" they said, "Ciutat". A lot of young people wore upside down crosses and when I asked about it, they confirmed Christianity wasn't popular there.

My friend Nia was really good at learning the local transportation, which I was terrible at. We took the metro to the Barcelona game and it

FC Barcelona game - Barcelona, Spain

was packed! We were sardines in there and no one cared. Messi was injured so I didn't get to see him play. Still, the experience was unforgettable. The stadium food was not the best, and there was no alcohol served for a reason. The fans were aggressively passionate, and like any Mexico game, I saw a few people fighting. Barcelona won 3 – 1 against Iberia. We arrived to our hotel room with a surprise on my bed. I found a birthday note, a bottle of Cava and a slice of chocolate cake, my favorite! The hotel staff were so kind to give me that gesture. The next day we took a bus tour to learn about the city and it was really good, it covered a lot of architecture. We stopped at a delicious bakery called Panet. It's probably like Panera for them but I thought it was amazing. We planned for what Flamenco performance we should go to, there were several.

  Before Flamenco, I went to the hotel bar to watch soccer and tapas before the show. Flamenco was unforgettable. The performers kept starring at me and one of the guys invited me to an after party, which I said no to. He called me "Cascabel" like the flower and it was too short of a conversation for him to give me a nickname, so that's always sus. The American lady that sat next to me was so annoying and policing everyone on rules when a lot of the people attending the performance did not speak English. The show began and the cave was silent. It was an incredible performance. The woman singing was so talented and they all performed in unity, even though the performance was unrehearsed.

  I noticed her strength. She was crying out in her song about a messed up relationship gone sour. I could relate. I asked God to change me. I wanted to live that passionately, the way she expressed herself. Strong and unafraid. Despite whatever pain she was crying out about, she still showed up and owned it. She stood firmly and with such boldness. I had never seen any woman perform that way. Everyone in the room disappeared. Ardent and undone, she owned up to it. She lamented the path that had brought her to that moment, and the depth of her anguish resonated powerfully in her performance. *'But she's still standing here now'*, I thought, *'She made it'*. Whatever tragic event she was mourning, she made it out on the other side. Like David in Psalm 23.

> *"Even though I walk through the [sunless] valley of the shadow of death, I fear no evil, for You are with me; Your rod [to protect] and Your staff [to guide], they comfort and console me." - Psalm 23:4 AMP*

I realized how God preserved my life. He consistently led me out of everything since I was a kid. His rod protected me from what should have destroyed me. He was my guide who brought comfort to see me through to the other side, every time. And then on the other side, it is not just survival, it's provision. Abundance.

> *"You prepare a table before me in the presence of my enemies. You have anointed and refreshed my head with oil; My cup overflows. Surely goodness and mercy and unfailing love shall follow me all the days of my life, And I shall dwell forever [throughout all my days] in the house and in the presence of the Lord." - Psalm 23:5-6 AMP*

Looking at the Flamenco singer, it was evident that literally nothing mattered to her at all. If I could be that passionate about God and be consumed with His love, that was success.

I admired her, and thought of how I wanted to live in zealous love for God, fully lavished by His love. I was convinced that was the greatest value to pursue. That was success.

Whatever that life looked like, that's what I wanted.

Flamenco

She approached the stage Broken...

Fragile...

and Alone...

...she surprised us all with the Strength of her Voice.

Her Presence shook the stage.

The depths of her Pain penetrated the earth.

Her Passion consumed and Overwhelmed her,

as her Story echoed throughout the place.

She was Undone,

yet Unphased ....Careless of who was observing,

Fearless.

She Stood her ground.

Despite her state of Brokenness, she presented herself with Confidence.

Her words, although few, conveyed a Strong sense of Authority.

Her thoughts were Fully Formed.

The Impact of her Presence was felt.

Her Message was received clearly.

She Changed.

She Owned it.

Suddenly I thought,

"Mmmmmmm.

If she can do all that because of mere romantic love lost,

I can live just as passionately, if not more,

because God's love won."

FLAMENCO

Author's Note:
The Triana district in Seville is considered a birthplace of flamenco, where it found its beginning as an expression of the poor and marginalized.

Seville's Gypsy population, known as Flamencos, were instrumental in the development of the art form. Flamenco is a national heritage symbol of Spain and for a time rejected by the elite.

I booked a show in Las Ramblas district of Barcelona. It was a late show, as it should be. The entrance was a narrow door that led to a lower ground level and it looked like we were ascending into a cave. Historically I had previously learned that many performances were made in caves. A typical flamenco recital with voice and guitar is comprised of a series of songs in different palos. Flamenco is made up of four elements, Cante (Voice), Baile (Dance), Toque (Guitar), and the Jaleo, which roughly translated means 'hell raising' and involves the handclapping, foot stomping, and shouts of encouragement.

Everything about it is tribal and I think it's why the elite hated it so much. As I walked in to find a seat in the dark cave like space, I found a seat close enough to center stage.

We were asked not to speak and not to record. The performance began, with musicians surrounding a beautiful woman in a flamenco dress and all the musicians looked like they were entering deep into their emotions. Each performance song had a story. The woman was crying about her lover who deeply hurt her, the stomping the clapping, the sharp guitar strums, all together supported the emotion of anger and pain. She bellowed, bent, her voice was strong and everyone was in sync even though it was improvised.

Mexican culture is very much in tune. I thought of Alejandro Fernandez's cry in "Como Cuando se Pierde Una Estrella". I thought of Juan Gabriel's entire song list, songs like "Se Me Olvido Otra Vez."

The performers that night left an impression in me. One in particular, a woman who sang with so much passion, who I observed very impressed.
She inspired this flamenco poem.

CHAPTER 23

Sojourner

I've never seen anyone work faster than an Italian barista during rush hour. I voluntarily threw myself at the sea of people in front of me. The morning crowd of Sicilians who all appeared to be late to work, were stopping for their morning espresso. Italian must be in my blood. People respectfully yelled out their order behind me raising their arm up and hovering over, one after another. Gorgeous fluffy croissants stacked up on display, and more bread I couldn't clearly see, but someone quickly asked for what looked like a croissant and I repeated, *"Cornetto cioccolato!!!"* and then again quickly, *"Un Capucco!!! Un Capucco!!!"* with my arm flailing up. So desperate and without the calm grace, because I had to get out of there fast. The tour bus was waiting for me outside. Observing the scene, trying to figure out where to pay, analyzing the workers to see which order was mine, completely distracted with the business and chaos. I snatched my coffee cup and bagged pastry and dashed outside to find that my tour bus had left me. I stood back starring at it drive off, with no way to get them back. I didn't have cell phone signal. I began to envision my life as a Sicilian, how I'd have to get a job there. I imagined staying. Then, as I stood there, and the bus was as tiny as an ant in my view, all of a sudden it made a u-turn. Hope.

You'd think I learned my lesson. Later that same day, there was a moment when I decided I was going to walk up a hill to a coffee shop. Prior to getting left at this stop, I had arrived by ferry traveling from the island of Malta that took us to the coast of Italy. From there I got on a stop and go bus tours where they have you stop at landmarks and places highlighting the city you're visiting. As the day progressed, I decided that I was going to walk up to a coffee shop that I spotted at the very bottom of a hill. I mean as soon as I realized it was a coffee shop, you couldn't stop me. It was picturesque. If you can imagine, it was a beautiful, gorgeous sunny day like what you would see in movies. The streets were paved in stone, the homes were ages old, just beautiful where everyone knows each other. It was a small, close knit town where not many people lived there. I approached this one particular home that was a coffee shop and a bakery. I stepped into the door, and fell in complete love. I looked at the woman and ordered my drink, *"Bonjo! Un cappucio per favore, di caramelo"*. I don't speak fluent Italian but I learned enough to ask for the important things.

The coast of Sicily. - Italy

I got lost in the entire experience. As I scanned the pastries I got lost in the place, I mean they had stuff I had never seen before. The choices were overwhelming, I was indecisive, and I kept telling myself, *Just pick one!* I couldn't choose. I urged myself to hurry it up because I didn't have much time there but did I listen? Absolutely not. I took my sweet little time. I got lost in the moment just admiring the entire scene and then shock hit my stomach like so hard, as I looked out the window and I realized that everyone in my travel group was gone. Oh no. Literally, I just got left that morning *for the exact same reason.* I grabbed my stuff, ran out of the café and asked myself – *'OH MY GOD WHAT ARE YOU DOING!!!?'* as I saw my bus leave me, again.

Your answer to the question, *"What are you doing?"* is one of the most important things you could respond to. Whatever you are doing right now is directing a path and determining what your future will be. So why don't we take more time to stop and ask ourselves what are we spending our time doing?

I find it amazing how people in the Bible would just get up and go places without knowing the itinerary or having a full plan. Think of Abram, before God changed his name to Abraham, and how early in His walk with God got everything together and left all he knew without asking a question and without knowing a plan. The people of Israel fled Egypt not knowing what awaited them on the other side of the Red Sea. All the way through to the New Testament where we see the disciples being told by Jesus to go to Jerusalem and simply *"wait on the Promised Holy Spirit".* They had so many unanswered questions and were just told by Jesus to go and wait. It's interesting because if you read the book of Acts in this one chapter it says

The pastries that took me, in the village, up the hill. - Sicily, Italy

Jesus taught them for 40 days. Jesus had *40 days* to prepare them and still left them with critically important unanswered questions. Jesus basically said don't worry about the important details you care about, just go there and wait. So frustrating.

Have you been in a place where you feel you're going a certain direction or trying to get somewhere in life but you're in a period of just waiting? Waiting for the opportunity to come up, waiting to finish your degree, waiting for the promotion, waiting to save up for that new house, waiting to move out, waiting to settle down, waiting for your kids hit a certain age, waiting for your family member's health to improve, etc.

Then there's people doing things, but being destructive. Proverbs 14:1 says *"A wise woman builds her home, but a foolish woman tears it down with her own hands."* I think of Joseph's brothers in Genesis 37. He had so many brothers working really hard to get rid of him out of jealousy and in the end had to beg for food at his feet. Some people work really hard to destroy the lives of others, put so much energy to come against them, move in deception, and still think what they are doing is ok. In Titus 3:10, Paul points out to Titus that there are people who work to cause division among the community of believers and in doing so, they condemn themselves. While they were harming other people the scripture reveals they ended up condemning themselves in all their doing.

Then, there are others pre-occupied and busy doing the wrong thing. Some even missing out on something good that God placed right in front of them. I remember the story of Mary and Martha in Luke 10:38.

"Now it happened as they went that He entered a certain village; and a certain woman named Martha welcomed Him into her

> *house. And she had a sister called Mary, who also sat at*
>
> *Jesus' feet and heard His word. But Martha was distracted with much serving, and she approached Him and said, "Lord, do You not care that my sister has left me to serve alone? Therefore tell her to help me."*
> *Luke 10:38-40 NKJV*

Some people are busy doing a lot of work they feel is productive and meaningful, but it's not fulfilling. Not only that they're miserable doing it and complain about it. Jesus pointed out here to Martha and said basically, why are you even doing all that? Her busy work was not necessary in that precise moment. He said few things are needed, actually just one thing, and Mary figured it out quickly. It would only be a short time period after that moment that Christ would be crucified.

The Italians have a saying, *'Dolce Far Niente'*, which means doing sweet nothing. It's the pleasure of doing absolutely nothing and nobody questions or bothers you about it. There was a clear reality that I was not in America anymore simply in this one detail, and it's everywhere. The restaurant staff didn't rush me, we sat for hours. Elderly people sat in benches in the public square doing nothing but people watch and talk. I remember the term *'Selah'* in the Bible and the importance to take a moment to pause. It is an invitation to rest in His refuge and strength. Maybe He is accentuating something in our spirits, as if saying, *'Wait, stop here.'* Some theologians believe that maybe Selah is a transition or pivot, a redirection away from harm or distraction and into God's perfect grace and purpose. Sometimes, you have to stop and do nothing.

I was completing my undergrad at the time at Dallas Baptist University (DBU). I went to Malta on a study abroad trip for a Marketing course. In another Business Management course, they emphasized the importance to take moments in the life cycle of all the work you do to pause and re-consider your strategy and what direction you are taking the business. Corporations all around the world find this a successful technique because they clear their minds to think things through and sort of step back from all the doing to see the bigger picture more clearly. Specifically, it was a good time to understand if the company activity was in alignment to reach future goals and in alignment with it's vision and mission. As I admired how Italians were not rushing through life (except for the coffee rush hours) on a daily basis, I became aware of the importance of stopping to do nothing.

Our main host in Malta was a middle-aged single guy who appeared to be committed to his career. He coordinated our schedule and was pres-

One of the coastal watch towers. - The island of Malta, Italy

ent for most of our activities. He had a full-time job in what would be the 'downtown' area. One day during lunch time we asked him, "Do you need to hurry back to work?" as he was already with us over 1 hour during his break. He looked at us so confused and exclaimed, "No!!!" but he left out the *'Are you guys crazy over there in America?'* part. That's really what he wanted to say, as he scanned our traumatized work-a-holic faces and laughed. He proceeded to explain that they can take as long as they need during mid-day break. We all thought that was amazing. He didn't have a boss on his back cracking an HR whip. He wasn't nervous or anxious to hurry up and finish his lunch or lose his job because of it.

Visiting the Island of Malta I found rich history and ruins of what communities of people left behind. The results of many members who came together to accomplish the task of building their city, and in all their busy doing, left ruins behind for us to enjoy and admire. Every site I visited was breath taking. We were greeted by a young adult Maltese woman who would be our educational guide. She was petite, polite and incredibly knowledgeable. She greeted us with a driver. The driver was a very short Italian gentleman about the age of my dad. His name was Mario and he said his name exactly how Mario from Super Mario Brothers says it. I just wanted to hug him so tight it warmed my heart, but I restrained myself. As we drove around sight-seeing we saw many watch towers, or fortresses. These were used by the locals to stand watch as postmen to notify the community of invaders. I learned that the job of watchman was the most important job to have at that time. The island was overtaken by so many countries and it was easy for them to see a foreign ship approach in time to warn the community.

During one site visit, we were able to see the ancient town that has The Ġgantija Temples. These ruins are older than the pyramids of

An ancient fortress - Malta, Italy

Egypt and known as the oldest surviving buildings in the world. One of the mysteries the guide explained is the size of the stones and how people were able to construct it. It's refered to as a town built by giants. Not simply that, but that it survived to its current condition all these years later and much of it remained in place. The Romans were one group that overtook Malta at one point. These buildings are ancient religious sites built with great detail and were used for worship. The stone slabs were decorated with spiral carvings and dotted patterns. One amazing fact is that the buildings were built with consideration of the seasons. It's position allowed in light to illuminate it in perfect alignment during the equinox and solstices. What they did in just building these structures alone provided for their generations in their lifetime and benefited even more people years later, including me.

    Looking back having witnessed these sites, I reflected on the hard reality that what we do individually as well as collectively, truly matters. We don't know any names of the people who built that temple, but what each individual did mattered significantly. The fact we don't know their names is irrelevant in full retrospect. I think some of us see our lives as fleeting and live as though what we do doesn't matter much. Convinced of this, many spend years of their lives wasting away, settle into complacency, and rest in mediocrity. We can't blame people for what they're doing or not doing, especially if they embraced the hamster wheel of a cycle. Ultimately we individually get choose to do what we are doing or choose how we spend our time.

    Some people are doing a lot of busy work and going in circles. Like the people of Israel when they fled slavery in Egypt. They were traveling, tired of their situation, doing things to maintain themselves and their household units, all the while traveling in circles not getting to their destination. They spent their time complaining, doubting God and in their bad attitudes they got nowhere. Many people today are stuck because of their bad attitude, unable to exit the mental set back, unable to break their thought cycle. They have work and things to do, but greet every year with no meaningful progress. In the Bible, the people of Israel eventually got to a point when God would finally lead them out of the cycle. Deuteronomy 2:2-3 *"At this time the LORD said to me, You have circled this mountain long enough. Now turn north."*

Isn't it also interesting that usually drastic change or a tragic event is precisely what it takes to leads us closer to things we should be doing? I hate that. I personally ask God to help me focus on doing what I should be doing without drastic changes or tragic events. In each story you read in the Bible, you'll notice the doing led the person into a path. For each person it was different, but in their doing they were led to a destination. Ruth, for example, even in her bitterness continued the path and it led to blessing. She was taken care of the rest of her life without a husband or her son's provision! Jacob, even as deceiving as he was, ended up correcting his relationship with God. It took him literally wrestling with God, but finally he was able to get right and enter into a blessing for himself and future generations. He finally learned his true identity and walked in it. In Genesis 32, Jacob received a new name, it reads, *"Your name will no longer be Jacob, but Israel, because you have struggled with God and with humans and have overcome."*

There are several stories of men and women in scripture that can help us reflect on our own lives and take in consideration what we are actually doing and re-consider the choices we are making. While many of us want a fast and clear answer to what the itinerary looks like and what the destination is, it's clear that we will most likely not get it. We're left really looking to God and trusting Him when we hear Him tell us where to go next. Most often it's a step by step instruction. Like any journey, there has to be moments where you have to make a complete stop. Sometimes, the best thing you can do for yourself is stop and do nothing. *Dolce far niente.* Stopping to do nothing can be progress if you were going the wrong way. Sometimes, the best thing you can do for yourself is let things be! I will be the first one to congratulate you for quitting if it means you finally allowed yourself the time to hear God about your life and future.

If you're someone who is currently at a point in your life where you have no idea what the path should be, or what it looks like, start with taking just one step forward, even without a path visibly ahead. October 28, 2010 I went jogging on campus at DBU. I used to run the Mike Arnold fitness trail by the Bush Pond. I loved running this trail, and I knew the path well. That night as I approached the start of the trail, I could not see the trail path anymore, *at all.* The path was gone. It was not only night time and dark, but there was no longer a trail, like it was completely gone. I just stood there wondering what happened, looking around in circles…blaming the Grounds Department. I was sure they drove over the trail with a John Deere. I stood there not knowing where to go or what to do.

Have you been in this position, where you know where you're headed and then all of a sudden the path ahead is completely removed and destroyed? You come to a halt, completely confused at where to go next? In that moment I felt that way about my life. I knew the trail, I had been running the path of serving God several years by that point. Symbolically, in the path of life I was in, I knew what that looked like, but in that season of my life, I couldn't see ahead. The path disappeared. The darkness was all I saw, the bad experiences I had gone through and all the questions I had about where I should go in my future. I broke off a long-term relationship with a guy, and started hanging out with new friends from other college church groups. I would graduate soon and felt I reached a ceiling at a job where I wasn't truly challenged or valued. There were still non-stop problems with my parents at home, that probably only I knew about, and kept it to myself. I wasn't plugged into a church serving anymore and wondered how long it would take me to heal enough to try again. But I honestly didn't want to serve in a church ever again. Finishing business school, hanging out with friends and the routine I had with a job that didn't callenge me was comfortable. God used this night to get my attention. Standing there in real life facing a path which was literally removed, I turned to the entrance and I felt the Holy Spirit say to me,

"Run it anyway…"

That is what God requires of us sometimes. When your vision is gone and you feel you don't see a path ahead, *run it anyway*. I turned around again, tire marks on the ground and grass was all I saw. As I took the first few strides into what I remembered the path was, I found my way and finished my run.

Maybe you're in a position right now where it seems like situations, events and things in life have marked over your path. Satan took that John Deere and just tore up that path ahead with his own plans in mind for your future – which left you in confusion, looking around and wondering where to go next. Instead of staying confused, indecisive or unsure, and with the easy option to just give up, I urge you to do what I did and run anyway! In your darkest moments run, and finish strong like I did that day, even if it means running without seeing the complete path ahead.

At the end of life, we each will individually stand before God alone. Read Revelation chapter 2, it's very sobering. Your mom and dad will not be standing by your side to excuse you before God when you face Him. Your spouse, your kids, your best friend, no one will be there to vouch for you or help explain to God how good of a person you were. No one will be able to stand next to you to excuse your behavior or take the blame for any of the poor choices you made in this life. All the missing out on God's will for you, impacting those who God sent your way, important appointments that would direct your destiny, ignoring God, doing your own thing - you will answer alone for all of it. We learn in scripture that God will even judge every word we spoke. Jesus said in Matthew 12:36-37, *"I tell you, on the day of judgment people will give account for every careless word they speak, for by your words you will be justified, and by your words you will be condemned."* Pastors, evangelists,

Mnajdra (Maltese: L-Imnajdra) is a megalithic temple complex found on the southern coast of the Mediterranean island. These ruins are older than the pyramids in Egypt. - Malta, Italy

ministers, teachers, leaders should heed the warning Jesus gave in Matthew 7:22, that while they think they're convincing people that they serve God, they actually face God in eternity and hear *"I never knew you."* It's very sobering to know Jesus said, *"Not everyone who says to Me, 'Lord, Lord,' will enter the kingdom of heaven, but only he who does the will of My Father who is in heaven. Many will say to Me on that day [when I judge them], 'Lord, Lord, have we not prophesied in Your name, and driven out demons in Your name, and done many miracles in Your name?' And then I will declare to them publicly, 'I never knew you; depart from Me..."* (Matthew 7:21-23).

Like the builders of Mnajdra, we too should build our lives up considering the seasons. Each season will require different roles and responsibilities. There are people who sow and those who go and reap. Also, there are steps to be taken within the process of each phase, and no stage of a season should be skipped over. Some people want to rush or skip a step, skipping over very important things that would help reach the best life decision. Some seasons of life require a time of waiting. For example, waiting to heal. After an offense or traumatic experience, many want to hurry up and heal. Taking the time to heal is very important in order to reach the next phase and to get to the right place. Healing is not something to rush or skip over. Also, you can't rush the production time to yield a harvest during a season. You can't reap a harvest early. Some people, as they're working and doing things, take on the perspective that they've been doing the right thing for x amount of years, consistent and obedient to God about something for so long, then demand to see results. You can't expect things to happen outside of it's opportune time, as you would not expect a harvest to produce ahead of its' time. Then, there are seasons where life is dormant and there is need for rest. You get what I'm saying. It's important you understand what season you are in and what God is asking you to do.

There's a silent affliction within many Christians that they need to keep doing more to be good with God, when in reality we need to do more of the *right things at the right time.* Instead of volunteering so much at church events, or greeting people or directing parking lot traffic on Sundays, maybe the right thing to do is I finally to forgive themselves for the mistakes they made x years ago. The best thing to do may be to spend quality time with their kids and families. Maybe the best thing they could spend their time on is to no longer carry the shame that keeps them from closeness with God. Maybe the best thing would be to use money they give to the church and help a family member in need, or use it to take their family on a vacation. Maybe the best thing for some to do is to make dinner for their spouse, ask for forgiveness and do the work with God to change. Some people could make better use of time by forgiving or making peace with a family member. You may be surprised to find out that doing one good and right thing

SOJOURNER

at the right time may get you closer to God than doing a lot of religious stuff that looks like ministry or charity and yet you stay separated from God and separated from people you care about.

When I got lost in Italy I'm surprised by how easily I forgot I wasn't at home. The Bible says we are sojourners on the earth. David is recorded to have lifted up a prayer to God and in recognition said the following.

> *"For we are strangers before you and sojourners, as all our fathers were. Our days on the earth are like a shadow, and there is no abiding."*
> *- 1 Chronicles 29:15 ESV*

That prayer David said is so beautiful. He said, *"...Yours, O Lord, is the greatness and the power and the glory and the victory and the majesty, for all that is in the heavens and in the earth is Yours. Yours is the kingdom, O Lord, and you are exalted as head above all. Both riches and honor come from You, and You rule over all. In Your hand are power and might, and in Your hand it is to make great and to give strength to all...but who am I and who are these people that we should be able to offer You (God) anything? For all things come from you, and of your own have we given you."*

The word Sojourning meaning we are resident aliens in a territory, we are on a temporary stay, just as I was sojourning in Italy. My home was Dallas, Texas, and I had an exact flight date to return. We can't get lost here, we can't live this life carelessly, being distracted by ideologies, chasing things that are enticing because they are new or attractive. You know, like how I was distracted by those pastries. We can't get so distracted where the end result leads to confusion, and we end up lost in this lifetime.

The tour guide had a limited amount of time planned. He said we can only stay at that stop a few minutes before returning. We have a tour guide during our lifetime. Jesus sent us a Helper, the Holy Spirit is our tour guide (John 16:7; John 15:26-27). He is the Spirit of God living inside you, once you decide to surrender your life to God. You can do that right now without thinking twice about it, without stepping foot in a church and without having anyone lay hands on you. In your own words ask God to direct the course of your life and manage everything you are currently doing. The Holy Spirit will begin to work in your heart.

What are you spending your days doing?

You give your soul away every day.

307

You give your soul, that is your mind, will and emotions, away daily to something. You spend hours of each day giving away your soul to a job, an institution, wealth-building, your image, addictions, an obsession, money, social media, beauty, a belief, a past mistake, a group of people or one specific person, an idea... you get the picture. The list is endless.

When you wake up each day take a few moments to pause and consider what you will be doing that day and to what things and what people you will give away your time to – because you will not get it back.

I want to gently remind you that you and I and every human on this earth is on a time clock, everyone has a set time limit of life here on earth. You and I can't lose sight of our tour guide as eternity waits around the corner.

CHAPTER 24
Work of Art

I stood in the middle of this busy city staring at my Parisienne map, back and forth, with my phone on the other hand. My long hair swaying in my face, and the gorgeous blonde ombre so perfectly fitting to the fall scene around me. My day was completely cleared up and I could do whatever I wanted. Alone. This felt so weird. To be in such an incredible place and just do whatever I wanted with no agenda. I walked along the sidewalk across the street from my hotel and noticed just how large and beautiful the fall leaves were, falling slowly to the ground all around me. Slowly, as if they needed to remind me to take it slow. *Let it go, and take it slow.* Have you ever taken time to be alone? I have felt comfortable being alone before this. I would spend hours at a coffee shop studying scripture or doing artwork for hours alone. I spent my entire childhood and teen life up to my twenties feeling alone. While I am very social and make friends easily, I can really enjoy time alone.

I decided to have breakfast outside at a restaurant down the street just walking distance of my hotel. Then I jumped on the public double-decker bus to wherever I decided I'd go. Surprisingly, shopping was the last thing I wanted to do — which also tells you I was at a different place in my life at that point. I planned to visit the Eiffel Tower, the Louvre and see the Mona Lisa, *finally*. I wanted to do the boat ride down the Seine River. Eat an eclair. Also, try the escargot, to see what all the hype was about. I'm tribal after all, my indigenous genes are strong, so I was down. Those were the only things I really had on my bucket list for Paris. I'm no basic Betty or simple Sally, but I was content upon landing. My friend Nia who joined me last minute on this trip went with me to the Louvre. It didn't turn out well. It was really surprising to have someone I considered such a close friend, all of a sudden feel like we were not close at all. She acted as if she was inconvenienced by all I wanted to do. It was my birthday trip. She flipped out when I asked for too many pictures. That's all I needed. We went our separate ways. It was God-ordained though, as if I had to spend that time alone. I had a lot of time to think about what I wanted my life to look like after returning to Dallas. I had ongoing conversations with God the entire trip, alone.

Some people hate being alone, especially in a place like Paris that you may think you'd want to share in company. But while you can be single and feel alone, you can also be married and *still feel alone*. You can be a single child and feel alone, and you can be a child of eight kids, and like me, *still feel alone*. You can work from home and feel alone, and you can work with a team in an office and still feel like you're in it alone.

Here is a serious warning which I contemplated. Being alone can bring good into your life, *but settling into feeling lonely consistently* can have a detrimental effect on your life. It is the root source that kills our relationships, our identity, our character and derail our purpose. *Being alone* though, can be a good thing. While some people hate being alone, the alone part is not the problem. God will get you alone to work in your life and mold you to who you were created to be. It's being in a state of loneliness that is the problem.

Moses heard God's voice alone, after leaving everything he knew behind and fleeing to a mountin. He heard God in a place where he knew no one and hand no family. God disciplined Jonah alone. Jonah in complete disobedience found himself isolated and alone in the darkness found in the pit of a large fish for three whole days. Mary accepted her calling alone. While she had a fiancée, she agreed with the angel God sent who appeared to her and told her she would carry God's son. She made that commitment alone. Elijah fled to a cave alone. He fled in fear to complete isolation, despite great victories he won on behalf of God in his generation. He still ended up in a cave alone. Embrace being alone but reject the feeling of loneliness.

The truth is that even if you find yourself alone, you're never left abandoned. Psalm 139 explains there is nowhere we can go where God is

View of Paris from the top of the Eifel Tower - Paris, France

View of the Seine River from the Eifel Tower - Paris, France

not present with us. Psalm 139:7-10 reads, *"Where can I go from your Spirit? Where can I flee from your presence? If I go up to the heavens, you are there; if I make my bed in the depths, you are there. If I rise on the wings of the dawn, if I settle on the far side of the sea, even there your hand will guide me."* No matter who enters or exits our lives, God's presence remains.

Don't allow yourself to settle into loneliness. It can bring out the worst in you. May God's love dissolve your loneliness where you never feel trapped in and may His light remove the darkness that comes with that feeling. Hopefully the moments we find ourselves alone in our lives teach us what we need to learn to develop in order to become who we need to become. In our alone time, God can create a clean heart and create a passion to pursue Him. In our alone time God can destroy idols and destroy addictions. There is purpose in solitude but loneliness will kill purpose so quickly.

On the double decker bus to the Louvre, as I stepped down I became awestruck. Seeing that large clear glass pyramid entrance in front of me seemed so surreal. *"Oh my God I'm here,"* I whispered to myself and released a deep breath all at once. This was my artist dream. Since I was in art school at Arts Magnet back in Dallas, I dreamt of one day seeing this place in person. All the relics. All the hall of famers, and the chance to see the Mona Lisa. The place was packed and security guards stood everywhere as I looked at a map that seemed to be a complete maze. I marked the path to the Mona Lisa. When I reached the place where the painting hung, it was complete chaos. A large crowd surrounded the area and huddled back and forth for the perfect selfie. It is so much smaller than I expected. I mean it was like an 8x10 painting in my eyes. Then, the shock hit me at the realization that such a small work of art could make that great of an impact in history. Also, the life lesson echoed hauntingly in my mind:

It will never, ever be exactly what you expected it to be.

I went back later that evening to revisit the Louvre a second time, and then afterwards I got on the double-decker bus to buy a ticket to ride a boat on the Seine River. I bought a one-way ticket across to take me back closer to my hotel. At that moment I felt it. Loneliness. It is not how I expected to reach this place. All of a sudden, never before had I been so aware of my alone-ness during the entire time and it sank in, that feeling of loneliness. Everyone who stood in the line had somebody, every person I passed on the interior of the boat had someone. Everyone was loud, busy, engaged, talking and laughing, leaning on someone's shoulder, taking group selfies, arguing with someone they loved and I stood there…alone. I walked out of the interior enclosed part of the boat and walked past everyone to head towards the outer deck. I don't know where all the people went. As soon as I stepped out to the deck, everyone stayed inside and it was just me out there. That was so weird, as you couldn't go anywhere in Paris without seeing people, whether locals or tourists.

There I was on an empty boat deck standing alone overlooking the water in a pitch dark night. The darkness started to look darker and when I looked on the water the glistening of the moon was a high glossy white. I mean beautiful. The moon's reflection looked like enlarged tears settling above and floating on the river. Suddenly I looked as far as I could ahead and saw the moon's reflection forming tear like shapes spreading everywhere on the river. *'Noooo…get it together sis, this is not the place.'* I thought, but

The Basilica of Sacré Cœur de Montmartre- Montmartre, France

The view from my hotel room. - Paris, France *Re-enacting art history. - Montmartre, France*

I couldn't stop it. The moon's tears formed quickly. Loneliness suddenly turned to sorrow inside me, deep. It took over me. Then, weeping. Out of my heart, from past memories I couldn't precisely point to because there were so many, questions I never had answers for, too many, and regrets of all the things I couldn't go back and re-do, all rose up like a massive wave and overpowered me. I couldn't. I gave up and let myself cry. My whole life of worries, disappointments, let downs, frustrations with everyone before this moment, the millions of experiences that created pain inside me, I just drug behind me in an invisible enormous haul just slammed in front of me on this boat deck. It was so heavy.

I just wished some things looked differently.

I wished a lot of things I went through would have looked differently. Maybe my story would have been...I don't know, *better*?

I did feel God's comfort though. I understood what David described in Psalm 34:15, 18-19. *"The eyes of the Lord are on the righteous, and His ears are attentive to their cry; The LORD is close to the brokenhearted and saves those who are crushed in spirit. The righteous person may have many troubles, but the LORD delivers him from them all..."*

Whatever God did in my heart, I felt a weight leave that night. God will set you aside and get you alone to work inside your heart. I remembered Elijah having accomplished so much on God's behalf, being so courageous and still suddenly cowering and fleeing to a dark cave. No one is spared. From the strongest leaders to the every day average person, we all must undergo this work. Whatever those alone moments are, God works in them to develop what He needs to develop in us. We have to be willing to not waste the alone time and allow for God's repair.

I collected myself after a few minutes. I closed my eyes and imagined letting go of all the invisible burdens I carried, watching them sink into the river. I pictured myself unable to dive in and retrieve any of them, letting them drown completely. People like to do that, you know. They struggle to let go, often rushing back to snatch their past with the desperation of hoarders clinging to worthless scraps that serve no purpose. This compulsion to hold on, no matter how burdensome, reveals a profound fear of loss and the deep attachment to the painful past. Well, mentally I did it, and it felt liberating. I wondered what my life would be like leaving everything I knew in Dallas and fulfilling a dream, among many, of living in Europe permanently. Maybe somewhere in Spain, but since I learned the economy in Barcelona was so bad, maybe Madrid. Or maybe the good economy side of Italy or France. Plans, plans, plans, I had to stop making plans.

Without much planning on another day, I journeyed up at the top of the Hill in Montmartre. Art was absolutely everywhere around me. I stopped to notice people too and everyone looked to be creatives working with art in some form in their private lives. They all looked and dressed like artists. You know artists have a way of being that I can identify and love. Whether a performing artist, a visual artist or whatever category, they carry a high level of *'I do not care'*. You know they will just naturally dress themselves unapologetically. I've worked with medical professionals, engineers, executives, entrepreneurs, educators and one thing I notice is that unlike those professions, artists carry an *'I am who I am, like it or not'* sense of being.

Walking around the Montmartre hill, you will see shops and shops of paintings for sale. They paint quickly and every painting is a complete work of art. From realism, to abstract art, everything looks to be a masterpiece. I walked over to a shop and saw a glass pane displaying the most perfect Parisienne pastries. I mean, perfect. I spotted the éclair and bought one. *"Éclair du chocolaté s'il vous plaît"*, I said to the woman in the tiny open shoppe. I handed her euros and didn't count my returned change. Because, éclair. I was fixated on its perfection. I thought of Uncle Phil from the Fresh Prince of Bel Air, and that episode when he spoke of his favorite pastries and emphasized his passion for the éclair. I turned over to observe my surroundings, the people, the perfect scene, the perfect day and this perfect éclair, and thought of absolutely nothing. I devoured it slowly and held the chocolate in my mouth for several seconds, the way you sample wine, before swallowing, with several *"mmmmms"*'s in between.

Then, I saw him. I spotted this artist working so focused on his craft. He was older, maybe in his 40s, and looked like he was just churning and burning paintings for the hustle. I know that intense look well. But the

The Montmartre artist's studio. - Montmartre, France

closer I looked, I realized he was really making copies of the same work. Most tourists wouldn't notice it, but if you truly took the time to analyze that painting, it looked like all the other ones he posted for sale. The same cottage like cluster of homes stacked together for that typical European Parisienne scene. It was copies on copies of what they must have thought every tourist would want to hang at home to tell their guests they bought the work of art while in Paris.

A different color front door on each house maybe, different color flowers on every other canvas, a slight hue difference on the combination of blues…cirrus clouds in one and a clear blue sky on another – but they all were truly a repeat composition of the same scene. I thought, *'No, I totally get it, the artist struggle is real and you need to make money. Those copy paste templates will get the job done.'* The real artwork was somewhere behind the entrance in his personal studio, because he probably thinks these tourists, especially Americans, won't get it and won't buy them.

But as I looked, I knew those masterpieces not for sale carried the imprint of the artist's heart and soul. So there he was churning and burning 10 copies before his lunch break probably. These were my thoughts. Obviously I wouldn't go up to the guy and tell him that. But yes, I walked up and starred as if I was an interested buyer, thinking about all of the above and analyzing the situation.

I work with clients doing illustration work aside from marketing. One client saw my previous work and asked, "Okay so I love what you did with this character you drew for your other client. It is just beautiful! I am in love with the boy's hair. Would it be okay if I use the same boy's hair for one of my pages?" I wish you knew me, and if you did, you'd laugh knowing I thought this question was so ridiculous. With all the respect in the world, I thought, *'What in the world are you crazy? I would never do that.'* But what I responded was, "Why would you want to copy that illustration over to your book? Sure he looks good, but wouldn't you want your own version, fit for your story?"

She then explained, "Okay but can we just take his hair and place it on my characters' head, I simply love the style and dimension it is perfect." I felt like laughing and tried to put the words together differently to explain to her something she clearly did not see. "I could... but I don't understand why you would want me to just copy the boy's hair over and use it in your story. I created that. I'm the artist. And sure it's nice, but I am capable of applying the same beautiful style to something new, that is customized for your book."

Why would she want something that had been created for someone else's book, while speaking to the artist who created it? Like in my mind it just sounded so crazy! She was so stuck on whatever she saw in her mind, that she couldn't hear me or see what I wanted her to see.

She couldn't see that I could create something better, something new and perfect for her story. She just had to trust me.

I heard God's voice echo inside me, *"Exactly. That's how I feel."*

Why do we beg for a copy of someone else's story? We come to God with our own image and ask Him to create a copy for us. Why do we wish for different circumstances, or a different past, when the scripture reassures us in Romans 8:28 that all things *work together for good* to those who are in Christ and are called according to His purpose? Why do we look at others and wish for a copy of just a tiny piece their story? Like that lady with the boy's hair. We show up to God, the artist and finisher of our story asking for a copy of something we saw in someone else's story. I believe he laughs too. The same way I laughed at her ridiculous request. God must laugh while hearing our version of a good life, our idea of a good future or our version of a good ending to every bad experience we've lived through.

I wasn't able to help that client. She was so stuck with her idea, that when I created any sketch, she became visibly frustrated and continuously wanted me to make copies of something else. I don't know if she ever finished her book. I believe the same happens with many people today. God can't help us if we stay stuck with our own idea of what we want our story to be.

When you come to God in prayer about your life, He will show you a sketch. A glimpse of what He has in mind. Pray and ask God to meet you in your heart about that specific things you've desired. Ask Him to meet you about all the disappointments, regrets and tragedies you've been through. Know today that it all serves a purpose in your complete life story. If you understand what I'm saying, I invite you to close this book and take a second with God. Decide to no longer desire less than the perfect masterpiece He has envisioned to give you.

The same way I felt about that client, all she had to do was trust me. *All you have to do is trust God.*

Without a complete picture from God, take time in solitude to tell Him you trust Him and are confident in all the amazing details He has prepared for your *perfect* story.

Don't be like that lady. Let God finish your book.

CHAPTER 25

Construction

"**G**reat." I said in complete disappointment. I was jet-lagged and tired, but still out late trying to sight see. It was completely drained, no water. The Trevi Fountain was on it's 16th month of reconstruction, having undergone a restoration project. I stood starring at the Trevi and saw it's present condition as a sign. It was ironic to show up to Rome and find construction.

A few months before I stood there in front of that fountain, I realized one day as I drove to work that the path to my job was trailed with construction. It wouldn't end. *"When will this be over? Why does road construction take so long..."* I wondered. Then, I arrived to my job and the commercial office tower I worked in was all of a sudden under construction in one of the wings. Hmm. Then, I drove to the Starbucks I frequented after work to do devotional time, and from one day to the next, it too was now completely under construction! *Are you kidding me?* I got off and noticed a sign on the window that read, "Yes, we're open!" I hesitantly stepped in. It was eerie, I asked God in my mind, *"God, why is everything around me under construction?"* I made my way to a table that looked good for study and ordered with the app to skip the line. I sat down and opened my devotional journal to a fresh blank page. As I opened the blank page I heard God tell me,

"I Am rebuilding you. You are under construction."

It hit my heart so hard I began to cry as soon as I heard it. Businessmen around me, moms with their toddlers struggling to hold conversations with each other, and college students studying all surrounded me, and I didn't care. I fell apart. Despite how busy my surroundings were, I sat there alone with God at the 6 o'clock hour in a busy Starbucks on a weeknight.

So there I stood in Rome, in the looming darkness, in a place that was usually full of tourists and I found myself enjoying this gorgeous masterpiece – under construction. I didn't mind that the water was not there. I didn't go for the water I went for the sculpture. The beauty and magnificence of the artwork was incredible. God told me again I was under construction and I felt it by the time I reached that construction site. *"No, I get it. I get the message loud and clear God. Construction. Tearing down. Re-building..."* I mean, I felt it inside.

Before arriving to Rome, I hit a breaking point. My friend Nia and I had a falling out in Paris. I felt I was in the right for being hurt by her actions, but I could have handled my response with words and not completely just checking out afterwards. We went our separate ways for the most part after that but were scheduled on the same flight to Rome. We had a long layover and she met some girl and left with her instead of waiting at the airport. She thought check-in would be easy, but she arrived too late and missed the flight as I boarded. I sat in my seat at the airplane alone, reading her text that she missed the flight. I felt so bad for her. I told her to be careful and asked about where she would stay. There was nothing I could do to help her. I couldn't put what I felt in words, but I felt God working in me. I was so tired and prayed to God for Nia, that she would be comfortable and safe wherever she stayed.

I recalled my reaction. I thought of how much I cared about her and how hard it was to think I wouldn't be friends with her again. I thought of how upset I was and how little patience I had at that point in my life. I was tired in general, and then I just started crying. That was probably the tearing down part of construction happening inside me. There was a muslim woman sitting next to me with her husband, or at least I assumed they were muslim. She asked me if I was okay in broken English and I shook my head yes. She looked really worried about me, but I didn't want to talk to anyone. I felt God tell me this was a time for me to reflect on seeing myself

The Pantheon - Rome, Italy

Well...The Trevi Fountain under construction - Rome, Italy

the way God sees me. I prayed about it and wrote a list of descriptive words in my journal. Daughter of God, light-bearer, evangelist, loving, forgiving, worshiper, creative, risk-taker, trailblazer, peacemaker, passionate, committed, consistent, reliable, courageous, focused…the list went on. I tied it all together in one word, God's *beloved*.

It was getting late as I stood reflecting on my trip and starring at the fountain. I walked in no particular direction but stumbled into an Italian restaurant for dinner. I sat alone and thought back on the idea of rebuilding myself, what that meant an what it would look like. What all that construction would be. I ordered a classic pasta dish with red sauce. After dinner I walked over to buy gelato for dessert. I looked at these amazing structures all within this one city, still standing after so many years. The Temple of Hercules Victor is the oldest building and dates to the 2nd century BC, which makes it the oldest surviving building in the city of Rome. That building was once used as a church. It's over 2,000-years-old and you have to wonder how it's possible that they are still standing, so many structures that survived all those years. I mean today, a storm can reach the Caribbean and totally destroy every structure in it's path. In Texas, a tornado will touch down and completely consume our million dollar neighborhoods. It takes just one storm. So, to see so many Roman ruins remain over 2,000 years later, is fascinating.

If you've been through seasons of difficulty, brokenness, lost relationships, uncertainty about the future, regret and feel years have been wasted, you may find yourself at that same position I did. In the hands of God and under construction. After all that, it's the best place to be: a point of restoration. In your own life, years you felt may have been wasted, that carried regrets and broken relationships, led to uncertainty. You look back and wonder what was the point of some things. Years wasted may look like your life not aligning to the promises of God, having lived through the same cycle without seeing progress or breakthrough. The pressure you went through, the heartbreak, the disappointments, the chaos, all of it was not supposed to destroy you, but shape you and build you up.

> *"So everyone who hears these words of Mine and acts on them, will be like a wise man [a far-sighted, practical, and sensible man]who built his house on the rock. [Luke 6:47-49] And the rain fell, and the floods and torrents came, and the winds blew and slammed against that house; yet it did not fall, because it had been founded on the rock.*
>
> *And everyone who hears these words of Mine and does not do them, will be like a foolish (stupid) man who built his house on the sand. And the rain fell, and the floods and torrents came, and the winds blew and slammed against that house; and it fell—and great and complete was its fall."*
> *- Matthew 7:24 – 27 AMP*

You have the tools you need right now to undergo rebuilding. Jesus explains that those who take action and do what Christ instructed and follow through with His teaching will be the ones who will not be destroyed by the storms of life. We are commanded to build ourselves up strong in Christ as the solid foundation.

The construction process requires tearing down. God has to tear down the damage and remove things in disrepair. What was no longer working has to go. It has to look like nothing before it looks like something. The work begins with the foundation first and in this case, we have to take the word of God, understand it in context, and take action to apply it to build solid foundation in our lives. It's so easy to build on sand, that is to build ourselves up on whatever the world and others serve us as truth.

When under construction, the structure looks bad. It doesn't look like what the plans show immediately. While we can read scriptures with all of God's promises for us in this life, it's hard to believe it when we see disrepair in ourselves. Even if we see nothing change as we apply God's word, in time we will step back and see ourselves standing strong.

I, more than most people, love a good book. I mostly read business

CONSTRUCTION

books on strategy, and memoirs of people who overcame adversity. I love books from successful leaders on how to improve interpersonal skills, and learn interesting topics in the area of business management and leadership. All of these incredible leaders and successful people give advice based on their own opinions, ideas, and the analyzed outcome of their experiences, but I have to be careful not to believe man's idea of building up a successful life. If I were to adopt their ideas as complete truth and implement them into my life, I will end up having built a life on sand. We run to everything out there, just to find out it's sand. We pay for expensive conference tickets, chasing the Tony Robins of the world, investing in businesses, purchasing assets, working on refining our ability to be the best versions of ourselves, attending events to connect with the right people, and we're chasing the life built on sand. To chase the acceptance from people, family members, friends, pastors, leaders, mentors, above the affirmation of God is building a life on sand. I had to go back to God with basics to fully understand what success meant from His perspective.

In view of the structures in Rome, they were built as an initiative by each Roman emperor who had an ambition to 'overshadow' his predecessor. They saw the building as making his own mark on the map of Rome and leaving their mark in history. This tells us that the intention and purpose behind the details on how each building was constructed was well thought out by one person.

Your future is well thought out by one person too, with specific details laid out in a master plan. I worked with engineers for a season in my life and learned that a quarter inch matters, a lot. I recall my co-worker once arguing on a call, "I'm looking at the drawings, and I don't understand where you got that quarter inch." You can't make a mistake when building structures and the details are so specific and precise. Then someone has to sign off on the final drawings. God is that specific and precise about the details in your life, considering how He wants to build up your life. The details of what the finished 'you' should look like are in His sight.

"Build your house on the rock." Jesus is the rock, our firm foundation. Notice Jesus said YOU build your house…it's your responsibility to do it. Let's acknowledge and own up to this fact. You get to build with Christ on your own volition, or you simply don't. Either way, it was up to you, not someone else and so we can't blame others for where our lives ended. Regardless of where you chose to build, the storm is coming. Not *if* a storm comes, but the scripture says, *"the rain descended, the floods came, and the winds blew and beat on that house".*

The storm is coming, how are you building?

Las Vegas, Nevada U.S.A.

CHAPTER 26

Henderson

omething's wrong. Oh God help me relax...Why am I so nervous?' I didn't know why but I knew something was wrong. The thought came that I would not make it to this Vegas trip before I sat on the plane. Although that's unusual, I felt uneasy about boarding. I talked to myself and prayed against anything bad happening. I sat in my window seat and closed my journal awaiting takeoff. Thirty minutes passed...then an hour passed and the plane was still parked with passengers inside. I began to pray, *"God, right now, if we are not supposed to be on this plane, do something to get me off. If there is something wrong with the plane, don't allow us to take off."* Passengers became irate and began to speak up to no one in particular, complaints about why it's taking so long. The flight attendant got on the intercom to apologize and offered passengers the option to exit the parked plane and be re-routed with another flight. Some passengers began to leave, but I stayed in my seat. I continued praying, *"Nope. Not clear enough. God, you get me off this plane. I don't want a vague sign. Do something now."* Just as soon as I said it, the captain got on the intercom and asked us to all exit the plane, and we would be placed on another flight.

That's clear direction. Relieved, I stood up and walked out.

Boarding the second plane, finally at 2:00 a.m., I kept thinking about freedom for the women I was to meet. It's no coincidence I ended up going on this trip during 4th of July weekend, a time when everyone in America is celebrating freedom. It was Thursday and I was so tired I actually fell asleep, despite my history of not being able to sleep on public places, especially planes. I looked out my plane window and saw a constellation of stars. I have never seen that before on a flight and was amazed at how beautiful it was! I tried to take a photo but the camera did not capture them well. I just soaked it in and thanked God for His beauty.

I really felt God speak to me to stop holding back from serving Him within a church. *'No, don't make me, I don't want to...'* I thought. I had been through a lot from church people and leaders that I backed out of church ministry and just shared God in ways I felt He asked me to. Which is not wrong. I did more for God in my opinion, when I left a church leadership roles than I did filling them. Something told me God would place me in a ministry to serve soon though, and I had to let go of the negative feelings I had about it. I landed in Vegas exhausted with little to no sleep.

Vegas is lively. It looks glamorous and alluring, with bright lights and the nonstop activity of events to attend. People were partying everywhere, and I noticed families as well as singles all ready for a fun time in the strip. Families were out late with little kids in the casino at midnight. My host on this outreach was Victoria, a friend I met in college in Texas. She was a young, single and gorgeous Latina in her 20s. She didn't look like what you would imagine a missionary sex trafficking ministry worker would look like. I don't know if you would have a picture of what that may look like. You may picture an older lady who wears like long skirts and comfortable walking shoes. Jehovah's witness aesthetic. Or a middle aged woman who doesn't use much make up and you question if she just rolled out of bed because she's so busy she looks like she didn't brush her hair. Because that's what I would picture if I heard "missionary for human trafficking workers." Meek, shy and reserved.

Victoria was none of the above. She was actually very young doing that type of work in her mid-20s and dressed very stylish. She wore trendy tops, fitted jeans and a high wedged strappy shoes that perfectly matched her outfits. She put on some ripped short shorts with wedges a few times, fit for the Nevada dry hot climate but not acceptable to most non-denominational Christian leaders in the south. She was a busy bee type of ministry worker, with a precise calendar, organized ministry tasks and fierce determination. The women she met in the industry became her friends, and she authentically shared the love of Christ with them as part of a large organization that focused on a mission to eliminate sex trafficking in the U.S.

I met Victoria in college as she attended another university. I was at DBU and she attended a seminary school called Southwestern Assembly of God University (SAGU). We became friends as we both went to the same church in Midlothian. We hung out a lot and I introduced her to many of my friends. She was so fun and always down to go out last minute. I once convinced her to break curfew and had her sneak back into her dorm at night. Christian colleges have strict curfew. It wasn't that serious. It maybe happened more than once, I don't know. She graduated and pursued the missionary life and I was so proud of her.

I arrived at her cozy apartment in Henderson, ready to hit the ground running. "Okay so we'll freshen up, I'll give you a Human Trafficking 101 session, then I'm taking you out to Night Observation, where I will show you the strip and how to identify victims," she said. She gave those trainings to groups who organized a missionary outreach in Vegas with her organization. She saw ministry leaders, mostly women, who attended churches and went through training and guiding them through an outreach experience in sex trafficking. Few men participated but those who did would stay in the sidelines waiting in vehicles outside or working behind the scenes while she took the ladies out on site to the strip clubs and brothels.

All I can tell you is that this outreach is not for the weak. I was convinced that even the most mature, experienced women in ministry would find it a challenge to handle that time of ministry work.

CHAPTER 27

Casinos

Night Observation was like a scripted scene being played out right before my eyes. Victoria walked me to a casino in the strip which she said was a common starting point in the working girls' night. Casinos are over-glamourized. They all looked the same to me. They all carried a stench and reeked of many different smells, as if all the money in town could not pay enough carpet cleanings to get it off. Cigar. Liquor. People's cheap and expensive colognes mixed together. Here and there, the smell of an antique store, Dallas Public Library, a whiff of bad decisions, I don't know. Victoria stopped me at a specific location inside, across from a large bar and began to brief me.

"First, just a reminder that out of respect for the women, we adopted the term 'working girls' for prostitutes, escorts and stripers. You'll see that working girls don't look like what people typically expect them to look like. You know, like what Hollywood shows them to look like, a tight mini dress and high heels. Actually, many of these women look like someone in your family, they are very normal, and carry themselves well and dress regular."

She was right. They looked like any other woman I would see in my circle of friends, co-workers, even church friends. One of the girls specifically reminded me of one of my best friends back in Dallas.

"Here in Vegas, we have different types of working girls, some charge less and some charge a crazy amount for their service." Continued Victoria. "Like how much is it for the expensive ones?" I asked.

"It depends on the service but it can be in the high thousands per night."

"And men pay that much!?" I replied completely shocked.

"Yea girl! Crazy right? So, typically we will find some girls start here in this casino, and they walk around in two's in the beginning of the night, looking for clients. We'll find them soon here it's about that time."

She walked me up and down this casino near the bar area and there we spotted two girls, dressed nicely, and like a light switch, began to flirt with a guy at the bar together.

The guy was clearly there alone, for business, wearing a stuffy corporate outfit. He wore a nice collared shirt with his coat hung on his chair.

He looked annoyed and stressed. He looked to be in his late 40s to mid 50s.

"He's the perfect client. He's here for work, so they will start saying something to flirt with him and see if he's interested in one of them." We watched them suddenly become animated, big smiles, touching their hair, leaning in on him. He was annoyed. "Aaaaaaaand...NOPE. Sorry girls, he's not a catch. Okay they're leaving don't look...let's keep walking," said Victoria as I followed after her lead. "So, he wasn't interested so now they are moving on to see who else they can find." We saw the girls giggle loudly, to cover up their embarrassment, after the man gently rejected their advance. They quickly paced over our direction to leave the area for the next opportunity.

"Wow they look young. How old do you think they are?" I asked. *"They are young."* she replied, "I'm telling you many of these girls start at the age of 14, they are underage probably. Let's follow them."

We followed them in the crowded casino past a group of about 4-5 guys who looked to be at least 25 – 30 years old. Like they were young guys, but not that young, and had some years of partying experience behind them. The guys quickly sniffed the girls out in the large crowd with drinks in hand. This told me they had solicited working girls before as they identified them without being approached. We were near the slot machines really close to them and the girls as they got closer to each other and saw them joke to each other pointing the direction of the girls. One guy from the group followed after them in front of our eyes, not realizing we were watching the whole thing. *'OMG don't do it. Please...don't do it.'* I thought in my mind, as if he could actually hear my thoughts over the explosive crowd. *'Just turn around, please don't...'* The girls were walking fast paced and we observed how the guy all of a sudden changed his mind. His facial expression changed suddenly for no apparent reason. He didn't see us notice him, he was looking at them as if they had a crosshair mark on their bodies and suddenly his facial expression turned into regret. I stared at him and we caught eyes near the end of his paced walk. I locked eyes with him. I simply don't understand. Part of me was upset with him, and the greater part of me felt sad for him. He stared back like my thoughts were so loud, despite the boisterous casino crowd. He turned around to return to his friends. He needed rescuing too.

By definition, human trafficking is the exploitation of a person through force, fraud, or coercion for the purpose of forced labor or commercial sex. Most are forced into it, with threats, lies and instilling fear in the victim. Pimps begin to build a relationship and 'groom' their victims early. Men groom girls by attending to their needs, telling them what they

CASINOS

want to hear, then beating them when they disobey. As a result the victim stays faithful. The average age of a boy or girl sold into sex slavery is 12 – 14 years old. The data points to broken families who fail to look after the girls at an early age. Parents are so worried about their jobs or other things and they neglect their kids. Siblings, like mine, who have no idea what is going on with their brothers and sisters when they walk home from school. Pimps frequent bus stations to find their next victim, as many are runaway teens and some even frequent schools to coerce a new victim. I learned that unlike what most people believe, prostitution is illegal in Las Vegas. Only certain counties in Vegas have a permit.

Many working girls I met on this trip didn't see themselves as a victim. Yet, I saw that they actually were enslaved. The chains were on their minds, not a physical binding. They didn't ask for help because many had already learned to be comfortable in the lifestyle. They learned helplessness, distrust, guilt, fear, shame and some even felt indebted to their trafficker. There were some who worked in the brothel and did not have a pimp, but began selling themselves out of a desperate need for money, not realizing what they were getting into. Also, they did not look like what you would think a working girl would look like. They looked like the average woman. I want to re-state here that they seriously looked like your mom, your sister, your aunt, your daughter.

One thing is for sure, for each woman I met, they have a very ugly perception of men and after the trip was over, I completely understood why. They sexually service every type of man you can imagine including men you and I may naturally admire, like church leaders. They engaged in sexual acts with married men, successful business owners, celebrities, ministers and everything in between. Regarding married men, the working girls told me the truth is that the way it happens, it's highly likely that their wives may never find out. Working girls view marriage as a complete joke at best. Their image of men in general is completely tarnished and all men are the same in their eyes. They truly believe, there are no good men out there.

We moved on to the second floor of the casino and Victoria explained this is where you can see a better view of the girls working the floor. We didn't find many on that angle so moved on to walk the path she says they commonly see them move on to, out of the hotel on to the Vegas strip to the next casino. As we walked, Victoria continued to explain, "The girls are usually posted up here walking up the street looking for their next client, and across this street her pimp is usually parked watching her work." She walked in a fast pace and continued, "Within this time frame of her walking the strip looking for a John, she is not allowed to go up to her pimp's car and talk to him as he doesn't want to be noticed or take up her time from another client... They move fast and can quickly identify the type of man that would solicit them. They just know." I struggled to walk fast enough, dodging the tight foot traffic on the strip.

"So once they have their client, what does the pimp do? Like does he stay there or ..."

"He'll leave, and she knows how to report to him after she's done." She said.

"And she doesn't take any opportunity to just leave him? I mean for a girl who was tricked into it and is desperate to get out, like she can't just run!??" I asked.

"Ugh...I know you would think, right.? But it's not that simple. They are usually threatened with their lives. You would think that a threat would not scare people but they are told things like, her pimp was going to kill her mom or family member she loved, so they cooperate. Many find it impossible to leave or even dare to leave. Many who actually got to leave, they were found again and received horrible beatings from the pimp. So they don't try it again."

I heard of a girl who had her pimp turn on the curling iron and burned the girls' private as a consequence some years ago in Cali. Other women had severe beatings where their teeth were knocked out by their pimp and suffered serious injuries where they had to be hospitalized and afterwards, because she was afraid, returned to her pimp.

"Okay right there, there's two." She said.

"Where..."

"Those two girls we are coming up to here, they're working together and it looks like they are getting approached by that guy. They're less aggressive than the last two."

The girls looked like just two girls dressed up on a girls trip.

"Yup...there he goes, let's see what the guy does."

We saw how they brushed together and the guy just lingered unsure.

"Here's another girl. She looks new." Victoria said, directing my attention to another girl accompanied by a guy.

"How can you tell?" I asked.

"Because, the guy talking to her like he's giving her a lecture, that's not her boyfriend, that's her pimp." Victoria said he was briefing her on what to do and what the plan was. It was like another world happening with the rest of the world around us completely unaware.

"Walk slow, walk slow, stay behind them." She said.

I followed her lead and in shock. The girl must have been not much older than nineteen, but knowing what I know now, she was probably just fifteen with a lot of makeup to make her look older. She looked scared. The closest I could describe her attitude to was those girls dating an abusive boyfriend. You know those pretty girls that didn't have many friends or a good family to give them a wake up call about the loser she's dating. The kind that are gorgeous on the outside but dying on the inside for many reasons. The ones that have a very controlling and jealous boyfriend, where she looks miserable and tortured but stays with him. Like that. Dirty blond hair, very slim figure, a tight fitting skirt that honestly I would wear, and a crop top appropriate for the Vegas heat. Cute elegant heels. The Christian girls celebrating their friends' bachelorette party earlier had skimpier outfits on. I'm joking. They passed the three inches below the knee rule. Kidding again. But seriously, the girl looked like today's average young adult. Just normal.

The guy was a white guy, and he looked like he was maybe in his 30s and he was young too. I didn't want to believe it. I was hoping Victoria was wrong and he was just a jealous boyfriend and we were not seeing a pimp leave a working girl on the strip for the first time.

"Hey, *maybe it is* just her controlling jealous boyfriend…" I said.

"No… That's a pimp, I'm positive. She's new. Keep watching."

I saw how he suddenly stopped her, told her a few other things in a way that looked like whispering, you know, like speaking under his breath. Which I thought, why in the world would he be whispering it's super loud out here. The girl listened attentively with an empty stare at a far distanced object, nothing in particular. She looked like she was having tunnel vision. We had to pass them and as I turned to look back, I saw him walk away

107 Sky Lounge - Las Vegas, Nevada

from her. She began to walk and look around. WOW.

"See?" said Victoria.

"Maaaannn…." I said in shock. She was right. "I say that's a wrap here." I said. That was a lot.

There was so much going on and a lot to soak in. It's a completely hidden world within the regular day-to-day world most people are living in. We were nearing the end of the route Victoria and her team had mapped out, where the girls finish their walk for the evening to pick up men. Then, we headed out to 107 Sky Lounge. It was a cute trendy place on the 107th floor that gave you an amazing view of Vegas. Overlooking the city, I realized Vegas is actually very small. We kicked our heels up and took a pic as a memory, talking about what we just saw, hearing more about Victoria's experiences and catching up on each others' lives.

When we got back to the apartment, I slumped down to bed exhausted. I fell asleep wondering how the girls night would end and prayed that God would protect them.

CHAPTER 28

Traffic

Boulder highway is a track for prostitution in Vegas. Victoria worked with a focus to find, rescue, embrace and empower working girls. The actual work of getting someone out of the sex industry is so incredibly complex. Everyone's journey is unique. The true definition of sex trafficking is the exploitation of a person through force, fraud or coercion for the purpose of forced labor or commercial sex. Most are women and the alarming reality is that we could get to a point of complete prevention if families did their job of loving and embracing girls at a young age. Just by showing them they are loved and valued at home, so many girls could be saved. Men meet them as young as pre-teens and begin a grooming process to begin to sell them on the streets. They tell them what they want to hear, and convince them they love them by attending to their needs of how the girl accepts love. Each pimp has a different style and they are labeled in different categories by how they coerce their victims. A *'Gorilla Pimp'* is violent and uses force on the victim. A *'Romeo Pimp'* uses charm to target girls desperate for love. A *'CEO Pimp'* uses charm to target girls looking for fame, to be models or entertainers in the industry and they use money and business talk to win them over. I was told some beat them and some don't get aggressive with them, but regardless, all place mental chains on them in order to make it a business. Not much different than other legitimate businesses in the U.S., but I digress.

"Society works against us when it comes to human trafficking" Victoria explained, "The culture, the music, much of society pushes the lifestyle in young people early so they think the lifestyle is appealing or ok." She proceeded to explain the term, *'The Game'* fitting into their culture is important to adopt as normal. Rap culture pushes this a lot into minority communities mostly, with those being the families that are most likely to not watch over their daughters. The language and terms are also important to use with how they communicate, the same as drug dealing. There's no *'eyeballing Johns'* when working as a standard that for the pimp shows ownership and loyalty. They don't get in the car with cops, ever, and never *absolutely never* come home without their quota. *'Daddy'* is a term male traffickers often require victims to call him. *'Wifey'* is how they describe the working girls sometimes, but it doesn't mean loyalty to one girl. A pimp can use that to manipulate them to make them feel important. He can have several wifeys. *'Johns'* are the clients identified as men with mother wounds, facing problems in their relationship with women, attempting to solve them with paying for sex. *'Family'* or *'Folks'* is a reference to describe the other individuals under the control of the same pimp. He plays the role of father (or "Daddy") while the group fulfills the need for a family. *'Bottom Bitc*'* is the woman the pimp trusts the most out of all of them to recruit other women. She works as his right hand and helps to manage the other women. An *'Automatic'* is not under pimp control and she operates without supervision. A *'Renegade'* works on her own will and I never met one in this trip. Branding them is also important, so they get a tattoo with a code that associates her with her pimp or trafficker. A *'Trick'* is sex for money. A *'Track'* is a street where prostitution is known to happen and a *'Circuit'* is a reference to cities along an interstate where transport of trafficked people happens.

They say it's an average of six months for the pimp to convert the victim using Maslow's hierarchy of needs and that's a very short time frame when you consider the years these women stay stuck in the lifestyle. For many it's the entire rest of their lives. Pimps use physical and emotional abuse to keep them bound, many blame them and convince them it's their fault. Many take away their documentation, do everything possible to get rid of their identity and any self-esteem they could have. They kill their light. Victoria explained that a female victim will return to her pimp after running away an average of 5 – 7 times. I was curious why men get to a point of being pimps. It had to be more than money, and I was told deeper reasons included men who come from environments where they needed a sense of power, control and respect. Some get into it because they come from a family that works in the industry.

The work involves so many facets. One is prevention, so Victoria works to partner with schools to bring about education. They go to the hospitality industry for help. I won't describe what they do in hotels, but if you'd like to get involved, there are several organizations in hospitality you could get involved with to contribute and help. Local hotels in your area and high-end restaurants may be part of a program to help prevent human trafficking and have ways you could help. You can also contact your local politicians and advocate for this effort, but we know how that goes. Volunteer in your local schools. Teach a values course for girls in elementary. Volunteer during school pick up to watch the area and report any suspicious individuals who don't have children in the school.

Victoria's organization tries to address the fight on the demand side regarding men and porn addiction that feeds into the industry. I was told very few organizations actually focus on reaching out to Johns though, and Victoria only knew of one. In the nearby area there were 300 massage parlors on the street managed and serviced by Asians. I was told it's a tragic situation where the women arrive from their country being told they will live in an apartment and work in restaurants or retail but they end up sex trafficked in an Asian massage parlor. They reported several are enslaved and some even kept to live in the parlor. They have them so isolated they can't escape or exit and they also don't leave out of just the fear of being in a completely new country where they don't speak the language.

We met with a woman named Kim. She has been working with sex trafficked women for years and teamed up with Victoria for many efforts in Vegas. This lady was impressive. I met her for the first time at a Starbucks in Henderson. She had long healthy fire-red hair, porcelain skin and gorgeous blue eyes. While she is beautiful in appearance and looks like she would be the sweetest lady, you realize very quickly she's not someone to mess with. You'd think that a woman putting herself out there in dangerous situations and trying to rescue women out of sex trafficking would be a certain way – maybe even just look tough. Kim looked like she wouldn't hurt a fly. But the moment she starts talking you realize, *man, this lady will shank a pimp.* Kidding. Only in the right circumstance. Joking. But seriously she was tough. She put up with no crap and tells you straight up how it is. "Men need to man up! They need to take responsibility for all the male issues that drive the sex trafficking industry. First, porn is male-driven. Second, pimps *are all men.* They need to step up and stop the demand. These women hate men, and can you blame them!?" I appreciated her passion.

Kim had been doing ministry for sex trafficked women in Vegas for 10 years. She was married a few times and every husband she had was unfaithful. She also explained she had a traumatic childhood of sex abuse, which naturally led her to become passionate about the sex trafficking industry. Also, her daughter was living on the streets for two years and died twice of a drug overdose. "But God brought her back twice!" She explained. This was not her field of study. She went to business college and also had an interest in homeopathic remedies. She identified as a Christian believer since the age of 12 and became a believer because of a woman named Gloria. Gloria worked at the brothel Rosie's Ranch, and she was still in the sex industry. That alone blew my mind in a way to think that the person who led her to Christ was a working woman.

Kim had a very incredible opportunity, however, to preach to women in the brothel and at one point even baptized them. She took that opportunity without hesitation and held a baptism ceremony for the women. The crazy reality is that when she was just preaching about Jesus one-on-one to the girls and sharing the gospel non-stop as a visitor, there were no problems. When women started saying they gave their lives to Christ, there were no problems. It wasn't until the moment Kim baptized them with water on the brothel campus that they kicked her out completely. What she really wanted to do together with Gloria was to set up a church service, and they were able to hold a few meetings until that baptism service day. "What happened Kim?" She proceeded to tell me the story. "We had service out back where the Bungalows are located and you know, that area is exclusive so usually someone reserves it for high paying clients. We didn't host the meetings inside, just outside the back area. 6 girls wanted to get baptized so we planned for a baptism Sunday. The girls got access to the exclusive part called *The Motel*. I was scared because it was like they were sneaking around in the way they did it. So that day, we went to have dinner at the brothel and waited for all the staff to leave. The girls were going to give me the sign that we could go out and when they did, all the girls came out in their bikinis to the pool area and six girls were baptized in the name of Jesus. When the owners found out they got baptized, that was it and we were not allowed back."

Kim described the service with nostalgia. Kim would bring pastries and they had a minimal program. It was very special. The girls arrived in whatever nightgown or pajamas they woke up in and when looking outside of the pool and started promptly at 10:00 a.m. on Sunday morning, during low traffic hour at the brothel. The women are called "girls" at every age and they would walk out of their rooms wearing robes and furry sandals. Kim arrived prepared with the praise and worship songs printed on paper so they could follow along and sing with her as she led worship. During that time, Kim had a woman visit from Australia to observe her process and launch a similar ministry program over there.

"I just preached God's love to them, and that is something they don't know. I did six sermons. I had six Sundays with the girls." And I saw the deep sadness and regret in her face and in her eyes. I thought she was going to cry, but she restrained herself. "I gave them Bibles. Every girl who came to the service got saved, a total of ten girls." Kim took anointing oil and said she placed it on brothel owners and the girls without them being aware. Some brothels were just trailer homes and some were really small.

Kim told me about this guy she knew who opened one years ago. His name was Paul. Paul's wife died and it was a great loss for him. "Paul was into nasty stuff," she said. "Oh really, isn't it all bad?" I asked. "Yes, but I mean the violent kind, at the end of the filming the girl gets murdered. It sets men up to kill women." Oh God, I thought, it was hard to even hear her say everything she told me about Paul, but I did not interrupt her. I'll leave those details out. She continued, "First thing you saw when you walked into his brothel was a bar. He had tiny TVs, three. One as you enter and others on a table. So, no matter where you turned you saw mess. When you walked in you had to keep your eyes down." She explained how Lisa, her ministry partner has to stay out because she refused to go into that brothel. Lisa *hated* Paul. "She stayed in the car to pray but she didn't want to go in the first place. Well, Paul told me, *'Don't ever buy TVs at home Depot, every time I go in and get a TV they break.'* And we didn't know that the women in the car were praying the TVs would break! The weird thing Paul did also was that he would give the women gas money after visiting for ministry work with the girls. He would say, here's for gas before they left. Kim wrote a book about the experience she had ministering to the girls in the brothels and Paul died reading it. Kim believes he got saved reading her book because at the end, she leads the reader to a prayer of Salvation. Two other women who worked in partnership with Kim feel the same way, that Paul surrendered his life to Christ.

"He liked Snickers." She continued...and paused as though she thought of other things about him but didn't say them aloud. He died of a heart attack leaving his beloved possession, a Chrysler 500. He called it "Shady Ladies" and gifted it to Kim in his will. I was like *wow*. "Yes he did. I changed the name to Church Ladies", she said with a giggle. "That's what the working girls call me and my team." That was amazing to me. You know, the detail that Kim would know so much about the brothel owners when most people would not want to have one conversation with any of them. She told me about another guy who loved home made peanut butter cookies.

The girls moved around and changed their names after they moved from a brothel. I sat at the Starbucks listening to Victoria and Kim talk about a few of the girls and give each other updates on how they were doing. One was 40 and she recently left the industry completely, but she couldn't find a job to support herself. That part was difficult because they made so much money in a brothel, that after they left, they were so used to that lifestyle of luxury and suddenly could no longer afford it. Another girl, Ana, was recently saved and was going to church on Sundays. Both Kim and Victoria explained how they would never disclose to anyone in the church that she was a working girl as a standard for how they protect them. Ana sold Mary Kay. Then they spoke of a woman who used to work with their organization who was newly assigned to disciple Ana.

Kim and Victoria work with women in strip clubs, massage parlors and brothels. They described two different strip clubs and focused on the foundation of entering into new clubs to introduce themselves and befriend the working girls. "Strip clubs are worse than brothels," said Kim, and Victoria agreed. They are sent from different cities to work other cities, from Dallas to Vegas, to Houston. They described how some girls did have to perform intercourse with men and some were shocked to realize they were required to. Some of the girls got saved and wanted to join them in the work they do. Many working girls face the reality that their exit plan has to extend over several years. They spoke of another woman, she was a Puerto Rican woman, who got married and sent money back home to her family in Puerto Rico. She put her nephew through college and bought homes in Puerto Rico and Thailand. She wanted to join the work in spreading the gospel but it sounded like she was stuck not wanting to lose all the financial benefits that the industry had to offer her. She was having difficulty giving up all the money that provided for her and her family.

Victoria and Kim do prayer cards that they share with a picture of each working girl and prayer notes like "Pray Psalm 141" on the back of the card. They wrote each girl's stage name and location and any details they knew about each one to keep track of how they're doing. Sometimes they included their age or any other detail about them and they prayed for 40 days at a time.

They used Neil Anderson's spiritual warfare training and Kim told me she used to also do drug and alcohol addiction counseling for them. She saw that God especially gifted her to pray for people who are healing from trauma, post-traumatic stress and anxiety. Kim called it 'prayer counseling with severely abused women'.

I left this meeting, *beyond impressed.*

CHAPTER 29

Free

"Okay, look at me," Kim said to Victoria, with a hard piercing stare. Literally, fiery flames blew out of her pupils. You know, the way a mom tells her kid something when they are dead serious. "I'm going to take you inside *this one time* but *do not ever go back in there*. Just this once. Unless you want a happy ending, don't go back there". Yes she was dead serious. I was preparing myself mentally for whatever we were about to see that Kim didn't want Victoria to go back in there for.

We headed to China Town. Kim said there were about 300 massage parlors just on Spring Mountain road. "They're all connected you know, the parlors in Nevada have connections to those in New York and other cities. The last time I went, I got a massage by a lesbian woman. I gave her a Chinese Bible but she still asked for her tip." Kim took us to one she goes to pray for people at that she felt was not so bad.

The plan was simple. We prayed in the car before entering and were going to each get a regular massage because there would be no other way to go back where the women were working. I asked for just a back massage, even though I didn't want one. Kim, Victoria and I were all three next to each other in the same room. The assigned a guy to me and he smelled of nicotine and greasy takeout. I prayed for him to let go of the nicotine and asked God to bless his hands. Nothing about it was out of the ordinary. I wrote his Chinese name down. I pulled my phone out to Google translate a message for him. I Google translated "Jesus loves you. May God Yahweh reveal Himself to you. May God Yahweh anoint your hands to teach and preach the Gospel of Jesus Christ." I asked Victoria to write it on a piece of paper and tore it off my journal.

The massage was fast, I gave the message to him with cash tip wrapped inside. I told the lady at the register, who was his boss, that I wanted to give him the note because I assumed I needed her permission. She was confused and I asked if he spoke Chinese. She said yes, as she took my note and read it. Then she said "Ugh…oh ok." Like she was annoyed it was a Christian note and handed it to him.

We walked out and Kim told us, "You know the brothel capital of the world is Israel? Tel Aviv. There are 300 brothels and maybe more." Kim does a lot of work. For example, she set up in an apartment and made it a

343

prayer room in a complex where she knew that women were working. She told me some people have even donated hotel rooms for her to do ministry in hotels. Kim said, "Some of the prostitutes, their own mothers or husbands are their pimps. There are others girls who made the decision alone and say their husbands don't know. They think she's just leaving 2 weeks at a time to work in Vegas at the casinos." The way she has conversations, was so rich in valuable life advice too. Kim would give you life advice just all of a sudden in the middle of an explanation of the sex industry work she did. At one point she said, "If you don't want someone to lie to you, don't ask them questions". I stopped her and said, "Why?" She responded, "Oh because they are most likely to be honest when they are ready to talk." So I said "What if you need to know?" Then she paused and looked at me really straight forward and very seriously said, "Then just ask the Lord. He tells you everything you need to know." I loved her so much.

 I learned it takes a lot for someone in the sex trafficking industry to be set free from that life. There are many things working against each working girl and the impact doesn't look like what most people would want to see when they ask about how many women see freedom. That is, there are no large numbers that Victoria can report at the end of the year to show proof of the effectiveness of their work, as some may think would be the case. Victoria explained with frustration how she raised money year-round to support the missionary work she does. After giving a presentation at a church, the pastors would ask her how many women she was able to 'rescue' out of the industry the previous year and she tries her best to explain

My morning jog. - Henderson, Nevada

to them how it's not that simple and the pastors are left confused. They seem to need numbers to measure the impact in order to provide her with funding. You really have to understand the full picture and take the time to learn about what the life of a sex worker is like in order to see why it's not as easy as a salvation prayer, and they're 100% out of the industry the next day. Victoria and Kim also expressed that many religious people would deny the working girls were ever truly saved, even after praying the same salvation prayer that, for example, a person would pray at a Sunday morning church altar. The reason being that in some religious people's opinion, it's not a true salvation because the woman is still working in the brothel.

Impact and progress looks like the list of all the girls who were willing to open up and talk to them. Impact looks like the list of those who prayed the prayer of salvation, which may take months after they opened up. Progress looks like a working girl putting together an exit plan, even if it spans the next several years. Impact looks like the amount of girls who started reading their Bibles on a regular basis, even if they were reading it at the strip club. Impact is a small seed deposited in their mind about being able to see themselves no longer working in the sex industry in their future. Also, impact is the faith watered within their hearts with every visit that these ladies make, to show them that they are valuable, that they matter, that they are loved and truly cared for by someone. I mean, loved and cared for without them giving away a piece of themselves or without someone wanting anything in return for quality time spent.

While these women who minister in the sex trafficking industry work year-round and bring the working girls gifts to make them feel special, I clearly saw that the greatest gifts they arrived with were unseen. Gifts like salvation in Christ, and words of comfort and support when they desperately need to hear encouragement. Gifts like not casting judgement on them for their decision to be a working girl, when many live in constant shame. Gifts like a friendship that offers a sense of sisterhood, when they are disconnected from their blood family. Also, they bring the unseen gift of sincere love that asks nothing of them in return. You know, the greatest non-tangible gifts, like showing up to meet them as the image of Christ.

CHAPTER 30
Working Girls

"Hiiiiii", we said sheepishly, necks bent, eyes batting. "Hello, may I help you?" She barely cracked the door open enough to poke her head through it. *Are you kidding me?* I thought, *She looks like a freakin' kindergarten teacher! What in the world are you doing here lady!?* You know, a kindergarten teacher. The sweet kind that takes her job seriously. The kind who actually cares about teaching and takes their sweet time with each child. The kind who speaks with a nice, high-pitched voice even when correcting a child for poor penmanship. The kind that looks like she bakes the best cookies for her half dozen grandkids. You know, like the kind of lady that says, "Spring showers bring May flowers!" That kind. She had rosy cheeks, thick and round shaped figure, and her rosy cheeks plumped up even more as she smiled. She had basic brown hair, styled in a 90s hairdo. Like she used a lot of hairspray but it still looked floppy. She was the brothel keeper, the woman who manages the brothel, also referred to as the Madam.

"Yes, we're here for lunch and have a few gifts for the girls." said Victoria.

"Oh-kaaaaaaaay...let's see what you have here."

She looked through the box of glass mason jars.

"These are inspiration jars, with words of encouragement for the girls to keep in their room," said Victoria.

"Okaaaaay, that's...nice," she replied.

I showed her my bag of jewelry that I brought from one of my boutique wholesalers.

"These are just jewelry sets with encouraging words like faith and strength...and-" I nervously described, as my manicured hand graced the surface of a large embossed pendant with the words Philippians 4. Noticing her kind smile turn into a frown of distaste, I felt nervous. Maybe she didn't notice. Did she see it...?

"Okay...I don't know about these..."

Yup, she saw the scripture on it.

"Oh but it's just jewelry - " I replied.

"I have to ask management if this is okay, give me just a moment before I can allow you to have these back. I will ask and in the meantime, walk you over to the bar."

I had prayed over that jewelry, and prayed for each woman that would end up wearing it. I began to ask God to do something, to let them approve it and allow us in.

We were at Rosie's Rodeo, a brothel.

"This has never happened to me before and I've been here with different gifts several times." Victoria said to me as we walked in. "It's okay, we'll get it to them." I responded.

We entered what looked like an old portable hotel, with vintage pure white curtains, Elvis Graceland looking details, glass light fixtures, and Victorian vintage furniture. The Madam walked us to the sports bar where we would have lunch, and it was like any other sports bar. Beer, drinks, T.V.s and greasy fried food. Unlike most other sports bars however, they had some of the working girls walking around in lingerie or barely there outfits mingling with clients. The bar smelled of burger grease and a vintage antique bookstore.

We ordered food in one of the booths and talked as some of the girls walked over to say hi and thank us for the gifts. One of them was a gorgeous blonde, an American girl, named Kristi. We asked where the jewelry was. The two girls rolled their eyes and said they don't know why they

Entering the brothel with gifts. - Undisclosed location, Nevada

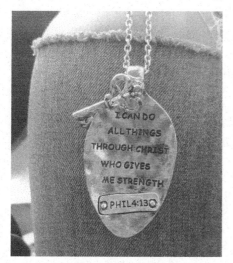

One of the necklaces I brought for the womeen.

did that because they don't usually care. I knew why. Kristi said she was going to check and shortly after returned with the bag of jewelry. She sat with us and I excitedly dove into my bag to show her the different necklaces and asked her to pick one. As we settled into conversation, I really wanted to know more about her and her story.

"How long have you worked here Kristi?" I asked.

"Oh, *a very long time*. I think I'm the veteran in this brothel. I started as a stripper 20 years ago. I retired and joined the brothel and have been here since 2003."

"Wow that is a good while." I said.

"Yes, and I like it here, it's safe and comfortable. We have the freedom to set our own schedules." She said that, not fully convinced of her own words. She was beautiful but seemed sad, even when she smiled. "I got into this work because when I was stripping, and then my regulars would frequently ask me if they could take me home, and that's illegal. So I thought, well maybe I should do it, but I want to make sure I do it the most legal and safe way. So I remembered how some of my frequent clients at the strip club told me about Rosie's and so I googled it and applied."

"I'm glad you chose to think of your safety. I've never been to a brothel before so this is my first time. I don't know much about it." I said.

"I really didn't either. I learned brothels started in trailers and back then, it was taboo so trailers were in the middle of nowhere and served mostly truck drivers on their long routs."

"Do you have kids? A husband?" I asked.

"No husband, but I have a boyfriend. Well this guy….And no I don't have kids. It is too late for me to have kids now." She replied looking like she really accepted it and was ok.

"What was that brothel that was on the news recently, you know the one that Lamar Odom overdosed at recently? It was all over the news, what was it called…" I asked them.

"UGH. The Love Retreat, that's that pig Damon Huff's place."

Another girl who sat with us jumped in to agree with an eyeroll.

"I hate that guy. Nobody in our industry likes him, he's an a-hole." the other woman added.

Kristi continued, "Yea, several of us don't like him, he's a disgusting human being. I would never work in any of his properties." If a working girl says a man is a disgusting human being, you should believe her.

"He owns more than one?" I asked.

"Yes, and it's not because I work here, but Rosie's is the best and cleanest brothel where they actually take care of the girls the best."

They told me that Damon Huff was a pimp and the owner of half a dozen brothels. I mean, first of all, if working girls say a man is 'a pig', that must be 100% factual information. They would most definitely know. They told me he had raped and had non-consensual sex with some of his brothel workers, without protection, and got away with sexually abusing the women that worked at his brothels. I learned there were several cases reported yet he never did any jail time, and still holds active licenses for all his brothels. One of the women that the ministry ladies met was one of those women who filed a case against him and she was told that her "paperwork was lost".

An Asian woman walked over and sat next to Victoria. She was beautiful and seemed well over 40, but looked like she hid it well with beauty treatments.

"What have you got here!? I love this jewelry! It matches my bracelet!" she said.

"Yes, pick a set! What is your name?" I asked.

"Gina."

"Gina, I like your make up," I said, "Thanks, it's porn make up," she replied playfully, yet I think she was serious. Her husband knew she worked in the brothel and said he was ok with it because it's just business.

Kristi stepped away and in our booth remained 3 women, Gina, and two other girls, Vienna and Ariel. We explained the meaning behind each gift and shared that we wanted to just visit and encourage them. They were so thankful and appreciative. We talked about how the rest of them got started in the work.

Vienna has been there 2 years, Ariel just 1 week. She looked to be the youngest of the group there that day. She said she had the idea to apply and work there to help pay her way through college. "I'm a little nervous, but it's just temporary. This is my first week and I'm learning a lot. But it's temporary, so as soon as I pay off school I'll be done here." We all silently said the same thing without saying it aloud. We knew she would likely stay stuck there like everyone else. I mean by God's grace and miracle maybe she would leave one day. I didn't think she had any idea what she got herself into. I screamed silently with a warm smile, *'GET OUT NOW. Get out before it's too late and your life changes forever!'* I mean, just a short time of work there would strip away so much from you – not only mentally, but spiritually. God. But all that came out of my mouth after the warm smile was a weak blab about how I commended her for her desire to finish school. She tried to study in the brothel in between clients whenever she could.

I was told that women serviced, on average, about 10 – 15 clients a day. It's hard to wrap your head around that reality. Their schedules were 2 weeks on and 2 weeks off. So for 2 weeks, they worked in the brothel and stayed there as you would a hotel stay. Some said they were allowed to go out of the property but only to buy groceries or toiletries they needed. They were not really allowed to just go in and out. The two weeks schedule was planned around their menstrual cycle. Some of them lived hours away and could easily slide back into their regular lives after each two weeks, without being noticed by friends or family. Each one gave their family their own story for why they disappeared for 2 weeks.

Vienna shared how it was difficult for her to have a boyfriend because they didn't understand and she waited a long time to trust them enough to tell them the truth. She said she started there by just looking it up and applying. She admitted she had no clue what she got herself into. But by the time she wanted out, it was too late and that she had been doing it for 2 years. She didn't see a way out and she said the money was really good.

Kristi returned to sit next to me and finish our conversation, but she had to go with a client. A new woman walked up and took her place next to me. I had noticed her trolling this one guy at the bar who was in front of my eyesight. She was a beautiful black woman named Karina. She was very animated, you know just super-bubbly personality and very animated mannerisms. As I observed her closer though, I realized she was coming off of a high when I starred at her eyes. I would later learn that many working girls can't do what they do without being on drugs and under the influence, because they can't feel anything and forget a lot of it. She had tattoos on her chest and body with a specific symbol on her chest. I asked her about it and she said it was a couples' tattoo she got with some guy.

"I have another boyfriend now. He's in television." she said.

"Does he give you problems for working here like the other girls?" I asked.

"Girl please! I don't care if he doesn't approve of my lifestyle workin' in here. No man can tell me what to do, I'm independent. I do whatever I want!" she exclaimed, with an impulsive eye roll. I believed her.

She looked at the jewelry and nudged it aside like it was cheap plastic made in China. I mean, it was just fashion jewelry and these women only wore designer everything! She nudged a stone necklace, then stood up to return to the floor to get a client. The other women were looking through the jewelry and deciding on which they wanted to keep. I noticed the bar full of men watching us wondering what we were doing there. We were so out of place in their minds probably and they could tell we were friends. They had stopped talking to each other to hear what we were telling the girls, but I doubt they could barely piece it together because we were too far away.

Gina, the Asian woman came back to sit with us and started to open up about her life. She said she was half Colombian and half Philippine. She was a very joyful person who enjoyed laughing and making jokes.

"I just got back from a vacation with my husband and kids." she told me.

"Cool, what did y'all do?" I asked.

"We traveled several states in a trailer, you know getting to see the country. It was a great vacation!"

"What about your husband Gina, does he give you trouble?" I asked just straight up, wondering how she was doing. Wondering if he was a pimp or where she may fall in the order of women if he had more.

"Oh no! My husband knows what I do and supports me! We like that we can do anything and everything together and we have a good relationship." she said happily.

Victoria later told me she had several conversations with her and has asked another worker about her before. Victoria believes her husband is her John who got her into the work and that is actually very common. Not all Johns are violent but the great majority are. She's not sure what type of John he might be, but she can tell Gina is very loyal to him and at least, depicts to be happy and okay with him. Victoria also told me that Johns may have an actual wife, along other working women. I suppose, anything is up in the air and each person is in a unique situation. Most often, the common situation seemed to be abusive for the working girl who was trafficked into the lifestyle.

As I write this, I still believe the majority of women would have chosen a different path, but are now unable to get out.

Karina returned to the table and looked very anxious. She interrupted by asking me,

"Hey, one of the girls I just saw has a necklace on that has a key that says faith. I want one, can I have one?"

"Of course girl!" I said, as I pulled the bag out again and showed her, "I have several, they say different things. I like this one, it says *Strength*."

"I need that one! Awe...which one do you think I should chose, it's hard to chose between the two!" she said as she held both in front of her.

"Take both of them. Here." I said.

"Really? Are you sure?"

"Yes girl, don't worry." I responded, handing both to her.

She put them both on and said, "Awe thank you! I want to sit here and talk to you guys more!...but that guy's waiting on me, I gotta go!" and she ran off. It seemed random and the ladies kept talking, but I stared at her run off to the man who was waiting on her far ahead of us. I realized, as she was talking to him to secure his service, she saw another woman wearing the *'faith'* key necklace and she came back for it before going in to service the client. She was wearing the keys of faith and strength. Right then when I put this together watching her walk away, I wanted to cry. That's the power of prayer and the Holy Spirit of God that will get through to the hearts of people with anything, even a cheap necklace.

One of the women walked back to our table and told the girls that the Madame asked for them to not linger talking to us and get clients. That is, the men who were there for lunch who sat around. We both apologized for taking their time and they said, "No don't worry we like talking to you!" Most went back to work but one last girl walked over to greet us. Her name was Melissa. Melissa was a beautiful fair skinned girl our age, a Latina in her late twenties. She walked over shyly and introduced herself. She had lovely colored eyes and blonde hair but she spoke perfect Spanish.

"Hablas Español!? De donde eres?" I asked where she was from.

"Yes, I'm first generation Mexican here in the US. De Aguas Calientes." We shared gifts with her and I could tell she was ready to share her burden because her eyes were watery as she began to talk to us.

"Is everything okay?" I asked.

"No." She began, and started to cry.

"What's wrong? Can you share?" I asked.

"I'm just going through a lot right now. It's like nonstop problems, one after another. I've decided to leave the brothel, to just leave this lifestyle. But it's like once I made the decision, things keep happening that prevented me from going forward with it because I have to pay financially for things now. One expense after another and I feel overwhelmed. I am a woman of faith, I believe in God and come from a Christian family...Of course they don't know I've been doing this. Only my boyfriend and one other close relative." She explained.

"That is great news though, God will make a way for you to leave! Stay encouraged!" I said.

"I know, I believe that. It's hard sometimes when these things are happening. Well I wanted to ask you a few questions." she said.

"Of course," I responded.

"Well I have a very religious uncle. I had an accident some time ago and he visited me at the hospital. They found a tumor and I was just devastated and confused. I didn't know what to think or do next. I was just, you know in shock. That Christian uncle came to the hospital and told me it was happening because I was not a real Christian."

She continued, "Well, that was years ago while in my early twenties, and he knew I partied."

I interrupted her to assure her, "Melissa, *he was wrong.*"

"Is he!? Because that has bothered me for years. I was very hurt when he said that way back then...I've been wondering if he was right."

She wanted to know if we as Christians, also shared her religious uncles' judgement and opinion about why she got sick and had a tumor. God opened the opportunity for me and Victoria to share love and truth with her. We both took our time to give her our input. This is what I told her, "I'm sorry. It sounds like your uncle maybe isn't a Christian after all. Maybe he is guilty of what he was accusing you of. Some of the ugliest, most hateful people I've met, considered themselves to be Christians." I told her I had my share of horrible experiences with people who were like her uncle. That her uncle did not speak on behalf of God. I encouraged her to pursue God in personal relationship and not worry about what anyone had to say. She began to cry and agreed. I really hoped she believed me and I hugged her.

"Do you have a Bible? You have to read the Bible and pray the scriptures over your life. So take for example, I just read Jeremiah 29:11, which says "For I know the plans I have for you, says the Lord, plans to bless you and not curse you, to give you a hope and a future." Your prayer conversation with God changes from begging God to give you a good future to, "God I KNOW You are a good God. You blessed Jeremiah and made a promise with him, to give him a future and a hope. You are the same yesterday, today and forever, I know your desire is the same for me, to give me hope and a good future. Help me to follow you as Jeremiah did and fulfill the calling you have for me."

I told her how I surrendered my life to God and how I experienced God's power in my life. How God set me free and that I started to read the Bible not understanding it all, but committed to know God more with each chapter. And that's exactly what happened. I shared how when she accepted salvation through faith in Christ, the Holy Spirit would take up residence in her life and becomes a teacher. That when she read scripture, the Holy Spirit would guide and teach her the same way.

"Arisbet, I don't understand why so many bad things have happened to me. I've been seeking God more than ever since I made the decision to leave. I don't understand then, why these things are happening. At one point, I became angry with God."

"It's okay girl. Those feelings are valid. You said you've been seeking God more and then suddenly, all these bad things begin to happen back to back. In my experience, when that has happened to me, it's the enemy trying to discourage me and keep me from pursuing God. Now *why* these things are happening, only God knows the full plan. But what I do know is God uses every situation, good and bad, to make us stronger and grow our faith. It's like growing pains. But God does not send those bad things, the enemy does. So decide today to grow your faith, get in the word and fight. Don't give up and don't get discouraged. You have to grow closer to God."

She agreed and I continued, "I see the heaviness on you, so much heaviness and worry, but God wants you to hand it all over to Him and this is how you do that. Say for example, I have this necklace in my hand, and then I hand it over to you. I'm no longer carrying it. That's how simple it works with God. Say to Him, 'God, this is beyond my ability and control, you deal with this, I can't'" and hand it over to Him." And I handed her the necklace.

She responded, "Another Christian relative said something similar to me recently. I know this is God speaking to me."

Victoria addressed spiritual warfare with her and the importance of her holding on to God as she entered the spritual battlefield daily. She shared how we all experience spiritual warfare, but she was definitely exposed on another level. God's presence was evident the entire time we sat there, despite the darkness surrounding that place.

I saw how the Holy Spirit was working in her and her burdens lifted. She looked like something came off her shoulders and her eyes looked happy! I felt the presence of God so strong. We finished our lunch and closed our tabs. Melissa stayed with us the rest of the time and we talked some more. Kristi walked over and asked if we were going to take the tour, and we said of course! Melissa volunteered to give us the tour.

"First, the client arrives, and are made aware of the rules. The main rule is that they have to use a condom. No matter what service is being rendered, they must use condoms. This is to protect her and the client from contracting an STD. This brothel has made it policy that even behind closed doors the client must use a condom or service will not be given." Melissa began as we walked to the main entrance.

"That seems hard though, I mean, behind closed doors the guy could say that he will pay her extra under the table to not use a condom. I don't know…how can they really control that?"

"Yea, that could happen. But that's her decision, and I would assure you nobody working here is willing to do that. I've had men ask me to service them without a condom and what I say to them is, "I may have a disease, I may not. You don't know that. So you're also at risk here." And he usually backs off after that and says, no, you're right."

Melissa then explained that the clients arrive and then the Madame will have the girls line up so the clients can choose who they want. Then, they discuss the service and price. "We have the ladies line up for him to choose which girl he'd like to book. From there, it's between the working girl and the client. They decide what services he will receive and at what price."

"What if she just doesn't want to? Like the guy chose her but she's grossed out or just does not want to service him. Can she decline?" I asked.

"No. She can't." She replied. I'll leave some details out to protect the girls. But you can get the general idea. Melissa continued walking us down a hallway. "Okay…so I'll show you only the few rooms that are vacant right now. This is the jacuzzi room…" The jacuzzi room looked like it hadn't been updated since the 70s. I was really surprised that the brothel was not more modernized with luxury finishes everywhere considering how much money they must have made.

There were many rooms. Despite the light coming in through the windows in the hallway, it still looked dark inside. The further we walked in, the darker it got. I got to see the bedrooms where the working girls stayed. They were like college dorm rooms and clients were not allowed in there. This was a firm policy to protect the girls and give them some privacy. The other rooms were rooms for servicing clients.

Melissa walked us over and pointed towards a window where we could see far outside. "Out there are the bungalows. Some clients reserve those with the working girl. They are used for private sessions." I realized they were the bungalows where Kim held Bible studies with the women. We continued to walk and I saw the pool where she had baptized several of the working girls. She held Sunday service with them and none of it was a problem with management, until the day that she baptized them in the pool. That day, management kicked her out and banned her from returning. The Sunday church services ended and now, all we could do was just visit, bring gifts and tour. I find that amazing.

WORKING GIRLS

Kim ended joining us, and was allowed in, despite having been kicked out of there in the past. We got to see rooms she probably hadn't seen before, including a dominatrix room. Melissa said the guys who liked dominatrix were the most successful men in business you would ever meet. They were so powerful and highly respected. No one would ever tell them no, so they liked women bringing them under submission and telling them no. Twisted. Melissa understood them somehow. The working girls stayed in dorm rooms that were small, I was really surprised considering the amount of money they brought into that place.

A lot of things may surprise people about brothels. One thing is that men sometimes don't get sex services and just pay to talk to the working girl. You'd be surprised how many married men, all kinds of men, of different backgrounds come to just talk to a woman and leave. Back in Dallas I had a stripper friend who does the same with some of her clients. She also told me some of her regulars at the strip club would want to hang out with her at the bar on her time off and just talk. I asked Melissa why she thought that happened so often. She explained, "Because they are lonely. They could be married and still are lonely. They talk about the problems they have with their wives. The main problem I hear is that their wife doesn't take the time to listen to them or they feel disrespected by their wife. Here, they can say whatever they want and the working girl will just listen, affirm him and they know they won't ever feel disrespected." I responded, "Well duh, because the working girl doesn't put up with all his crap at home!! She can just tune him out and get paid!" We all busted out laughing, because it was so true, and continued walking.

"This is the dominatrix room. Clients who enjoy that type of service are booked here with a licensed dominatrix." This was the darkest room, spiritually and literally. The lights were dimmed very dark. If I remember correctly, the walls were black or dark red. There were chains mounted on the walls and a stripper pole, with seating in front of it.

"What do you mean a *licensed* dominatrix?" I couldn't believe there was a license for that. "That's right." she said, "So I'm a licensed dominatrix and there is one other girl who is also licensed. We are trained to do different commands that bring the client under submission. We use things like whips and chains. It can get violent, so you have to be licensed to do this properly." She said it can be fatal to the client if the person is not properly trained. *Phew.* I asked her how it affected her and she said, "No, I was trained to do this, so a lot of it is just, you know, a process. I follow a process of behaviors to get them under submission and accomplish what they are looking to get out of the experience." But as she said that, I knew she wasn't fully aware of the spiritual darkness she was engaging in each time. I wondered about soul ties involved with each guy, aside from the regular clients, just by her engaging in that process with them. She continued talking but I couldn't hear her anymore as I reached for the wall and began to pray over the room. Victoria asked a few questions but I don't know what she asked. I prayed and stopped paying attention to what was said. I prayed for Melissa, the girls and those who would visit in the future.

    This was the end of the tour. We ended it in the dominatrix room. I took a deep long and loud breath. I can't share everything we saw here, mainly to protect the working girls. We sat in these chairs in front of a stripper pole. "That's so wild." I said just aloud as I sat in front of the stripper pole, slumped down in the audience chair, together with Kim and Victoria next to me. "Yea...it is," Victoria responded. I thought that although she already knew a lot of the information, it was still overwhelming for her. Then, Kim got up off her chair, stepped up to the stage, and did something even *wilder*. She grabbed the stripper pole and began to dance. Victoria and I looked at each other at the same time with eyes wide, like *what is going on here??* Kim did a worship dance that you would see at a non-denominational Christian church where the women wear the long white dresses with hints of a purple ribbon and hold prayer flags or something, arms flailing and twirling all around. "Kim what are you doing?" I asked, as if I had no idea, but I wanted her to explain. "Well, I'm going to go ahead and worship God on here and declare, Satan, you are defeated in the name of Jesus. You let these girls go..." then she stopped talking to me specifically as she continued talking, it became just a prayer aloud as she twirled and danced holding

The drive back to Henderson in the Nevada desert. - Somewhere, Nevada

the pole every so often, until Melissa got back.

My heart was broken. Not just for the working girls, but for the condition of these really broken men. We said goodbye to the girls we saw on our way out, including Melissa. I told her I'd continue to pray for her and hope to hear from her in the future and hear the good news that she made it out of the brothel. As we walked out to the car, I felt so tired! Physically exhausted. I told Victoria, "Wow girl, you are doing such an awesome work for God out here! I mean what you are doing for these women is, *just...priceless!*"I said to her with joy and excitement in my voice. Then, Victoria fell apart in the drivers seat of her car and began to cry. It was not the reaction I expected.

"Why are you crying?" I asked.

"Because, you understand. And…like…people don't understand. I have heard so many people say so many different things and like you're one of the first who seems to get it." She explained.

"Like what do they say?" I asked.

"Like for example, you know how we host the summer missions groups? So we get different Christian ministry groups each year. This one year, I brought a group with their pastor's wife joining them. And you know men are not allowed to go in here with us. So it was the pastor's wife and some of the other legal aged girls from the church group. Well the pastor's wife, she saw everything you just saw. She sat there at the bar, and took the tour. And when we got back in the car, I asked what did she think and she said, "UGH. They are so disgusting!"

"What!? Who is disgusting? The men?" I asked.

"No, she said the working girls are disgusting. She saw everything you did and in the end…" She wiped her tears and held more tears back. "She didn't get it...Like *how* could she say that. Church people are not living the life of the Kingdom of God. I speak at a lot of churches. I spoke at two churches and I see they're ready for me to go, like to wrap it up, get out and so they can go eat their lunch and they're just living a routine. I realize people are not really living for God, they're living a religion." I heard her frustration loud and clear because I saw the same thing in my experiences.

"I agree... I'm sorry she said that Victoria. That pastor's wife was wrong. So many people would never have the chance to step into the ground you are covering right now. Praise God! You are making such an impact just by talking to them, by being their friend. You're the only Jesus these women may ever meet." I reassured her and hugged her. It couldn't be easy to do what she was doing and at such a young age. I believe that was her first ministry job after Bible college.

"I know. Anyway…I know you're tired. I had on the plans for today to go to church. My church has service on Saturdays, which is usually when I go. But we can skip it." she said.

"No girl, I'm good, I'll sleep later, let's go to church." I responded.

I saw a rainbow in the rear-view mirror and took a picture of it from my passenger side of the car. I knew it was God. No rain, complete sunshine, just a random rainbow in the hot, dry desert. That was God telling me He was there and I was so happy and felt peace. We took the beautiful scenic ride back in mostly silence.

I wrote about this for awareness. Wherever you live, you should know this is going on in your area. Someone is being trafficked unwillingly or is working in the sex industry trying to make a good life for themselves yet stuck in work they probably wish they didn't do. Please take care of the kids in your family, especially young girls. Show up and volunteer in your public and private schools. Look for opportunities to give of your free time to causes like these. We can't expect law enforcement, the local politicians or national government, or any organization to come to our rescue with this issue. It's up to each one of us as a community to put in our part.

Before leaving, I asked Victoria to give my Bible to Melissa. It was my favorite Bible, a NKJV compact Bible in faux leather with flap closure which I never found again online. I'm over it. I began reading Kim's book a day or two prior to leaving Henderson. I finished the book on the plane back to Dallas and just started crying. It was so beautiful to see the results of just one person who decided to give her entire life to the work of sharing the gospel with her community. Kim lived for the ministry of reconciliation. She took the gospel seriously and lived to see many reconcile back to God in one of the most dangerous industries. Kim and Victoria gave their lives and worked restless hours to see women in sex trafficking set free.

At that Saturday church service, I felt God speak to me and told me to stop holding back regarding ministry work. I was really kicking back after all the mess I had already experienced in my life at that point. I felt God told me to just be myself and serve Him. I left so inspired and motivated to keep going.

Wherever you find yourself in the world I want you to know there is one true God. He is the Creator of Heaven and Earth, YHWH, The Great I Am. He is the LORD, and there is no other; apart from Yahweh there is no God. While all heaven and creation declare His glory, He deeply loves you and longs for a personal relationship with you.

God reached me at the age of fifteen. Or better yet, I finally surrendered to Him. I fell in love with Christ. The Holy Spirit became my best friend. I ran after Him and got to see God meet thousands of people with the same passionate love. I had the privilege of seeing many lives ahead of me transformed by His unrelenting love. I hope you're convinced of this one thing: God loves you and God wants to consume your heart with His perfect love. He is not a distant, far off God that cares little about you. You, individually and specifically, mean the world to God. He gave His best for you when Christ came to die for our sins. He is a good heavenly Father. I can assure you that He will chase you down, and at all costs, get your attention throughout every season of your life. To follow is the Salvation prayer. My hope is that you accept the invitation to make Christ Lord in your life and surrender your life completely over to God.

Also, I hope you don't stop at that decision and undergo discipleship at a local church. I hope you suit up with the Armor of God daily to overcome any attack you will ever face. I hope you use all of the gifts and talents God placed in you to give God glory. I pray that after you live your last breath on Earth, you meet God face to face in Heaven and hear the words in Matthew 25:21, "Well done, my good and faithful servant."

Today, I want you to stop and look around you. All the faces you see every day, wherever you find yourself to live in the world, all of those people you see daily are *your mission field*.

You're not meant to be religious.

On the other side of Salvation, we are all Christ's ambassadors, sealed with the Holy Spirit. He promised He will never abandon us and equips us with everything we will need daily. Every believer is called to the Ministry of Reconciliation, as the Bible describes, and we are all handed the responsibility of carrying out the Great Commission to those around us.

There is a lot of work to do.

So, you have to keep going.

AFTERWORD
A Call to Salvation

The key to salvation is faith. This means trusting God, and believing even when you can't see. It's an action out of your own free will. If I met someone and after everything they told me I'd respond with "I don't believe you", they'd be so offended with me. Not simply offended, but my lack of trust would not allow for a good relationship simply because no matter what they do or say, I would be unable to get close. I'm directly affirming deep down that I believe they are a liar.

This is what we do to God.

We stand in the position of questioning His character and doubting the truth of His words in the Bible. God gives us no reason to doubt Him. We call God a liar daily in the way we make decisions and choose to live our lives. 1 John 5:10 says *"He that does not believe God has made God a liar..."* and when we don't believe Him, Hebrews 3:12 says *"there is in you an evil heart of unbelief"*. Further, Hebrews 11:6 says, *"without faith it is impossible to please God."* I saw this being the position of many people I've met. They can be presented with the truth of God's word, but deep within their spirit they still say to God internally, *"I don't believe You"*.

To be fair and clear, when I step back and consider every country I've ministered in, with people in and out of the church, everyone who declines the decision of salvation in Christ stands on that same ground. Internally they say, "God, I don't believe You." Ministry can be summed up as the activity in which we use everything we have to convince the world around us that what God said is true, and that you *should* believe Him to the point of entrusting your entire self over to Him. This is freedom. When people get to the point to say deep within their spirit, "I choose to believe You God, I accept Christ as Lord and Savior," and take the step of salvation, they find freedom. This is where I see the transformation occur in people's lives instantly.

If you reject the position of believing and trusting God, that's simply you remaining spiritually stuck at the beginning, in position with Adam and Eve at consuming the fruit. That is, spiritually unalive, because the reconciliation came through salvation and being spiritually alive in Christ. This is why you hear the term, 'born-again Christian'. You are born again spiritually.

The offense that Satan committed when he deceived Adam and Eve in the garden was not a direct offense against humanity. The offense was against God. Think of our legal system. If there are two parties involved in an offense, you can't use a witness to take part in remedying the crime. In other words, f two parties are involved in an offense, a witness cannot participate in remedying the crime. Since the witness was not a party to the offense. Non-involvement disqualifies a witness from making restitution. A witness *has no authority* to rectify the situation. This is why in the Bible, none of the prophets, kings or priests God ordained throughout all those generations in the Old Testament (the witnesses to the offense against God), not one of them was able to remedy the spiritual separation between God and humanity perfectly and finally. Jesus, came down as a party to the offense as He was God in the form of man. Jesus said, *"All authority in heaven and on earth has been given to me..."* (Matthew 28:18) King Jesus came to remedy the crime and reconcile us back to God the Father. What prophets, kings, priests and religious leaders could never accomplish by default, was accomplished in the life of Christ's ministry, death and then resurrection. Jesus declared on the cross, *"It is finished."* (John 19:30)

God doesn't love us because we are sinless. If that were the case, he would love none of us. If anyone claims to have no sin, that would make God a liar and we deceive ourselves. Your sin, my sin and that of the entire world is the reason Jesus came down to Earth to extend God's saving grace. Jesus is the only Way, the Truth and the Life. Christ is the Narrow Gate that leads to Heaven and eternity with God. Make no mistake, the Bible is the true word of God and Christ is the only one who can reconcile you back to God the Father.

If you are waiting to give your life to Christ until God proves Himself to you, like a certain miracle, it's likely you could see that miracle and *still* not commit your life to Christ. Many saw miracles in the Bible and still didn't follow Jesus. If you're waiting to understand everything about God and the Bible, or compare it to other religions, I promise you, *you will never be able to understand or learn enough.* If you're waiting to get your life together before you come to God, well guess what, *you'll never get it together without Him.* If you're waiting until you are ready to stop engaging in sin before you commit your life to God, I have shocking news. You'll never stop endulging in sin without Christ as Lord. In fact, you'll actually go deeper the more you allow years to pass. None of us can conquer sin on our own will power. Without your life being entirely perfect and without you understanding it all, I urge you to make the commitment today and surrender your life to God in salvation through Christ. *Today* is the day of salvation. If you would like to make this commitment, I invite you to pray the following prayer:

A CALL TO SALVATION

God, I come to You in the Name of Jesus. I repent of my sin, which kept me separated from You (say anything you'd like to include here regarding your past sin.) I believe the Bible is the true word of God. The Bible says in 1 John 1:9-10, "If you repent of your sin, God is faithful and just to forgive all your sin and to cleanse you from all unrighteousness."

The Bible says "Whosoever shall call on the name of the Lord shall be saved" (Acts 2:21). I repent and I call on Your name Jesus and accept the gift of salvation today. I pray and ask Jesus to come into my heart and be Lord over my life. According to Romans 10:9-10, "...if you confess with your mouth the Lord Jesus and believe in your heart that God has raised Him from the dead, you will be saved. For with the heart one believes unto righteousness, and with the mouth confession is made unto salvation."

I confess that Jesus is Lord, and I believe in my heart that God raised Him from the dead. I renounce any pacts with any other contradicting spirits, demonic authorities, idols or religions. I renounce any soul ties that keep me enslaved to sin and separated from God. My life belongs to you God and I want to bring You glory. My citizenship is in Heaven, as the Bible says, and I know my name is written in the book of life.

Thank you Father, in Jesus Christ's name I pray, AMEN!

Congratulations! I'm overjoyed for you if you prayed that prayer. Remember, it doesn't end at this commitment. You barely just approached the Start line in your race of faith. You are now a disciple of Christ. Keep growing in your faith as you embark in the process of sanctification. Find a good Bible teaching church and connect to a good Christian community.

If you consider yourself to already be saved, stay vigilant. Every believer has been given the responsibility of the ministry of reconciliation and to undergo the process of sanctification. If you are not currently ministering, take time to consider where you stand in your relationship with God. We're all supposed to be ministering to the world around us, whether we have a title in a church or not. Consider the gifts and talents God has given you, the things people compliment you on, which you do easily. You are not called to hide your talents, but to use them for the glory of God. This is true life success. Many people will miss out on blessings and a life of salvation in Christ if you fail to use your talents for the kingdom of heaven. Consider re-committing your life to Christ, and hit a reset today. Remember the words of Paul in Philipians 1:5 – 6, *"...because of your partnership in the gospel from the first day until now, being confident of this, that He who began a good work in you will carry it on to completion until the day of Christ Jesus."*

"In My Father's house are many mansions; if it were not so, I would have told you.

I go to prepare a place for you.

And if I go and prepare a place for you, I will come again and receive you to Myself; that where I am, there you may be also. And where I go you know, and the way you know."

- Jesus Christ

John 14:2-4 NKJV

Monterrey, Nuevo León, México

For more resources on how to grow your faith, visit
www.OverflowAris.com

You can also listen to Arisbet's podcast, Overflow with Aris on Spotify.

SPOTIFY PODCAST

WEBSITE